PSYCHIATRY IN TROUBLE

Psychiatry in Trouble
Narrative from a Damaged Profession

James C. Beck, M.D., Ph.D.

IPBOOKS.net
International Psychoanalytic Books

International Psychoanalytic Books (IPBooks)
New York • http://www.IPBooks.net

Psychiatry in Trouble: Narrative from a Damaged Profession

Published by IPBooks, Queens, NY
Online at: www.IPBooks.net

Copyright © 2020 James C. Beck

ISBN: 978-1-949093-67-4

For Ariella, Maya and Jesse

Preface

I have many people to thank. First, my wife Elisabeth who put up with me during the seven or eight years I was writing this book. Anyone who has lived with a first time author will have an idea of what she went through. I am deeply grateful for her support.

I am grateful also to my family. With hindsight, writing this book had the quality of an addiction. I was driven to do the work at the cost of ignoring almost everything else and everybody. When I finally surfaced, my family was kind enough to forgive my absence and take me back.

I thank my editors. Betsy Haggerty did the heavy lifting. Her problem as an editor was that I did not know how to write for a general audience, and I did not know that I did not know it. So Betsy had the twin tasks of editing my prose and holding my nose to the grindstone (which is what it often felt like). Eventually, I understood the problem and after that the work went more easily for both of us.

At a late stage, John Barstow helped a great deal with the organization of the book and provided valuable support as I struggled through the final stages of the writing. Gabrielle Guarracino was engaged as the copy editor, but she became a second content editor and the book greatly improved as a result. Heather Pixley was my research assistant, and I cannot say enough about her contribution.

I thank my trainees and my colleagues who were kind enough to let me interview them. Some of their stories are in the book, and some did not make an editorial cut, but I am equally grateful to them all.

Lastly, I am grateful that the work is done. I enjoyed the writing while I was doing it, but it was much harder than I could have imagined. This is the book I wanted to write; it is written, and I do not think I will ever write another.

Note: All trainees and colleagues have given their permission to be included. The names and identifying information describing patients have been changed to insure that the originals cannot be recognized.

Table of Contents

Introduction

Chance can change a life, and it certainly changed mine. As a third-year undergraduate at Harvard, I overheard a conversation about a college volunteer program in the local state mental hospital, and for the next two years I volunteered on the back wards of the hospital. Each week I would talk with Mary, a gray-haired, tired woman who had been sitting quietly in a corner for three years. Over the academic year that we talked, she regained enough function to leave the hospital, and I believe our conversations were part of what made that happen. My experience with Mary would prove to change the course of my life.

After graduating from college, I went on to graduate study in academic psychology, but I changed direction as I realized how much I missed the experience with Mary and other patients. I went on to medical school and from there to psychiatry. Now, more than fifty years later, I have two stories to tell: my own, and how psychiatry changed during my working lifetime.

I spent my career as an academic psychiatrist working in a public hospital, where I taught young physicians and other trainees to take care of sick, poor people while also caring for patients myself. I loved my work; but at the same time, I saw

1

how psychiatry was changing, and I was troubled by what I saw. When I trained in the 1960s, psychiatrists cared for patients as individuals. Now, they push pills and promise more than they can deliver. In this book, I describe that change and I offer a proposal for a different and better psychiatry—one that returns psychiatry to its roots and is more helpful to patients and more fulfilling for psychiatrists.

I start with a personal narrative because I think that the writer Joan Didion was right: "We are uneasy about a story until we know who is telling it."[1] I write about my education and training in the 1950s and '60s at the University of Chicago, Harvard, Yale, and at the hospitals where I was an intern or a trainee in psychiatry. I describe these institutions in the belief that their history will be at least as interesting to the reader as mine. I was fortunate to train at the Massachusetts Mental Health Center (MMHC) in the 1960s, when it was among the best psychiatric training centers in America; I have drawn freely on my colleagues' experiences as well as my own.

The second narrative thread interwoven through the text is some of the history of American psychiatry since 1950, drawn largely from my own experience. I write about professional ideas and practice and about institutions where I worked: The National Institute of Mental Health (NIMH), community mental health centers, and teaching hospitals.

In reflecting on this history, and in considering what psychiatry is and is not, it helps to remember how young the field is—less than one hundred years old in its present incarnation. Until the

---

1 Joan Didion, *A Book of Common Prayer,* 1977.

early twentieth century, psychiatry was a hospital-based practice that dealt with the insane. There was essentially no outpatient psychiatry before Freud's visit to this country in 1909. His lectures at Clark University led directly to the psychiatric acceptance of psychoanalysis and jumpstarted psychiatry as a treatment resource for less impaired patients. Psychoanalysis liberated the practice of psychiatry from the asylum, and it offered a unified theory of human psychology.

Just as importantly, it suggested that psychiatric illness could be treated. This infused my fellow practitioners and me with optimism. For a time, we believed we could treat the whole range of mental disorders with psychoanalysis; but, to our sorrow, we eventually learned better. I tell that story in this book.

Some psychiatric explanations for the causes of mental disorders have been found to be not just wrong, but pernicious. Treatments that we thought were effective have been shown to be worthless or even harmful. I try to present a balanced account of what psychiatry has achieved and where it has failed. Mainstream histories of psychiatry document our successes; rarely do they talk about our failures, both professional and ethical.

Psychiatrists as individuals are as culture-bound as everyone else, and this history illustrates how our beliefs have reflected the times in which we live. In the 1950s, white men dominated American social thinking, and most psychiatrists were white men. White male psychiatry blamed women for causing mental illness, and the profession knowingly tolerated the sexual abuse of female patients, as I discovered firsthand through my private practice in forensic psychiatry (about which more later). Only when women entered the profession did this change. Similarly, psychiatry persisted in its belief that homosexuality was pathological long after attitudes in society started to change, We were not a neutral force—we were part of the problem.

Although mainstream psychiatry discarded psychoanalysis as a theory and a model for therapy in the 1980s, solid research support exists for the efficacy of psychodynamic therapy, and psychoanalysis still has an important, if limited, role to play in treatment. Many knowledgeable people who have options choose a psychoanalyst for their own treatment. Psychoanalytic thinking has continued to evolve, and it continues to make important contributions to our understanding of psychological function in health and disease, as well as to our understanding of the process of psychotherapy.

* * *

In the late twentieth century, as psychiatry moved away from psychoanalysis, neuroscientists began to better understand the brain—and psychiatrists became enthusiastic about neurobiology. When Eric Kandel, who had trained as a psychiatrist, won the Nobel prize for his work on the molecular basis for how new memories are created, psychiatrists became even more enthusiastic. Research on the genetics of mental illness showed that schizophrenia and bipolar disease have strong genetic determinants. These advances and others generated great optimism that, soon, we would be able to understand the nervous system well enough to treat people who developed severe mental illness. But the imagined breakthroughs in treatment have not yet arrived, and our understanding of the biological determinants of mental disorders remains limited. To date, neurobiological research has made virtually no difference in how we treat patients.[2]

When these scientific advances first appeared, the institution of psychiatry was not alone in its enthusiasm for neurobiology: government was equally enthusiastic. Two presidents declared the decade of the brain, and NIMH increasingly devoted its resources to neurobiological studies, rather than balancing them with psychosocial studies. Critics complained—reasonably, in my opinion—that studies of psychotherapy and other psychosocial treatments were being starved for government support.

Excitement about neurobiology is just one of the reasons why American psychiatry has been transformed over the last forty years. Today, to a great extent, institutions external to psychiatry—pharmaceutical and insurance companies—control the way we practice. The last section of the book documents how contemporary psychiatry relies to an unhealthy extent on medication and how insurance companies, through managed care contracts and electronic medical record requirements, have industrialized the medical profession, diminishing and degrading the care patients receive. When there is a conflict between good clinical care and the bottom line, the bottom line wins.

The end of this book argues that psychiatry should return to its late nineteenth and early twentieth centuries roots, with training and practice concentrating on the severely ill: people with schizophrenia, bipolar disorder, severe P.T.S.D., and major depression. Primary care physicians now prescribe medication for

---

2 What is true for psychiatry is not true across other subject areas. By 2019, in one study Alzheimer's disease was treated under a protocol developed from basic neurobiological research.

patients with less severe mental health issues, and psychologists and social workers provide them with psychotherapy.

I have added a practical appendix to this history for the many Americans who will seek treatment or will know someone who does.

#####

PART ONE

PREPARATION

CHAPTER 1

EARLY YEARS

My father, Samuel Jacob Beck, was the oldest son, one of three children in a poor Jewish family living in Tecucci, a small town in Romania. His father, Avrom, was a stonemason. In 1900, when my father was six years old, his father took him to register at the local school.

> *Avrom: "I have come to register my son for school."*
> *Official: "Are you a foreigner?"*
> *Avrom: "No. I have lived here all my life."*
> *Official: "Are you a Jew?"*
> *Avrom: "Yes, I am a Jew."*
> *Official: "A Jew is the same as a foreigner. Your son cannot go to school here."*

And so, in 1900, my grandfather came to America. A labor hustler met him at Ellis Island and convinced him that a wonderful job was waiting for him in Racine, Wisconsin. The "wonderful job" turned out to be in a tanning factory, where, over time, the chemicals badly damaged his health.

Avrom saved enough so that two years later he was able to send for his wife and their three children: my father, aged eight at the time, his older sister, and his younger brother. Another brother and sister were born in the United States. The family moved to Arpin, a small town in Wisconsin, to participate in an idealistic program to retrain immigrant Jews as farmers. The program was poorly conceived and badly executed; ultimately, it failed, and Avrom had a hard time earning a living.

In hopes of a better education, my father left his family at the age of fifteen. He moved to Cleveland, Ohio, where he lived with relatives and hawked newspapers on the street to pay his board. A high school guidance counselor encouraged him to apply to Harvard. He applied; Harvard accepted him, and he entered as a freshman in 1912.

He spent two years at Harvard, where he majored in Greek and Latin, but money was scarce. He once told me that he had no winter coat, only a heavy sweater, even when the thermometer hit two degrees Fahrenheit in the winter of 1913. He persevered through both cold temperatures and difficult courses, but when his father died the next year, Sam went home to help support the family.

From 1914 to 1924, Sam worked in a variety of jobs, such as life insurance salesman and city reporter for one of Cleveland's daily papers. Throughout that decade, he was determined to return to Harvard. He saved nickels and dimes—literally—and in September of 1924, he returned to Cambridge. He graduated from

Harvard in June of 1926. Later in life, my father was recognized internationally for his work as a psychologist, but obtaining his Harvard degree was the achievement of which he was most proud.

After he graduated from Harvard, my father went to graduate school at Columbia University, obtaining a PhD in psychology in 1932. He then spent two years in Zurich, Switzerland, studying Hermann Rorschach's new inkblot test, followed by two years as a postdoctoral fellow at the Boston Psychopathic Hospital. In 1936, he accepted a position at Michael Reese Hospital, the Jewish hospital in Chicago. He was the first clinical psychologist in a general hospital in the United States, but he felt keenly that physicians at the hospital treated him as second class, not with the same respect they gave each other. His story is important because it has meant so much to my own: memories of his account would lead me years later to medical school.

Our family lived on the south side of Chicago, walking distance from the University of Chicago. My younger sister Louise was born there in 1936, and I lived there until I left for college in 1952. My mother, also a psychologist, worked at Bruno Bettelheim's famous (later infamous) Orthogenic School, where she performed psychological testing.

I went to the local elementary school and to Hebrew School at our synagogue, where I was Bar Mitzvah at thirteen. At fourteen, I went on to Hyde Park High School, where I was—well, mostly bored. I let my parents know how bored I was, and my father finally said, "That's enough. You're going to the University of Chicago." The Chancellor of the University of Chicago was Robert M. Hutchins, widely regarded as the *enfant terrible* of American higher education. He decreed that

11

the undergraduate college would admit high school juniors and seniors as first-year college students. This program attracted two kinds of high school students: *bright* socially awkward kids who were seriously unhappy in their local high schools (me) and *very bright* kids who just wanted a college education as soon as they could get one. I entered the university in February of 1951 and spent the next three semesters there, leaving in June of 1952 with a high school diploma.

The program for these high school-age 'college' students seemed designed to get us into trouble. The year's grade in each course depended entirely on one exam taken at the end of the school year. I was one of many students who did not do well with this freedom.

The university itself was in a ferment of intellectual and educational change. Many of the faculty had lived through the Great Depression, a social cataclysm that had led many Americans to conclude that capitalism was a failure and that communism was the answer. That the Soviet Union was our ally during World War II, and that the Russians had suffered twenty million casualties, only strengthened the sense of common cause with Soviet Russia. Rebellious adolescents at the university, of whom there were many, were attracted to the political left organizations that flourished in that intellectual milieu.

I shared this rebellious left-leaning political thinking. I was never sympathetic to what little I knew of communism, but my sympathies were with the oppressed. When my friends in the Socialist Youth League (a.k.a. Young Communist League) and I demonstrated against Jim Crow in the adjacent black neighborhood, we were motivated by the idea of working toward a more just and equal society.

I later attended a meeting at which a self-identified Communist Party member told us that "the unconscious does not exist," because, he explained, the Party said so. I vigorously rejected that thinking. At the time, my course readings included Freud's *Introduction to Psychoanalysis* and Erik Erikson's *Childhood and Society*. Based on my reading, I accepted that the unconscious exists. Even more important than the content of this disagreement was the relationship between the Party and its members. The idea that an organization proposed to tell me what to think about anything offended me. No one was going to tell me then—or ever—what to think. I valued the freedom to reach my own conclusions, and I had come to value Freud and psychoanalysis.

My unwillingness to lend credence to this Party dictate came also from my experience as a patient. While I was engaged with my coursework and involved with my political friends, emotionally, I was a mess. Being young and small for my age did not help.

In those days, heterosexual adolescent social life meant going on one-on-one dates, and the girls I asked out almost always said no. To escape my misery, I spent most of my time playing cards in the student lounge, often arriving home late for my family's rigid six o'clock dinner hour—the reason, ultimately, that my parents sent me to a psychiatrist.

In 1951, seeing a psychiatrist meant seeing a psychoanalyst, and I saw one twice a week for eighteen months until I left for college. At each session, I lay down on his office couch, an ashtray beside me, smoking at will throughout the hour. I don't remember much about what we did, but I have a clear memory of one of the doctor's remarks that I found very helpful at the time: "You know, James," he said, "your parents are very strange people."

I did not know that. They were the only parents I had, and I had no basis for comparison. With that comment, I was able to make a good deal more sense of my situation, and my life at home improved. On a typical night, my mother washed the dinner dishes, and my sister and I dried. My father lay on the couch reading the paper briefly until he laid it on his face and fell asleep. When he awoke, he went upstairs and began to work, typically until two in the morning, often reading Greek at the end of his night. He continued to read Greek for pleasure until almost the end of his life. Unless they were working together, my mother went to bed around nine o'clock while my father worked. I never knew them to go to bed at the same time.

Later, my best friend and college roommate, Paul, who got to know my family well, commented that he had never seen my parents kiss. I had never thought about that, but then it occurred to me that I had never seen them hug or touch each other except in the most casual, offhand ways. If my parents ever took a vacation together, I never heard about it.

My father was limited emotionally. The only time I ever saw him cry was when he talked about an event that had occurred 2,500 years earlier—the death of Socrates. His great strength was his intellectual integrity. Identifying with him, I understood that the integrity of the investigator is the core value that makes science possible. In his professional work, he stressed the importance of grounding theory in verifiable data. These are among my core values, and I owe them to him.

14

As an adolescent, I was aware that my parents were socially isolated. I think my father's single-minded focus on his work was a big part of their isolation, but in hindsight, I think my mother's character also played a role. My mother had one friend I remember, but after she moved away my mother never made another friend that I know of. Much later, I would learn that her experience at the Boston Psychopathic Hospital had been quite different.

My early memories of my mother are positive. I remember her as warm and loving until I was about six. My memories from grammar school years are neutral, except when I was sick. During those times, she was always nurturing. Our relationship changed when I was an adolescent. She became actively critical of me, often hostile. Looking back, I think this was evidence that my mother had become progressively unhappy with her life. As I see it now, I think she was profoundly disappointed in her relationship with my father. Unlike him, she was an emotionally vigorous person. When I reached adolescence, she complained to me in so many words that her sexual relationship with my father was unsatisfactory. She was overtly jealous of any interest I had in girls, and she teased me about my interests in a bitter and demeaning way.

She had a strong sense of social justice, and she always took good care of my father, my sister, and me. She managed money well and cultivated relationships with men who gave her excellent financial advice. She was a woman for whom status and appearance were important, and I think the status that came from being the wife of a professionally distinguished person helped her deal with more fundamental disappointments.

15

These were my parents; this is the family in which I grew up; and this was my experience at the University of Chicago and in therapy. All of these had a major part in molding me into who I was as an eighteen-year-old ready to enter college. When I left for Harvard in September of 1952, I was in much better emotional shape and much better able to function than I had been eighteen months earlier when I first started treatment. I thought then, and I still think, that my success in college would not have occurred without my own experience in psychoanalytic therapy.

As I left home for Harvard, America was going through a period of economic growth with resulting social stability. The post-World War II economy provided consumer goods that had not been available during the war. Cars, refrigerators, washing machines, toasters, the new TVs—all powered the new economy. In tandem with this economic well-being, the government functioned well, as Democrats and Republicans worked collaboratively, and with respect for one another.

America was fighting a war in Korea, but except for the young man of draft age, the war made little impression on American life. Socially, white males ruled from the top of the heap. Whites expected people of color to stay segregated and impoverished. Men similarly expected women to stay in their place as obedient homemakers, sexually compliant wives, and mothers. Gay people were so deep in the closet that they could not even see the light in the crack under the closet door. This was the larger world in which I lived as I left for Harvard in September of 1952.

#####

CHAPTER 2

HARVARD COLLEGE: UNDERGRADUATE YEARS

Harvard College had been in existence for more than 300 years when I arrived as a freshman in 1952. Admission then was far easier than it is today. Harvard admitted nearly a third of its applicants to my class (versus less than five percent in 2018) and an even larger proportion of alumni sons. The class was all male and almost entirely white; more than half my class were graduates of prep schools and about a quarter was Jewish by quota.

Intellectually, I was a good fit at Harvard. I loved the work, and I did increasingly well at it over the next four years. My social fit at Harvard was another story. During my first year, I made only a few friends, and I was still awkward with girls. My first attempt to woo someone produced my first heartbreak. Early in my freshman year, I was attracted to a girl in my required basic writing course. I still remember my opening line: after class, I said to her, "Come downstairs and see my new (actually secondhand, but new to me) ten-speed bicycle." It was a perfect early fall New England day, bright and sunny. She came downstairs and threw herself down on the grass next to the bicycle, her circle skirt spread out around her. She was enthusiastic about the bicycle, and I soon became enthusiastic about her. To the extent that an eighteen-year-old can fall deeply in love, I fell deeply in love with her. A man in the class ahead of us was also interested. She rejected me in favor of this man, whom she later married.

That rejection threw me into a profound funk that I recognize in hindsight as a modest depression. I was taking a course in writing poetry that spring, and I wrote, "Five flights up and ten hearts down, my heart is as cold as a smooth, round stone." I suffered, but this experience also taught me something useful about suffering and perhaps prepared me—more than I knew at the time—to respond to the suffering of others.

In the 1950s, the social class of every undergraduate was immediately obvious because the college charged for dormitory rooms according to their desirability. Rooms on the second floors cost the most, followed in order by third-floor rooms, then first-floor rooms, then fourth-floor rooms, and finally fifth-floor rooms, where I lived in a spartan space with old, whitewashed plaster walls; a splintered wooden desk and chair; and a narrow bed with an iron frame. I had little spending money, and I always worked.

If our residences hinted at our economic situations, the regulations governing the dining hall made us all appear equal. Freshmen ate in a common dining hall wearing coats and ties, a strictly enforced requirement. The dining hall was an imposing space where several hundred of us could eat at one time. The ceiling was two stories high, and heads of large animals shot by Theodore Roosevelt lined the walls—truly lions and tigers and bears.

I always worked, and one of my first jobs provided my introduction to the world of psychology. For a few months, I fed pigeons in the laboratory of B.F. Skinner (of Skinner Box fame)—until one morning when I did not. B. F. Skinner was one of the great psychologists of his generation, and he believed that all behavior was conditioned by reinforcement, by which he meant reward or punishment. Behavior followed by a positive reinforcement—food, for example—would increase in frequency. Behavior followed by a negative reinforcement, such as an electric shock, would decrease in frequency. Skinner's experimental work tested how different schedules of reinforcement would influence the learning of new behaviors. For example, he studied the difference in how quickly animals learned if the new behavior was reinforced always versus intermittently, and, if intermittently, on some regular schedule or randomly.

The Skinner lab was in the basement of Memorial Hall, an imposing Gothic revival building. In contrast to the beautiful upper floors, Skinner's basement lab was dark and dingy. My job was to move the pigeons one at a time from the coop where they spent most of their lives into the box where they worked for food. Each box was big enough for one pigeon, and on one wall of the box was a disc that the pigeon could peck. In response to a programmed number of pecks, the pigeon would receive a food pellet. After a designated amount of time, I would take the pigeon out of the box and put it back in the coop. I did this for several hours every Saturday and Sunday morning.

In 1953, I went to New Haven for the annual, much-vaunted Harvard-Yale football game. In those days, undergraduates drank a great deal. After The Game (as it is known to this day), we drank a lot to celebrate if we won, or to drown our sorrows if we lost. With the exception of amphetamines at exam time, alcohol was our only drug. Today, Harvard "cards" students strictly at any social function where alcohol is served; but in my day, Harvard served us all.

The morning after The Game, I was in no shape to travel back to Cambridge. I called the Skinner lab to tell them I would not be in to work that Sunday. Skinner's assistant fired me on Monday, telling me, "You are temperamentally unsuited to taking care of pigeons." The precipitant for my firing had nothing to do with my temperament, but he was right: I really did not like the pigeons, and they did not like me. I was sorry to lose the job but glad to have nothing more to do with those birds.

I did have one minor triumph as a college freshman involving the famed poet E. E. Cummings. During that academic year, Cummings gave a series of six endowed lectures at Harvard. His lectures lasted only half the expected fifty minutes, but he filled the time reading from his own poetry. He had a wonderful reading voice, and I used to imagine that he might be my father so that he could read to me as I fell asleep at night.

In one of his lectures, Cummings remarked that when he had been a student, it was a privilege reserved for seniors to live in Harvard Yard. He wondered whether today's freshmen, who were now the sole occupants of the Yard, could properly appreciate the experience. I loved living there, and I thought to engage Cummings based on our shared love of the Yard. I sent Cummings a letter. "Dear Mr. Cummings," I wrote, "Although I am only a freshman, I live in the Yard and I like it very much. Several of my friends and I would be very pleased if you would come to tea in my room," and I named a date and time. Cummings accepted. A postcard, which I have to this day, came back written in his signature style, "thank you. will be there & then. e e cummings." I was more than a little excited and invited several friends who had literary interests or aspirations. One of my new friends came from a Boston Brahmin family, and we borrowed a silver tea set and a white bearskin rug from his home. My friends and I prepared as best we could.

On the day of the visit, Cummings and his wife trudged up the five flights of stairs and arrived at the appointed time. The bearskin rug was on the floor; the tea set was on the table; and I had made a fire in the fireplace for the first time. When I lit the fire, I forgot to open the damper, and, as a result, I smoked up the entire room. We all, including the Cummingses, had to sit on the floor until I opened the damper and windows and cleared out the smoke.

As it turned out, the Cummingses enjoyed the afternoon. My impression was that they had very little contact with undergraduates, and they were glad for the opportunity to spend time with us. I remember only one remark he made. One of my friends earnestly asked him, "Sir, what do you think of the criticism of poetry?" Cummings replied in his dry, laconic tone, "It's alright if you do it, so long as you know you're killing the poem dead."

For me, the follow-up to this social event was as important as the event. I came home for Christmas quite pleased with myself. "Well, Father," I said, "I had tea in my room with E. E. Cummings." And I sat back to wait for his response.

My father: "Who is E. E. Cummings?"

Me: "You know, Father. Modern poet. Writes all in small letters."

My father: "No, I don't believe I do."

Me: "Harvard, class of '14, Classics major."

My father: "Oh, *that* Mr. Cummings. We had Greek 2 together with Parker and Greek 6 with Post. C Plus Post we used to call him. Ask him if he remembers me?"

That was my father—no clue about modern poetry, but a clear memory related to his own intellectual interests from almost forty years earlier.

My friends and I did see the Cummingses one more time, and of course he did not remember my father. Now, many decades later, I recall Cummings and his wife sitting on the only two chairs, with five earnest undergraduates sitting on the bearskin rug at their feet. I learned that I could make an unlikely connection by recognizing common ground, and I learned something about myself—what I could do if I tried. From the follow-up, I learned something of my father's limitations, and I resolved to separate myself from what I saw.

* * *

Each freshman class was required to move out of the Yard at the end of the year to make way for the next year's freshmen. Since the 1930s, when Harvard built the upperclassmen houses, all undergraduates were expected to live in university housing, and, with rare exceptions, all do. In September, I moved into Kirkland House with Paul Sperry and Al Levin, two classmates whom I knew, but not well. Sixty years later, Paul and I are still best friends, and Al and I remain close.

A Harvard House is not just a dormitory—it is a community of 350 to 400 undergraduates, and approximately 20 resident and twenty nonresident graduate students or junior faculty who serve as tutors. The tutors advise some students, but their chief role is to enrich the social and intellectual life of the house. During my time at Harvard, I saw them as a resource, and I got to know some of them well.

Many went on to distinguished careers—Zbigniew Brzezinski was a counselor to President Johnson, the National Security Advisor to President Carter, and a powerful voice in foreign policy for the next forty years. Sam Huntington became the most distinguished conservative political thinker of his generation; Tom Kuhn introduced the concept of paradigm shift, perhaps the most important idea in the philosophy of science during his working lifetime. There were others, equally distinguished, but not as well known.

These men taught me what I could not have learned any other way. Based on his experience in the Office of Strategic Services during World War II, Carl Kaysen told me, "War is the biggest opportunity for fuck-up that there is." Fortunately, I never had to experience that personally. More directly relevant to my life, he advised me never to get in the habit of writing bad papers. I took that advice to heart, and I have tried never to do that.

Bob O'Clair, the assistant senior tutor, and I became good friends. We drank a great deal together. Bob was a big man with a hearty manner and a florid complexion that I later realized was a result of alcoholism. More than was true in my relationship with other tutors in the house, I never had a sense of difference in status between Bob and me. He was older than I was, but that was all.

Bob told me a story from his service in World War II that I have tried to live by ever since. He was among the troops liberating Germany at the end of the war, and as the American army advanced, Bob learned of a group of Russian women slave laborers who had been working for a German farmer. Russian soldiers, advancing from the east, liberated the farm. They were about to kill the farmer when the women formed a circle around him. They told the soldiers, "You are not going to kill him. He is a decent man. He treated us well." The farmer lived. The lesson I drew from Bob's story is that everyone can treat people as decently as conditions permit. Few of us have the power to change those conditions, but we can all try to do what that farmer did.

* * *

Undergraduate life at Harvard was incredibly insular. As far as we were concerned, the world outside the college barely existed. To get our attention, news either had to be very special or directly involve us. Occasionally, something made an impression. In 1954, the Cold War with Russia was at its height. Americans saw communism as a huge threat to the United States. Senator Joseph McCarthy came to prominence as the chairman of a Senate committee that investigated suspected communist infiltration into government and other important American institutions. He was a favorite among citizens with conservative views; the liberal left vilified him as a witch hunter.

When he attacked Harvard's president Nathan Pusey, elected just a year earlier, we took notice. The *Harvard Crimson*, our undergraduate paper published daily since 1875, covered the story in depth. Pusey had been plucked from the relative obscurity of Lawrence College in Appleton, Wisconsin, where he had stood up to McCarthy on McCarthy's home turf. At Harvard, there was even more at stake: one of McCarthy's targets was Wendell Furry, an untenured associate professor of physics. There was considerable political pressure from McCarthy and from conservative alumni to fire Professor Furry. President Pusey refused, and his judgment was vindicated when Furry went on to become a tenured professor who made important contributions in his field.

Academically, I majored in a broad field that included much of psychology, sociology, and anthropology. I wrote my honors thesis on word association using a word list that Carl Jung had studied extensively in the early 1900s. I did well academically, and I graduated with high honors. During my junior and senior years, I volunteered at a local state hospital, an experience that would shape my career, described in the next chapter.

In the summer after my sophomore year, and again after my senior year, I had a job as a research assistant at the Association of American Medical Colleges (AAMC) in Chicago. Getting that job illustrates that "it's not what you know, it's who you know." When I was home from college in the spring of my sophomore year, I had relentlessly pestered my father to ask his colleagues about possible research assistant jobs for me. I say "relentlessly pestered" because my father kept not asking.

He finally yielded to my repeated requests and heard from one of his younger colleagues about a research assistant job at the Association of American Medical Colleges (AAMC). I applied and was accepted. I liked the work, and I did it well. At least as important, my boss and I forged a close working relationship. That summer job would shape the entire course of my later professional life. It helped get me into medical school, and it equipped me for a position at NIMH that led me directly to community psychiatry.

By the time my four years in college ended, I had been accepted as a graduate student in psychology at Yale, expecting to become an academic psychologist. Entering the College, I'd thought academia was my only choice. I knew I was smart and could think clearly, but I doubted that I had the experience or personal characteristics that would fit me for any other career.

My opinion of myself improved by the time I graduated. I had made meaningful friendships and was beginning to be more successful with women. I had done quite well academically, and Harvard recognized my achievements in public ceremonies that were good for my self-esteem. By the summer of 1956, I could imagine other options, but they were not enough to change my choice of a career—yet. I had decided to pursue a PhD in psychology, and I had chosen to go to Yale because at that time Yale offered the best psychology research training in the country; but my undergraduate work in the mental hospital had changed me. In time, that experience would lead me away from psychology and toward medicine. The mental hospital story comes next.

#####

CHAPTER 3

FIRST EXPERIENCE IN A STATE MENTAL HOSPITAL

Picture a high-ceilinged room, perhaps forty feet long and eighteen feet wide, and almost completely bare—a few radiators with ugly covers; light green paint of a particularly bilious shade peeling off the walls; old, tired wooden rocking chairs too heavy to throw; high, barred windows that opened only a few inches; no clock, no calendars—just a blaring radio for entertainment that the staff controlled. Picture also patients smoking in an enclosed outdoor gallery off this "day room," and sleeping dormitories with one bedside table holding all a patient's belongings open off the long interior wall.

A nurse or attendant sits in an office at the end of the day rooms—one for the men, another for the women. Thirty patients sit silently or mumble quietly, endlessly rocking or lying on the radiators. A few patients pace from one end of the room to the other. On the men's ward, some patients openly masturbate. The only conversation: "Got a cigarette?" or the occasional expletive.

This was the scene I encountered in 1954 as a college junior when I walked into a state mental hospital to begin working as a volunteer. Early that school year, I'd overheard a conversation about this new program at Metropolitan State Hospital in Waltham, Massachusetts. I was intrigued, and I volunteered to work one afternoon each week in this 1,200-patient hospital. The conditions were appalling, but I was drawn to the patients. I volunteered at the hospital my entire junior and senior academic years and worked primarily with two patients: Mary O'Regan and John Arillo. My work with Mary was particularly meaningful to me—and to her. The volunteer experience was important for other students as well; many went on to become mental health professionals. My group of five Harvard undergraduates included two future psychiatrists (myself and one other), one psychologist, and one social worker.

State mental hospitals were a backwater then, a world apart from mainstream psychiatry. They were deliberately built far away from population centers, where they would not call attention to the plight of the resident insane. These hospitals ("hospitals" in name only) were always underfunded, understaffed, and, from the 1890s until the 1960s, desperately overcrowded. By 1955, there were more than 540,000 patients in American state and county psychiatric hospitals. Only in the 1960s, with the development of new medications and the advent of community mental health centers, did these institutions begin to empty out.

"Met State" was marginally better staffed than others. In many state mental hospitals in the U.S., individual psychiatrists were responsible for more than 200 patients. In Massachusetts, the average caseload for a state hospital physician at that time was 100 patients or more. Since the state hospitals had no affiliation with medical schools, the American physicians who worked in these hospitals were often the walking wounded or otherwise limited people. An example: one day, I saw a group of patients playing cards at a table. One older woman looked particularly bizarre. Her hair was wild and unkempt, and she had stuck a multitude of paper curlers in it. I thought to myself, "They shouldn't let the patients look like that." Then I looked again, and I realized she was the ward physician.

Many of the physicians were trained at medical schools outside the country. A few idealistic physicians did not fit this description—men and a few women who had a calling for the care of the severely ill—but these exceptional physicians were rare.

Dave, a young, idealistic social worker on the hospital staff, supervised the five volunteers on our team. We each spent an hour with the patient Dave assigned to us. Then we met with Dave as a group for an hour to discuss our experiences. He worked to help us understand the patients we saw and our relationships with them. I recall endless discussions about the differences between friendship and psychotherapy. (We were not trained therapists, so our role was to make meaningful personal connections with the patients.) We learned about the original illnesses that brought our patients to the hospital and the demands the hospital staff made on them once they arrived. Most, but not all, suffered initially from psychosis.

Psychosis is a generic term for a condition in which a person has delusions (persistently false beliefs not shared by others) and hallucinations (false perceptions experienced as real). Major psychotic disorders include schizophrenia, bipolar disease, and major depression. When I first volunteered at Met State, new medications were being introduced but were not yet widely in use. For many psychotic patients, staff could only try to control their behavior physically or chemically. On rare occasions, some staff person would try to understand what was troubling a patient. Our job as volunteers was to listen as best we could and show our patients that we cared. In the time it took to travel back and forth between the college and the hospital, we talked about our patients, the hospital conditions, and our conversations with Dave, and we bonded strongly with each other.

State hospitals, including Met State, were custodial environments operated with minimal staff effort and maximal staff comfort. They did little to help patients; most patients became shells of their former selves. The staff socialized them into compliance with the rules of the institution: "Be quiet. Do what you are told when you are told to do it." Threatening harm to the self or others led to physical restraint or removal to a "quiet room," a.k.a., a padded cell. An acutely disturbed patient could be kept in isolation for days.

Some patients were pressed into service, essentially as slave laborers. They were made to work, for example, in the hospital laundry or in the kitchen for regular hours, with no pay. Staff called this "occupational therapy." I once observed a chronic patient who appeared to me to be functioning quite well. When I asked whether he might be ready for discharge, the head nurse on his unit dismissed the idea out of hand. "Oh, we couldn't possibly discharge Alan. He has been working in the laundry for twelve years, and we could not possibly do without him."

Patients entered Met State for different reasons. Some were admitted when they did something bizarre, unsafe, or threatening in a public place, or they acted out at home, leading their families to seek help. Some were admitted after a more insidious, deteriorating course. They had simply stopped taking care of themselves in the most basic ways: not eating, not washing, and not communicating with anyone as they became increasingly involved with the world in their heads. For many of these patients, suicide was a serious risk.

The discovery of chlorpromazine (trade name Thorazine) in the 1950s marked the dawn of modern psychopharmacology. Thorazine's importance for the treatment of psychosis is comparable to penicillin's importance for the treatment of infectious disease. It is effective for the most dramatic symptoms of major mental illness, blunting the delusional fears and frightening hallucinations that drive many patients to weeping, screaming, occasional violence, and self-destructive behavior. The patients I met who were being treated with this drug told me the voices were still there, but muted. The delusions persisted, but they had lost much of their power to frighten the patient and to influence their behavior.

For many, Thorazine was a miracle drug that promoted enough recovery that the patients could be discharged safely into the community. But there is no such thing in medicine as a treatment that has power only for good. Any treatment potent enough to affect an illness can also cause negative consequences, and Thorazine is no exception. Even when used in recommended doses, it has serious side effects for some patients; used in high doses, it turns patients into shambling, mumbling zombies. Too often, doctors would rely on high doses of Thorazine to get angry or otherwise disruptive patients under control. If they became something less than fully human, staff saw this as unfortunate but necessary. Some of the patients I observed were like this, but I never knew whether or not they were medicated.

Mary O'Regan, the patient I met with twenty-five or thirty times during my junior year, was neither medicated nor psychotic. Like other Met State patients who had less severe mental disorders, Mary was sent to the state hospital because her symptoms caused problems for others in the community, and there was nowhere else for her to go. Her problem was obsessive cleanliness: she was excessively fearful of germs. To control her anxiety, she repeatedly washed her hands and arms with Lysol. She managed her life in spite of the raw skin on her arms until she stuffed up all the plumbing in a three-story building with paper towels. That was enough to get her involuntarily hospitalized. She had been at Met State for three years when I began meeting with her.

Mary was a single woman in her late forties whose hair was beginning to gray. She was about five feet four, slightly overweight, and clad mostly in hospital-issue, scrupulously clean, shapeless cotton dresses. When I first saw her, she was sitting quietly in one of the rockers in the day room, bothering no one. Her ability to converse appeared to be in mothballs, but as she realized that I actually wanted to talk with her, she responded.

We met each time during midafternoon in a corner of the big day room and talked mostly about her daily life in the hospital. Her speech was soft, with little variation in emotional tone. I was struck by how barren her life was—quiet all day, sitting in her corner, interrupted only for meals. I learned that she had no close family, and I was her only visitor. She said she understood why she had been sent to the hospital and gave the impression that she accepted her situation. I saw her as resigned but not defeated.

I never learned why she had been so fearful of germs, but as our weekly meetings went on, Mary became more comfortable with herself, and she reported less need to wash. (Certainly, the unavailability of Lysol was helpful to her skin.) We began to talk about the possibility that she might leave the hospital. She told me that she thought she could take care of herself if she had the opportunity to be free again and acknowledged that it might be nice if she could leave the hospital. I talked with Dave, the social worker, and he said he would look into possible placements.

In the meantime, Mary began one of our weekly conversations by telling me that she'd had some female complaints and had been scheduled to see the doctor. At that time, the hospital relied on part-time medical specialists to provide medical or surgical care beyond what the hospital psychiatrists were capable of providing. Several weeks later, Mary told me that she had had an operation related to her female complaints. I asked, "What operation?" Mary could not tell me because she did not know. She knew only that she had been sent to the doctor, put to sleep, and later sent back to the ward.

My moral sense was grossly offended. I was outraged that this woman had had something done to her body but was not told what. I refused to accept this as an unknowable fact. I made strenuous efforts through contacts in the hospital administration to find out what operation had been performed on her. My efforts were a complete failure. Neither she nor I was ever able to find out what the surgeon had done. Mary and I did the best we could to put this unfortunate event behind us.

She continued to do well in the hospital, and Dave agreed that she might do well in a suitable setting outside the hospital. He arranged for her to be interviewed for a position as a maid at a local Catholic college. I took her to her interview. She got a tour of the facility and an account of her duties and her working conditions. She would clean, she would live in a dormitory with the other maids, she would receive all her meals in the institution, and she would be paid fifty cents an hour for her work. When she came out of the interview, she told me, "This place is so clean you could eat off the floors." At that moment, I knew this placement would succeed. Before the end of the academic year, Mary was discharged to this new situation. I spoke to her on the phone one year later, and she told me she was happy and doing well. Looking back, I think that Mary probably would have sat in the corner for the rest of her life if not for my meetings with her, along with Dave's skills at researching community resources in order to match Mary with the right situation.

My experience with Mary was deeply meaningful for me, for I felt that I had connected with a person who had been connected to no one. Moreover, I had been instrumental in helping her make a profound improvement in her life. She was able to leave the hellish situation in which she had lived for three years, and she was going to a new, better place with the hope of a similarly new, better life.

My senior-year experience was important to my education, but less satisfying to my emotional state. When Dave assigned me during my junior year to work with Mary, he could envision a hopeful outcome, since she clearly had the potential to improve. The following year, he asked me to work with a seventy-two-year-old man. John Arillo had limited intelligence and was hospitalized because he could not manage on his own.

John was round-shouldered, slack-faced, and slumped in a chair when we met in a corner of the men's day room. He made minimal emotional contact with me. Our sessions were matter-of-fact and lasted only about twenty minutes. He told me that he went home periodically to visit his mother, who was in her nineties, and we sometimes talked about how often he went and how he traveled there. There were clear problems between them, and as a college student, I was amazed that a person in his seventies still had issues dealing with his mother. I had problems with my own mother, so I could appreciate something of his situation, but at that stage in my life, I figured it was something one would get through while relatively young. Meeting with John was a very different experience from the previous year's meetings with Mary, and I know that Dave assigned me to work with him because he wanted me to learn about the difficulty and disappointment of dealing with a limited patient who would not change.

Volunteering at Met State changed me, but I did not realize just how much until I started graduate school. I found that I had a new definition of meaningful professional work. Learning about how the human mind functioned was no longer enough. I had to be doing something that directly helped other people, in a process that was emotionally meaningful both to them and to me. That is as good a definition of psychotherapy as any, and ultimately, I became the kind of doctor who provides psychotherapy.

#####

CHAPTER 4

A YALE TALE

I began graduate work at Yale University in September of 1956, comfortable with my choice of psychology and with my new roommate, a friend from my undergraduate years in Kirkland House. Our graduate fellowships allowed us financial stability, but nothing more. Our apartment was a third-floor walk-up with heavily used furniture in an old, moderately ramshackle wooden building. If we wanted hot water, we had to light a gas boiler in the kitchen—constantly flirting with the possibility of an explosion—but we each had our own bedroom, and we could afford the rent.

The apartment was an easy walk to the psychology department in the Institute for Human Relations. The institute was a five-story brick building planned in the 1920s and dedicated in 1931. The Yale president, medical school dean, and law school dean had envisioned an institution that would provide medical students with a holistic view of their patients.

To that end, it housed faculty from medicine, psychiatry, psychology, anthropology, and sociology.

By the time I arrived, the interdisciplinary promise of the institute was history. The psychology department was physically and organizationally isolated. Our laboratories were in the basement, and our offices were two and three flights up. We had almost no contact with other faculty, but we could view psychiatric patients from a distance when they exercised in an outdoor area of their locked ward. That was our only contact with anyone beside ourselves.

At the outset of my graduate career, I enjoyed my work, but six weeks into the academic year, I realized that I intensely missed the work I'd done with patients at Met State. I'd always told myself that if I wanted to do clinical work I should go to medical school, because I had seen the doctors at Michael Reese treat my psychologist father as a second-class citizen. I considered dropping out of graduate school immediately in order to take the required premedical courses in one academic year and one summer, but I abandoned this idea because the academic year was already too far advanced.

As the year progressed, I also realized that, despite missing clinical work, I had not lost my interest in research. I proposed to my department that I continue to work toward a PhD, with a focus on research training, while also taking undergraduate premedical courses. I was doing well enough that my department agreed to this plan.

One of my first big decisions as a graduate student was choosing an area of study within psychology. I chose child psychology because it offered both unique research opportunities and intellectual stimulation. I was particularly interested in developmental issues, and William Kessen, the program's developmental psychologist, was my faculty advisor. He and a colleague were writing a book on the language of psychology, so he was not doing any research. I enjoyed learning about his work and doing further reading on my own in the philosophy of science, but I learned little about research from him.

Nonetheless, I got very good training in research at Yale, and my premed courses were excellent, but my social life was a nightmare. My fellow graduate students and I thought of New Haven as a social wasteland. The Yale undergraduate men spent many weekends driving up to Smith or Vassar or Wellesley, but on my budget, that was a luxury I could not afford.

As a result, my social life consisted largely of dancing with the wives of married graduate students at department parties until I developed a relationship with one of the research assistants. We enjoyed each other's company until we didn't and broke up after a year. In hindsight, this was a relationship with very little content; I had initiated it out of a desire for an intimate relationship, and she was quite literally the only woman I met who was a potential candidate for the position. Some time later, the department, unaware of our history, placed the two of us in one office. I've had few experiences more uncomfortable than sharing an office with a woman after we'd ended an intimate relationship.

I took graduate courses in statistics and research design, and I participated in research seminars. I was fortunate to work as a student intern with Dr. Sally Provence when she was a young physician in the child study center. Later, she became a professor at Yale, nationally recognized for her pioneering neurodevelopmental assessment of newborns. I was able to watch her careful methods of observation as she examined the infants. Her meticulous recording of her observations taught me the importance of a data-based approach to clinical work.

I also learned a few things about myself. At the age of twenty-three, I was a callow youth, and working in child psychology offered several opportunities to demonstrate this. The first grew out of my observations of newborns. I thought up an independent research project to study the relationship between newborn activity and how they were placed in their cribs. In those days (as now), newborns were typically placed on their backs for the fear that they would suffocate if placed on their stomachs, but there was anecdotal evidence that babies slept more quietly on their stomachs. I decided to test this at the newborn nursery in the Grace New Haven Hospital, directly across the street from the Institute for Human Relations.

I crossed the street with an ordinary cardboard box, walked onto the delivery floor, told the nurses in the newborn nursery what I proposed to do, and set up the box on one of the scales on which the nurses weighed the infants. The scale was delicately balanced so that it would move up as the infant moved. I proposed to place some infants in the box on their stomachs, and some on their backs, and then observe and record those scale movements as a measure of the infant's activity. Formal protocols to protect human subjects during research did not exist until the 1970s, and I was unconstrained by any formal oversight.

When I described my project to one of my fellow graduate students, a woman a few years older than I, she was appropriately appalled, telling me that I simply could not take any old cardboard box over to the newborn nursery and put these infants in it. Reluctantly, I saw that she was correct. As a result of that and other practical problems, I abandoned the project.

Another illustration of my immaturity came when I spent a semester observing four- and five-year-olds in the Child Study Center nursery school. I had no more idea of what I was doing there than if I had been on Mars. I sat in the corner of the room and watched the children go about their nursery school activities, chattering to each other. Occasionally, one of them would look over curiously at me. I could have spoken if I'd had any idea of what to say to a four-year-old, but I had none; so, I remained a silent observer in my corner, never a participant in the several months I was there.

Research itself was taught in several seminars, and through work with faculty members in their labs. After the first year of graduate study, there were relatively few course requirements, so I took the premedical courses I needed without conflict with my psychology studies. The Yale psychology department of the late 1950s had a remarkably laissez-faire attitude toward its students. If we worked, we worked, and if we didn't, we didn't, and no one noticed. One of my fellow students sank into what I later recognized as a depression, and he basically did no work at all for one entire academic year. The next year, he got back on track, and after eventually completing his doctorate, he went on to run a successful practice as a clinical psychologist in Boston.

I took required premed courses along with a full graduate load, and this limited my time for organized social activities, so I often just drank with my roommates. My limited finances similarly limited what I drank (but not how much). I drank either home-brewed beer or laboratory alcohol (ethanol) cut with tonic and lime. The tonic and lime elevated the taste from awful to barely tolerable. Who knew that my ethanol intake would change the course of my entire future life?

Medical schools used the premed grade in organic chemistry as the primary marker to assess whether a prospective student could do the required scientific work in the first two years of medical school. My laboratory grade in organic chemistry at Yale depended entirely on identifying six unknowns. Coming down to the last day of the lab, I had identified five of the six. The last unknown was a liquid that I'd had no time to analyze. I smelled it, and I recognized it only because I had smelled it so often when I drank it. I told my instructor, "This is ethanol." My instructor, God love him, gave me full credit for the identification. This raised my grade for the year from eighty, which would not have been good enough for many med schools, to eighty-eight, which was.

I applied to medical school in my second graduate year, hoping to be admitted for September of 1959. Both the University of Pennsylvania and Harvard Medical School offered interviews. The Penn interview was not a success; Harvard's, fortunately, was a different story, in spite of an inauspicious start. The Harvard interviewer's first question was about my undergraduate honors thesis. I had finished that thesis close to three years earlier and had not thought about it since. I did what later in medical school we would have irreverently referred to as "pulling it out of my ass." From more or less nowhere, I managed to remember enough about my honors thesis to respond intelligently to his question. The remainder of the interview passed off pleasantly and uneventfully.

At Christmas in 1958, I got the acceptance letter from Harvard, meaning I'd be back at Harvard in September 1959.

I got into Harvard Medical School partly on my record of achievement, but also on who I am and who I knew. Helen Gee, my old boss at the Association of American Medical Colleges, and I had liked each other, and we had stayed in touch. Helen knew George Packer Berry, the Dean of Harvard Medical School. Helen told me, without saying it in so many words, that she had strongly urged the dean to accept me as a student in the medical school. This was just one more example of the adage, "It's who you know, not what you know, that gets you in." It's worth adding that staying in depends on what you do after you get there.

* * *

Because I took undergraduate premedical courses at Yale, I had a unique opportunity to compare the undergraduate experiences at Harvard and Yale. The latter had the reputation of committing greater discretionary resources to undergraduate teaching, and I saw that this was true. When I took organic chemistry at Yale, 160 students had signed up for the course. The course was taught in morning lectures and afternoon labs. Yale thought that 160 students was too many, so they split the lectures in half, and the same professor delivered each lecture twice to a group of 80 undergraduates. I was impressed.

That would never have happened at Harvard. At that time, Professor Louis Fieser, the inventor of napalm, was teaching organic chemistry, which at Harvard was also a lecture and laboratory course. Several hundred undergraduates typically took his course, but Harvard would no more have thought of splitting this up than they would have thought of changing the rules to allow male undergraduates to entertain women in their rooms at all hours!

I was comfortable as an undergraduate at Harvard, but less comfortable with the Yale undergraduates I knew. The Yalies I met were white, mostly Anglo-Saxon, Protestant prep school graduates, who came surprisingly often from Long Island. As a group, they appeared to be remarkably self-satisfied. That would not have bothered me, except that, as I talked with them, I got the impression that they came into Yale with a particular set of ideas and values that went unchallenged during their undergraduate experience. As far as I could see, they graduated fundamentally unchanged. In contrast, the Harvard students I knew were a somewhat more diverse group. Harvard's education challenged many of us, and we changed as a result. In the ways that mattered most, I thought the Harvard undergraduate experience was far superior to that at Yale.

* * *

During my third year at Yale, I focused on my dissertation and my last two premed courses. My goal was to complete the dissertation in one year so I could earn a PhD and begin medical school the following September. I had a clear idea about the best way to do that, as I had observed other students working on their dissertations. Some got their degrees with a minimum of aggravation; others suffered through a painful process, often requiring years to complete. Based on this, I formulated a strategic imperative that I applied in my own case, and that I passed on later to other graduate students. The nub of my wisdom was this: a graduate dissertation is a political act. The most important decision that any doctoral candidate makes is not the choice of a topic, but rather the choice of a dissertation advisor.

Advisors vary enormously in how helpful they are to their advisees. The good ones, or the ones I think of as good, understand that their role is to help the student do a piece of work that the dissertation committee will find acceptable. These advisors can think clearly about their field, are generally motivated to be helpful to other people, and understand the politics of their department. They have a pretty good idea of which topics are likely to find favor with a committee and which are not. This is the advisor to look for when it comes time to write a dissertation.

The second imperative is that the student must not imagine that the task is to make a contribution to the field—that is far too large a task. In science, the true task is to conduct a good, independent piece of research, and in the humanities, it is to write an original piece of analysis or criticism. After a student gets a degree, he or she has decades to demonstrate intellectual heft and to make a contribution to the field. The job in writing a dissertation is to choose a topic that, first, will appeal to a faculty committee and, second, is doable in something less than geologic time. If the doctoral candidate follows these precepts, the chances of getting through reasonably comfortably are good—otherwise, look out.

I followed my own precepts for my dissertation and asked a kindly, much-loved senior faculty person with a solid scientific reputation to be my advisor. That he was alcoholic and long past his intellectual prime was irrelevant. I chose concept formation as my topic because it offered a problem that was methodologically within my reach and a project that I could reasonably complete within one calendar year. My research addressed how people come to recognize and understand a concept they know nothing about—specifically, how they use positive and negative information to reach conclusions.

My advisor and I discussed the work as it progressed, and after he reviewed an initial draft, he approved my work as appropriate for submission as a dissertation for a PhD in psychology. My 110-page paper included background information, a literature review, hypotheses, methods, analyses, results, and a discussion of my findings. I submitted my final bound copy to the department on the day before I was due to begin medical school.

The usual expectation was that a three-person faculty committee would review a dissertation after it was submitted, and the candidate would then appear before that committee to defend what he had written. Given the tight time schedule I was on, we agreed that this committee review would take place at the department in the 1959–1960 academic year and that I would appear to defend it then.

I was in my second semester of medical school when I learned that my dissertation was in trouble. I should have taken into account developments in information theory analysis that neither I nor my advisor knew anything about. One Yale senior faculty member did know, but he had not read my dissertation until after it was bound because he had been on medical leave. When he did ultimately read it, he correctly criticized it because I had failed to measure the amount of information in negative versus positive instances of the concept I had studied. During spring break in my first year of medical school, when I should have been studying the central nervous system, I was in New Haven redoing my analysis and rewriting my dissertation. I was awarded my Yale PhD in psychology in June 1960.

I consider my three years at Yale well spent—not much fun, but I got what I came for. Yale strengthened my understanding that empirical data form the bedrock on which theories and beliefs must be based. It also provided me with the intellectual tools I needed to conduct my own empirical research as a psychiatrist; I have used those tools ever since. They are a critical part of who I am professionally, and, more broadly, they are the basis for many judgments in my personal life.

#####

CHAPTER 5

TRIAL BY MEDICAL SCHOOL

September 6, 1959 was my last day in New Haven, or so I thought. I handed in my dissertation, packed up my apartment, and drove to Cambridge to begin medical school. The next morning, I called Harvard to ask when school started. The woman at the other end told me, "I hope you're not too far away. It started an hour ago."

I got to the medical school late, but still in time to hear Dr. Herman Blumgard, the chief of medicine at Boston's Beth Israel Hospital, welcome us. He told us a story of his time as an examiner for the internal medicine board certification exam—a story that I have not forgotten. During the exam, candidates were required to examine live patients and present their findings and diagnosis to the examiner. One particular patient was an enigma that candidate after candidate diagnosed incorrectly. Finally, one candidate told Dr. Blumgard that the patient had lupus erythematosus—and she was right. Dr. Blumgard asked her how she had arrived at the diagnosis. She told him she had asked the patient, "What do you think is the matter?" The patient said, "Doctor, I have lupus erythematosus." Dr. Blumgard ended his talk, saying, "Listen to the patient. He is telling you the diagnosis." This wise advice has informed my teaching and my clinical work ever since.

My medical school classmates were almost all white men: one Asian man and just five women comprised the minority population, less than six percent of the total class. As a group, we were accomplished, talented, intellectually curious, friendly, and cooperative with one another. We shared a task to which we were all dedicated: we were there because we had a calling for medicine. For most of us, that meant patient care; for others, research was the goal. Whatever our background and whatever our intellectual interests, we were united in a determination to prepare ourselves to become physicians.

The faculty were almost all white and male as well. The teaching was by lecture in the morning and through laboratory work in the afternoon. The lectures gave the faculty the opportunity to present themselves as well as the material. Raymond D. Adams, a distinguished neurologist at Massachusetts General Hospital and a professor at the Medical School, gave us our first lecture on the brain. He was a trim man wearing a white shirt and bow tie who gave a formal and decidedly dry presentation with few gestures and little emotion—just the facts. He began by telling us, "You are competing with your classmates, be they good or be they bad." This struck me as odd. "Well, no," I thought, "I'm not competing with anyone. I'm here to do the best I can, however good or bad that turns out to be."

There was a wide cultural gulf between some of my Boston Brahmin professors and me. One quintessentially WASP surgeon lectured us on taking a history. He told us admiringly of a long-time patient who came to his office with the chief complaint: "In the morning, I am having my bowel movement one or two minutes later than usual. Do you think this could be a problem?" The patient's question led this surgeon to a diagnosis of an early, curable stage of colon cancer. He presented the case as an example of how a person with the right sort of character and regular habits could triumph over adversity. As I think back on this, the cultural gulf between the surgeon and me comes flooding back, and I am still appalled by anyone who kept track of his bowel habits that obsessively—and by anyone else who admired a person who would do that.

If an institution can be said to be arrogant, then Harvard Medical School was arrogant. We got the clear message that Harvard was an academic leader and that we, as Harvard graduates, were expected to be academic leaders in our turn. On the same first day that Dr. Blumgard spoke to us, we also heard from the dean, who informed us in sonorous tones, "One sixth of all the medical school faculty in this country graduated from Harvard Medical School, and one quarter had some portion of their training here." The message of how we were expected to use our Harvard education was clear.

In fairness, the school had a lot to be arrogant about. Two of our professors, John Enders and Thomas Weller, had already won the Nobel Prize for their work on poliovirus when they lectured on tropical medicine. Two young assistant professors, David Hubel and Torsten Weisel, lectured to us on vision and the brain, work for which they also would win the Nobel Prize. Our faculty almost always had done original work in the area on which they lectured.

The teaching was generally first rate, but at its best, it was superb. My course in tropical medicine was so good that even though I never imagined I would practice in the tropics, I learned the material thoroughly and went into the final exam feeling confident that I could answer any question they would ask me. That was the first and only time I had that experience in medical school.

The medical school held its faculty to the same high standards that they expected of us. After a lecture by a junior colleague on the drug treatment of one intestinal parasite, Tom Weller came bounding down the aisle from the back of the lecture hall where he had been sitting, and he came to the lectern. "We are going to have an exercise in integrative teaching," he told us. With the lecturer standing beside him, Weller told us the lecturer had been all wrong, and then he explained the subject correctly. The shame of the junior colleague was visible to the entire class.

Going to medical school with the intent of becoming a psychiatrist narrowed my focus. I did not always see the point of everything I was asked to learn, and in my first year, I rebelled in a small way. All first-year students were required to dissect a cadaver, working in a group of four. Deciding that a psychiatrist did not need to know the anatomy of the foot, I refused to dissect the foot or to learn any anatomy below the ankle.

Later, I learned that anatomy could be useful—even for someone with my narrow focus. One of my classmates brought our anatomy professor a small bone to identify, which he had found in his dinner at a local Chinese restaurant. Several days later, our professor told us the bone was a cat's rib. This led the city health department to make a surprise visit to the restaurant, where they found a freezer full of dead cats! Case and restaurant both closed.

* * *

It may be hard for someone who has not gone through medical school to appreciate just how consuming those four years are. As a medical student, I devoted almost all my time and energy during the academic year to trying to learn what the faculty was trying to teach. Even my religious observance dropped off. As a secular Jew, my observance was limited, but I normally had gone to services on the high holidays, fasted on Yom Kippur, and avoided leaven during Passover. All these things fell by the wayside while I was in medical school. (I later resumed them.)

The momentous changes going on in the world during those four years barely touched my fellow students or me. I never heard the morning news program coming out of anyone's room as I walked down the hall to the bathroom. In college, we had read the *Harvard Crimson*, but in medical school, I never saw a fellow student reading a daily newspaper over breakfast. We were only vaguely aware of the civil rights movement and the beginning of women's liberation. Our drug of choice when we had the leisure to indulge was alcohol.

Medical school presented challenges different from those of graduate school. The faculty taught us new material every day, which we had to digest and understand in order to be ready for the next day. I experienced some culture shock, and I had my share of difficulties in the first two years. Some came with the territory, but others, like my choice of living situation, were self-inflicted. After living independently for three years as a graduate student, no one could have persuaded me that I would want to live in a dormitory.

When I moved from New Haven to Cambridge, I lived with an old friend from Chicago. The medical school was across the Charles River in Boston, and my commute took time away from my studies. Bob was a working businessman, and when he came home after work, he wanted to socialize just when I needed to settle down to study. The apartment was laid out so that the only way to get to the kitchen was through my bedroom. The experience was, in short, a disaster. After the first semester, I moved into Vanderbilt Hall, the medical school dormitory, and life improved—somewhat.

But I still had other problems. I had a part-time job that ate up time I could ill afford to spend away from my studies. I was not especially well prepared for the first-year courses, and the work was a struggle, not made any easier by my initial living arrangements and job. I passed all my courses—barely—and I badly needed a break. Thankfully, the medical school gave us the summer off. I worked that summer as a research assistant for Dave, the social worker I'd worked with at Met State, who had a grant to study the undergraduate volunteer program at the state hospital.

Working on this research and knowing what the volunteer experience had meant to other undergraduates, I thought the program had potential value for improving the lives of state hospital patients. An international congress on mental health put out a request for papers for its conference in Paris the following summer. I doubted that an international congress would accept a paper from a medical student, but the possibility of a trip to Paris to present our program was too good to pass up. I wrote a paper describing how our program worked, who participated, what it meant to the volunteers (many of whom went on to graduate school in the mental health professions), and what it meant to the patients. I was surprised and pleased when the paper was accepted.

I returned to medical school with my batteries recharged. My second year started on this high note and was overall better than the first. I completed my shift from a graduate school orientation to one appropriate to medical school. I had the intellectual capacity to do the work, and when I understood that I had to do it every day, my academic performance improved. I began to enjoy the experience of medical school. I moved out of the dormitory and rented a house that was an easy bike ride away from the medical school. I lived with three classmates, and we were a compatible group.

The summer after second year was also free, and I had the leisure to pursue intellectual interests in the college library and prepare my Paris talk. I also got to know a few girls who were there for the summer school. Jewish girls were notorious, at least among Jewish graduate students, for coming to the summer school only to look for a Harvard husband. Susan Schwarz may have been the only one who came for the education. She and I happened to be standing next to each other in the checkout line where our books were inspected before we could leave the library.

"It's a nice place to study," I said. Susan looked at me as if to say, "Who are you, and what are you talking about?" As a Wellesley College student, Susan was unfamiliar with the security checkout that was standard Harvard procedure, so I explained why we were in this line, which she appreciated. After we checked out, we talked on the library steps, and I got up the nerve to ask her out. The conversation went something like this:

Me: "Would you like to have a beer?"
Susan: "I don't drink beer."
Me: "Would you like to go for coffee?"
Susan: "I don't drink coffee."
Me: "Well, come with me to Cronin's and I'll buy you a lemonade."

We had a beer and a lemonade at Cronin's, a favorite bar of Harvard students, and we began to get to know each other. After the drink, we took a walk, and I showed her a favorite alcove in the Radcliffe academic quad with a small fountain in the center. I asked her what she thought of it, and she said, "I think it's pretentious." That independence of thought and her willingness to contradict the opinion of someone she had only just met made a great impression on me. I left Cambridge for Europe knowing I had someone important to come back to.

In Paris, I attended as many sessions as I could, and I was impressed that the speakers were often people whose works I had read. The focus of the conference was on public mental health services, and I thought my paper would be of general interest. Apparently, the organizers thought so too, because the room where I presented held easily 100 people. I was crushed when only 7 people came to listen. The older man who chaired the session kindly consoled me afterwards.

I made a side trip to London to visit the Maudsley Hospital, the premier psychiatric training center in the United Kingdom, to explore the possibility of psychiatric training there. They offered me a position when I finished medical school that I later regretfully declined when the American Board of Psychiatry refused to give me credit for the proposed year. Already three years older than average, I felt that I could not afford an extra year.

After I returned from Europe, I rekindled my new connection with Susan. I asked her to go to the beach, and she accepted, but she told me later that she only accepted because she had a new bathing suit. She was dubious about this relationship with an older man. She was nineteen and had just finished her freshman year at Wellesley, and I was twenty-six.

I continued to pursue her and invite her to events that we might both enjoy. When I learned of a string quartet playing the Beethoven late quartet cycle, I invited her to join me. She wanted to hear the music, so she accepted that invitation as well. As the summer wore on and we spent more time together, it became clear that, despite the difference in our ages, we shared common interests and values, and we cared about each other. Little more than a year later, I asked Susan to marry me. Her immediate response was, "Who, me?" When she got over her surprise, she accepted, and we were married on August 26, 1962, just before my fourth year. I was twenty-seven and she was twenty, headed into her junior year at Wellesley.

Aside from my burgeoning relationship with Susan, the third and fourth clinical years of medical school were a huge improvement over the first- and second-year lectures and lab-based instruction. I loved talking with patients and learning about their diseases. As I began my third year, I became a resident proctor in one of the freshman dormitories in the Yard. This was a sought-after job open to graduate students throughout the university. Our role—as academically successful, friendly older students—was to be available to our freshmen, to help those who got into academic or emotional difficulty, and to keep order in the dorm. In return, we received free room and board. I lived in an elegant three-room suite in a dormitory in the Yard, with all the meals I cared to eat in the freshman dining hall.

When Susan and I married the following year, Harvard appointed us as the second-ever married freshman proctors at Harvard, and we lived in one of the new freshman dormitories, a renovated apartment building just outside the Yard. It was a dramatic innovation for Harvard to allow a married couple to live in a freshman dormitory. Men and women were still largely separated at Harvard, and there were strict rules on when women could visit undergraduates in their rooms.

The university did not think through our situation well. Our apartment was in the basement, and the students assigned to me lived on the third floor, so I hardly saw any of them. The students who lived directly above us often lifted weights and dropped them heavily on the floor. We were seldom able to take advantage of our free meals in the freshman dining hall because, in those benighted days, Harvard did not allow women in that dining hall except on weekends. On weeknights, when Susan was commuting to school, we preferred to cook our own food and be home together.

In the last semester of my fourth year I did a research elective, which meant that my life was more like graduate school and less like medical school, and I had time to prepare for the comprehensive exam at the end of fourth year. Preparing for the exam, I asked myself, "What would I ask if I were giving this exam?" I thought acid-base balance would be an excellent question because it covers a wide range of both basic science and clinical material, and so I reviewed it. Sure enough, discussion of acid-base balance was one of two possible choices for the three-hour essay. The other choice was a subject I had blown off in the first year before I had even understood that I was expected to learn it.

Acid-base balance refers to the mechanisms by which the body maintains the chemical composition of the blood at exactly the right balance between acid and alkaline. If you have a glimmer of memory for your high school chemistry, this means at a pH between 7.35 and 7.45. The mechanisms for maintaining this balance include chemical buffers in the blood, cellular metabolic processes, and the function of the kidneys and lungs. A good answer to the question requires the student to discuss all of this, which I did. I performed well on that exam and in my courses generally, and I graduated with my class in 1963.

Medical education at Harvard in the 1960s was not the financial burden that it is now. Back then, Harvard policy stated that no student should graduate more than $2,000 in debt. When a student's debt reached $2,000, the university gave the student a full scholarship. Between that scholarship aid and my part-time jobs and proctorships, I graduated with only $2,000 in debt. Now, even with substantial financial aid, the average Harvard student's debt at graduation is just over $100,000. This compares with the average medical school debt nationally of just over $200,000.

Medical students apply for postgraduate training—internship and residency—during the last year of medical school. Susan and I had agreed when we married that I would apply only for Boston internships so that she could finish at Wellesley. In the 1960s, the major Boston teaching hospitals required their interns and residents to work every second night and every second weekend. Mount Auburn Hospital in Cambridge was a community hospital with an academically respectable teaching program, and its internship required only every third night and every third weekend.

I applied there and listed it as my number one choice. One day in April, the algorithm that matched applicants with training programs spat out the results. This was, and still is, called match day, and at Harvard, after the relief of finding out where we would go the next year, many of us ran around shouting "FUBIGMI." That stood for "F... you, buddy, I've got my internship!" Then we settled back down to work. I graduated in June but missed commencement, as Susan and I used the three weeks between medical school and my internship to go to Europe. On July 1, 1963, I began my internship at Mount Auburn Hospital.

#####

CHAPTER 6

I BECOME A PHYSICIAN

Throughout my working life, I have loved being a physician. That love began during my internship. Medicine, I found, is not just something you *do*—being a doctor is something you *are*. The process of becoming a doctor changed my character in important ways that medical school had not. Medical school required that I assimilate a large body of new knowledge, learn better study habits, and develop more capacity for extended intellectual effort. Working with patients during my internship taught me things I could never have learned from books or lectures.

The Mount Auburn Hospital internship was a one-year training program. It would have been a poor choice for anyone aiming for a career in medicine or surgery who needed a multi-year program with their internship followed by residency, but the single year was perfect for physicians who intended to become psychiatrists. We were six interns that year; five headed for psychiatry.

61

Senior medical residents from the Harvard service at Boston City Hospital and surgical residents from the Tufts service at New England Medical Center rotated through the hospital. They and the staff physicians who cared for patients at the hospital were our teachers, roles in which they excelled. We also attended medical grand rounds, the teaching formation in which an expert would discuss a particular clinical problem in depth. This internship is where I learned to be a doctor.

David Hurwitz, the chief of medicine at the hospital, was committed to maintaining an excellent teaching program for the interns. He was warm, cared about his house staff, and had a becoming humility. At one grand round, he chose to present a patient of his own who had died from a rare brain infection after Dr. Hurwitz had missed the diagnosis. Few chiefs would have made the same choice. In later years, the hospital honored his memory, naming its auditorium after him.

We five nascent psychiatrists bonded. Surprising our faculty, we cared deeply about our work and tried hard to learn everything we were taught. The cardiologist who taught us could not understand why we worked hard to learn to read EKGs, since we would never read another one after June 30. We told him, truthfully, that we wanted to do the best job we possibly could for our patients during the year we had with them.

The Mount Auburn was a private, nonprofit community hospital that maintained two charity wards for the sick poor at a time when Medicaid did not exist. We interns had primary responsibility for the care of the charity patients, both in the hospital and after discharge, at the hospital's outpatient clinic. We cared for our patients under the supervision of senior residents and staff physicians. These latter were men primarily in private practice who volunteered one month each year to teach and supervise the interns and residents.

There is a huge difference between working every second night and every third night in an internship. My impression from talking with friends at the Massachusetts General or Beth Israel Hospitals was that working every second night ground them down physically well before the end of the internship year. We six interns at the Mount Auburn had an easier time. On the nights we worked, we often got between four and six hours of sleep. Even when we had little or no sleep, we had the next two nights at home to recover. That worked well for those of us who were going on to psychiatry: we learned to be doctors, and when we were not in the hospital, we had our own lives. Between Susan's commute to Wellesley and my long but manageable hours, our life represented what would become increasingly common in American society: the two-career family.

* * *

Working primarily with charity patients opened my eyes to shortcomings in the healthcare system. Before the passage of Medicaid, people who could not afford private medical care depended on charity. For people who were proud, this could create serious problems. A story from my internship year that has stayed with me to this day illustrates such problems. I cared for a middle-aged single mother who was hospitalized on our charity ward with a bad case of asthma. After her discharge, I followed her as an outpatient, with supervision from one of the medical residents.

While hospitalized, she had been on high doses of steroids to control her severe asthma. Steroids can have bad side effects, so as she improved, we decreased the steroid dose as quickly as we could while controlling her asthma. This seemed to be going well until I got a tearful call from her two adolescent daughters: "Dr. Beck, we are calling to tell you our mother is dead."

I was devastated. How had this happened? Nothing we knew about her condition suggested that she was at any risk of death. Her daughters told me she had a serious asthma attack after I'd lowered her steroids, and she had gone to Cambridge City Hospital for treatment. "Why didn't she come to see me?" I asked. Her daughters told me that she had not paid her bill at Mount Auburn, and she was too embarrassed to come back owing money. Instead, she went to the city's other hospital, where she was grossly mistreated and died.

Cambridge City Hospital's roots date back to 1917, when local physicians told the City Council that they would take care of indigent patients in the city free of charge if the city would build a charity hospital. The city accordingly built the hospital. By 1960, however, Cambridge City Hospital was in such deep trouble that it was the subject of an NBC White Paper episode addressing the crisis in American health care.

Working as a house officer at a hospital without a university affiliation amounted to a term of indentured servitude. These hospitals typically attracted two classes of physician: the dregs of American medical school graduates who couldn't get into any other training program, or foreign-trained graduates, and often too few of these to fill their program. The doctors who treated my patient were not up to the task, and whoever had treated my patient was directly responsible for her death.

I wanted to know what happened. One of Mount Auburn's best staff physicians worked part-time at Cambridge City Hospital as a public service, and he found out what had happened. The story was pitiful: the house staff at Cambridge City Hospital had killed my patient, pure and simple. To understand how, it's important to know that the adrenal gland manufactures steroid hormones that are essential for life, but when doctors give steroids to a patient, the body stops making them. The Cambridge City Hospital doctors stopped her steroid medication cold, which meant she was not making any and therefore not getting any. She went into metabolic crisis, which they failed to recognize, and she died. Every second-year medical student in America is taught that sudden withdrawal of steroid medication can be life-threatening. The emergency room house staff at Cambridge City Hospital apparently didn't know that or did not know my patient's history. Had they recognized it, restarting her steroid medication would have easily treated her condition. The failures of her doctors were gross, but this is not a full or adequate explanation of the tragedy.

At least three deficiencies led to my patient's death. The first and most obvious was the ignorance of her doctors at Cambridge City Hospital. Second, and related to the first, the whole country had known since the NBC documentary four years earlier that this hospital rendered grossly inadequate care, but nothing had been done about it. No government agency had intervened to shut the hospital down until it improved enough to render at least minimally adequate care. The third deficiency was the absence of an insurance scheme that would have paid this woman's medical bills. It was this failure that, jointly with the others, led directly to her death. Had her outstanding balance not embarrassed her, she would have returned to Mount Auburn Hospital, where she was known. Had Medicaid been enacted, she would have lived.

* * *

My internship provided me with an invaluable education, but some of the lessons it taught me came at a cost to patients. During my rotation on the charity ward, two of my patients died, partly as a result of my inexperience. The first occurred in July—always a dangerous month for patients in teaching hospitals, because the doctors who treat them—residents and interns—are new and inexperienced. I treated a man in his eighties who had pneumonia, with an antibiotic that was ineffective, and he died. My supervisor consoled me by saying that this was just my inexperience; with more experience, I would have changed antibiotics sooner.

The second patient died as a result of my inadequacies as a physician. In my two clinical years at medical school, I had relied largely on my interviewing skills in evaluating patients. I got most of my information from their history and relied little on the physical exam, which I performed rather poorly. As an intern caring for patients who were too sick to give a good history, this approach was insufficient.

The patient in question was a man in his forties who came in with a fever and difficulty breathing. I had listened only to the base of his lungs, where I heard decreased breath sounds. A thorough examiner would have listened all the way to the top

66

of the lungs; without doing so, I diagnosed pneumonia and treated him with what I assumed was an appropriate antibiotic. The patient, however, continued to decline. When the resident examined the patient, he listened to the patient's chest more thoroughly, listening all the way up to the top of the lungs. He heard decreased breath all the way up. He diagnosed a pleural effusion: excess fluid in the pleural cavity, the fluid-filled space that surrounds the lungs. This killed the patient before we were able to treat it effectively. The resident's comment to me: "I assume you did a careful physical exam."

That memory is still painful. At the time, it taught me, with a sudden, severe shock, that I was not a good doctor. I resolved to change my ways, and I did. I developed the capacity to do careful, thorough physical exams, and I became a much better intern. Then I began to love being a doctor, because I could see that I was doing work that helped my patients. I began to imagine that I might go on after my internship to be a general practitioner in Vermont. I knew this was just a fantasy, but it was meaningful at the time.

Equally meaningful was the emotional education I received as an intern. My experiences were not all negative or difficult: I had another case where something I did routinely prevented a death. A Harvard professor, the head of one of the undergraduate houses, was hospitalized with a cardiac arrhythmia, and his cardiologist had started him on a new anti-arrhythmic drug. On morning rounds, I listened to his heart and noted that it was beating dangerously fast. I telephoned the cardiologist, but he was unavailable. Routinely, I wrote the order to stop the new medicine and went on to the next patient. Later that day, when the cardiologist was in the hospital, he told me that I had done the right thing, and he thanked me. When I next saw the patient, he said to me in a tone of deep gratitude, "You saved my life." The experience taught me two lessons: first, to trust my own judgment when I thought a situation warranted it, and second, that the same experience might have very different meanings for the two people involved. Something that was routine for me had meant a great deal to someone else. Experiences like these helped build my capacity for empathy.

A practical note: people staff hospitals. We try hard, but like all people, we make mistakes. New physicians will make more mistakes in July than later in the year. If you get your health care from an institution that trains interns and residents and it is possible to delay your hospitalization until later in the medical academic year, then I would suggest you take that course.

Another practical point: every hospitalized patient needs an advocate—an independent person who can look at what is going on and raise questions when it appears that something is not quite right—when we are either doing something that we shouldn't, or not doing something that we should. You, as the patient, are by definition in a position of vastly inferior power in relation to your doctor and all the other people taking care of you. The last thing you want is to alienate your doctors by questioning their judgment. As a patient, you are isolated from your clinical team. Social isolation is a risk marker for bad outcomes across many contexts, and none more so than during hospitalization.

One last experience that I had as an intern taught me an important lesson about the different perspectives that may impact a patient's care. During my rotation through the surgical service, I interviewed a nineteen-year-old woman who had almost bled out from her uterus before the surgeons saved her. She described in moving detail her near-death experience. As with any patient, I took a social history. She and her mother both worked giving out towels to students at the swimming pool of a local university. In addition to providing towels, this young woman also provided sexual favors to a number of the young men. When I presented the case at surgical rounds, I included the social history. My description offended the chief of surgery. He thought this did not belong in the presentation of a surgical patient, and he told the chief of medicine I should be fired. The chief of medicine soothed him, and the conflagration subsided. I learned from this experience that surgeons and psychiatrists can be very different kinds of people, with very different ideas about the practice of medicine.

The year of internship changed me. The deaths of patients changed me the most—not just the two I caused, but also the ones I witnessed. As doctors and nurses, we are uniquely privileged to share the experience of dying with patients and their families. To be there, to be part of the process, to do what we can as life ultimately ebbs away, is to share most deeply in the experience of another. These intimate moments developed, or perhaps even created, whatever capacity I have to share emotionally with others. At the end of my internship, I had acquired some expertise as a physician, along with a corresponding feeling of confidence that I could be helpful to patients. I graduated with my fellow interns and went on to my psychiatry training.

* * *

A digression is necessary before I describe my psychiatric residency. In the 1960s, psychoanalytic theory provided the intellectual underpinnings for psychiatric training and practice in most academic centers on the East Coast, including the Massachusetts Mental Health Center, where I trained. For this reason, a chapter on psychoanalytic theory and practice follows so that readers better understand my experience as a resident.

#####

Chapter 6 – Epilogue

I include this story because it illustrates a characteristic of mine that is useful to patients.

Every hospital ward has a support person usually called the ward secretary. The secretary is the public face of the ward. Her workstation is usually placed near the entrance, so she is the first person a visitor is likely to encounter. Especially on a charity ward, where the families may be less knowledgeable and may also feel the power differential between themselves and the doctors especially keenly, the secretary is an important person.

Laura was our secretary on the charity ward. She had just graduated from Radcliffe, and she was earnest and responsible about how she went about her work. Not infrequently she was uncertain about some medical fact or about some hospital procedure. As I got to know her over the course of the year, I encouraged her to ask me what she wanted to know. I had no ulterior motive; I just wanted to be helpful.

Twenty-five years would pass before I learned how the bread that I had cast upon those waters would come back to me. My daughter Emily in her last year at Lexington High School had applied to Harvard where she very much hoped to go. My office phone rang, and a voice at the other end said, "Dr. Beck you don't remember me, but I remember you." She went on to introduce herself as Laura and reminded me that she had been our ward secretary when I was an intern at Mount Auburn Hospital. She was now working as a mid-level staff person in the Harvard admissions office. "Whenever I had questions you were always helpful to me, and tried to answer my questions," she said. "So, when I saw that your daughter had applied to Harvard, I was particularly interested in her application."

Laura told me that Emily's application appeared to be doing well until she was interviewed by a group of male undergraduates. Emily had told them that she wanted to be an elementary school teacher, and these young men had raised the question of whether Harvard should admit someone with these rather low career aspirations. Without saying so, Laura made clear that she had shepherded Emily's application past that rough spot. Emily did go to Harvard and she did become an elementary school teacher where her work has repeatedly been recognized as outstanding.

#####

CHAPTER 7

PSYCHOANALYSIS AND AMERICAN PSYCHIATRY: THE LOVE AFFAIR ENDS

Speaking of Freud's writing, a graduate student in psychology recently said to one of my colleagues, "no one reads that shit anymore." Her comment reflects the fact that many people today view psychoanalysis as an old, discredited theory and practice not worth knowing, largely because organized psychiatry has said so for the last thirty years. I disagree—in my opinion, psychoanalysis still has much to offer as a treatment and as a theory.

The history of American psychiatry between the 1920s and the 1970s is the story of how psychiatry first embraced psychoanalysis, became disillusioned with it, and finally initiated a nasty divorce. The break came as it became clear that the psychoanalytic understanding of major mental illness was wrong and that its treatment of psychotic disorders was inappropriate— and at times even harmful. None of this invalidated Freud's understanding of human psychology, nor did it change the value of psychoanalytically based treatment of people with neuroses.

Psychoanalysis, as Freud developed it, is one of the great intellectual achievements of the late nineteenth and early twentieth centuries. It encompasses a theory of human psychological function and a set of therapeutic techniques firmly grounded in that theory. After Freud brought psychoanalysis to America in 1909, the broad sweep of this theory and the depth of its approach led American psychiatrists, as well as social scientists, to embrace it enthusiastically.

Many of the first practicing psychoanalysts in America were immigrants who fled Nazi-dominated central Europe. A large percentage were Jews, as were many of the American physicians who went into psychiatry in the heyday of psychoanalysis. Most of us went into psychiatry expecting to devote ourselves largely to the practice of psychodynamically oriented psychotherapy. My cohort and I are the basis for the one-liner, "A psychiatrist is a Jewish doctor who hates the sight of blood." Speaking personally, there is some truth in this. The large Jewish presence in the field also produced an undercurrent of anti-Semitic hostility to psychoanalysis that persists. In 1967, I first heard the phrase "psychoanalysis is a Jewish trick," and I heard it again in 2015.

Before 1920, American psychiatry focused on caring for the severely and persistently mentally ill—those the nineteenth century knew as the insane. Almost all of these unfortunates received their "care"—what care there was—in state hospitals, the godforsaken institutional descendants of nineteenth-century asylums. Psychiatry had no effective treatment for any of these patients, and they suffered accordingly. These were the institutions where society stored and ultimately flushed out some of its least desirable citizens. In a very real sense, they were outhouses.

Psychoanalysis breathed life into a moribund profession. It offered a unified, coherent theory of personality development—how infants become children and then adults, and why some people suffer from severely distressing mental symptoms while others do not. What's more, psychoanalysis offered the promise that we could remove the sources of psychological distress through our efforts.

Beginning in the 1930s, practicing analysts formed professional associations called psychoanalytic institutes, in New York, Boston, and Chicago. These institutes were independent of organized medicine, and they exerted total control over who could be trained as an analyst. Only physicians were admitted to analytic training. Those of my fellow residents who wanted to become analysts went through an extensive training process at the Boston Psychoanalytic Institute.

Psychoanalysis offered psychiatrists a high road out of the asylum, allowing us to practice in the comfort and safety of an office, where we could treat people who were suffering, but not so impaired that they had to be institutionalized. The process helped many healthier patients who could afford it but attempts to treat people with more severe mental disorders were not successful, and the efforts to treat schizophrenia, as you will read later, were irrelevant for those patients and damaging for their families.

* * *

Psychoanalysis and psychodynamic psychotherapy, or 'dynamic psychotherapy' for short, are both based on a dynamic understanding of human psychological function. A dynamic process is one that involves active change. As such, a psychodynamic understanding of human psychology describes an active struggle between contending forces, some of which are unconscious. This is the foundation upon which Freud built his theory and the practice of psychoanalysis.

This practice relies on free association. The analyst sits behind the patient, who lies on a couch. The analyst instructs the patient to say, as nearly as they are able, whatever comes to their mind, however irrational, nonsensical, or rude these associations may be. Associations about the analyst are especially important. The process of free association helps patients retrieve memories that have become unconscious because of the anxiety or guilt associated with them.

Freud understood much of mental life as an ongoing dynamic conflict between sexual or aggressive impulses and the conscience, or superego, a conflict mediated by a structure he called the ego. Freud wrote that the individual develops unconscious psychological structures he called defenses in order to ward off the conscious experience of anxiety or guilt. Defenses bind anxiety, but they can exact a price: they may prevent the person from fully experiencing relationships with others, and impair productivity, or both. Thus, Freud understood conscious experience as representing a compromise between impulse and defense, and he postulated the ego as the structure that attempts to balance these forces as they contend within the person.

The process of confronting defenses in treatment produces resistance and giving defenses up and experiencing the resulting anxiety demands work, as well as courage. The patient draws the strength to do this work from their own internal resources and from the developing working alliance with the analyst or therapist. The patient gains insight as they and the analyst come to understand how previously unconscious conflicts have produced symptoms, defenses, and impaired personal relationships.

Freud's psychoanalytic theory not only explained human psychological function, but it also explained how treatment works. Freud developed the concept of transference in order to explain much of what went on between the patient and himself as the therapist. He observed that his patients attributed to him all sorts of motives, beliefs, and characteristics that were unrealistic or not true at all. Further, these attributions varied with each patient. Freud wrote that, based on their own early experiences, patients developed expectations of how they would be treated as adults. The patient would project these expectations onto any adult who remained present, but only as a neutral screen. Freud thought that the transference would develop most clearly when the patient had little realistic sense of the analyst against which to compare his distortions, which is why he proposed that the analyst should show no personal characteristics, but rather present as a neutral screen.

Current psychoanalysis represents a vibrant intellectual tradition. Although analysts have rejected the scientific method as a basis for developing new understanding of their field, they have continued to think and write based on their clinical experience. Perhaps their most fundamental change is a rejection of Freud's view of the analyst as a screen, revealing nothing of himself. Analysts now understand psychoanalysis as a process that occurs between two people. They replaced the original formulation with an understanding that the analyst as a person is always fully present, and that the analyst must recognize their own responses to the patient either as based in reality or as countertransference—distortions based on their own, not fully recognized early experiences.

The analyst's main work is to interpret the patient's transference. An example of a transference interpretation might occur when the patient complains to the analyst that he is angry because the analyst has failed to understand what the patient has just said. The analyst might say something like, "I wonder whether your anger at me has anything to do with how angry you were at your father when he . . ." Or, when the patient is bitterly disappointed in the analyst, the analyst might make the connection, "It sounds a lot like what you told me about your mother's response when you came home so upset from kindergarten and . . ."

Freud suggested that the patient would give up distortions as they became consciously aware of them. As this uncovering occurs and the patient begins to understand what they can accomplish with the analyst, patient and analyst develop a working alliance. The patient can then use this alliance to confront anxiety and examine repressed wishes. Through this analytic process, the patient comes to understand how early wishes and fears continue to influence or even control their adult mental life. In a successful analysis, the patient can then give up the defenses that have constricted them and achieve a more open and satisfying life. This is a process that typically takes four to five years.

The great strength of successful psychoanalysis is that it gives the patient a set of tools to deal with the vicissitudes of life. Instead of having to push thoughts out of mind because they cause anxiety, the patient can recognize this process when it occurs. Using a self-conducted process of free association, the patient can then understand where their anxiety comes from and deal with it consciously.

As the monied and troubled began to experience psychoanalysis as patients, psychoanalytic thinking entered the mainstream of American intellectual life. Freud's ideas began to appear in high-end magazines and in some of the most fashionable drawing rooms in American society. It became a trend in socialite circles in New York and a few other intellectually and socially sophisticated cities to be able to say "my analyst" to one's social intimates.

Society built further on what Freud had taught to develop new institutions. The mental hygiene movement in the 1920s aimed to prevent mental illness rather than treat it. Parent education would help parents raise psychologically healthy children, and teacher education would ensure emotionally healthy learning environments. If a troubled or damaged child was more likely to grow into a troubled or damaged adult, then it stood to reason that addressing problems in the child might prevent adult problems later. In the 1930s, this new interest in childhood emotional difficulties led to the development of child guidance clinics and to child psychology as a subject of scientific investigation. These were the roots from which child psychiatry as a specialty later developed.

Psychodynamic psychotherapy also evolved from psychoanalytic theory. Psychodynamic therapists, of whom I am one, practice within this theoretical framework, using techniques derived from formal psychoanalysis. Classical psychoanalysis involves four or five sessions a week in which the patient lies on a couch, and the analyst sits in a chair behind the head of the couch, but near enough that when the analyst speaks, they are clearly present. Psychodynamic psychotherapy typically occurs once or twice a week, with the patient and therapist sitting up facing each other. This therapy is widely practiced today.

Not only psychiatrists, but also historians, writers, and social commentators in a broad range of disciplines applied psychoanalytic theory in their own work. Historians reinterpreted history through the lens of the psychoanalytic theory of instinct and defense. Social commentators speculated that world peace could be achieved if only our political leaders would undergo psychoanalysis. Psychoanalyst John Mack won a Pulitzer for his biography of T. E. Lawrence, *A Prince of Our Disorder [1]*, a speculative psychoanalytic interpretation of the subject's life and character.

John Mack was an important person in my own professional development and later work. He was the ward chief at the Massachusetts Mental Health Center where I had my first year of training, and he was the architect and first chief at the Cambridge Hospital Department of Psychiatry.

* * *

Over time, psychiatry and the larger intellectual community gradually recognized the limitations of psychoanalytic theory and treatment. At the same time, organized psychoanalysis went through a process of introspection that led to important changes in theory and technique. Further on in this book, you will find much to criticize in the history of psychoanalysis. Those criticisms are only part of the story. Many patients have been greatly helped by their experiences in analysis or in therapy, and I am one of them.

Over the course of my life, I have had three experiences as a patient that were of great use: one as an adolescent, one starting at age 55, and one in late life when my wife Susan developed Lewy body disease, a particularly nasty dementia. The analysis in mid life had accomplished what, classically psychoanalysis is supposed to do. By the end of this analysis, I described the change that had occurred in me, likening my new thought process to the motion of an elevator. In this metaphor, I had an elevator inside me that went from somewhere in my lower abdomen to somewhere in my head. When troubling or anxiety producing thoughts arose deep within me, the elevator would bring them up to where I could process them. This was in sharp contrast to my experience before the analysis, when I had spent a lot of effort blocking these thoughts from rising to consciousness.

Skepticism persists, but psychoanalysis is alive and well today. Psychologists and social workers have broken the MD monopoly on psychoanalytic training, starting additional new training institutes. There are now more than thirty analytic institutes in the U.S., as well as additional programs that offer training in psychodynamic psychotherapy.

There is a strong, continuing demand for psychodynamic psychotherapy from the social class that can afford it, but this—essentially a testimonial—takes the place of scientific evidence for the effectiveness of treatment—evidence that is dismayingly scant. Nevertheless, mental health professionals who can choose their profession actively choose to become psychoanalysts or psychodynamic psychotherapists; troubled adults choose to become their patients and find the therapy helpful. The critic may call this superstition and ritual, but those of us who have been therapists or patients will testify to its value.

#####

CHAPTER 8

"THE PATIENT IS YOUR TEXTBOOK"

I have spent much of my professional life working with psychotic patients or teaching younger people to work with them. My residency at the Massachusetts Mental Health Center (MMHC) was my first experience with this work. In 1964, Jack Ewalt, the chair at MMHC, selected me as one of twenty-four first-year residents at MMHC. I was fortunate to be chosen; MMHC was one of the best psychiatric training centers in the United States.

The hospital had opened as the Boston Psychopathic Hospital in 1912, and at the time, it represented a breakthrough in psychiatric care. Three years earlier, in response to citizen-led pressure, the State Board of Insanity had introduced a bill in the state legislature to establish an acute-care hospital for the care of the insane. The bill passed, and the legislature appropriated money for the project. The Boston Psychopathic Hospital, later called "The Psycho" by all who worked there, was deliberately built within a five-minute walk of Harvard Medical School to encourage scientific research on mental disorders.

Unlike the badly understaffed state hospitals of the time, the new hospital was well staffed. Clinical services included an outpatient department, an innovation at the time. Professional staff, in addition to doctors and nurses, included psychologists and psychiatric social workers—a brand-new profession. By the time I began my training, the hospital's somewhat forbidding name had been changed to the Massachusetts Mental Health Center.

Psychiatrists have four years of training after they graduate from medical school: one year of internship, usually in general medicine, followed by three years of psychiatric training. Trainees are known as residents, a term that goes back to the early twentieth century when doctors in training lived at the hospital and were, literally, residents. Coincidentally, I had already been a "resident" at the Psycho for two years as an infant, starting in 1934. My father had a two-year appointment as a postdoctoral fellow in psychology, which included housing for him and his family above the Southard Clinic, the outpatient service named after the hospital's first chief.

* * *

When I began at MMHC, the hospital's primary function was training—specifically and most importantly, training psychiatry residents and medical students. The faculty trained the residents, who in turn trained the medical students. The hospital also trained student psychologists, social workers, and nurses.

84

On our first day as residents, Jack Ewalt told us what was expected of us. He said we could take as much vacation as we wanted, and whether we met our patients was up to us, but if we did not meet with our medical students, we would be fired. Dr. Ewalt was not your typical psychiatrist. He was a Texan in his early fifties who drove a red Jaguar and was comfortable with his own aggression. Hanging on his office wall was a realistic painting of two pearl-handled Colt .45 revolvers. During his tenure, he took up with the wife of one of the residents and divorced his own wife. At our weekly grand rounds, a critical teaching formation that all staff were expected to attend, Dr. Ewalt frequently preceded his introductions of distinguished guest speakers by providing a graphic update of his divorce, a performance we residents found particularly distasteful

Ewalt did have a sense of humor. It is a tradition at MMHC for residents to put on a show with parody-portraits of the faculty. In our show, one of my fellow residents performed a slightly modified "Balling the Jack." He instead sang, "That's what we call *de*-balling the Jack." Some faculty worried how it would go over, but Ewalt absolutely loved it.

Shortly before I arrived at MMHC, Ewalt took administrative action that illustrated his independence of mind and willingness to act. The MMHC inpatient wards were all locked at a time when more progressive institutions were beginning to unlock theirs. Ewalt wanted the wards opened, but most staff were opposed. Ewalt accomplished it directly and characteristically. One weekend, he simply ordered the hospital carpenters to remove the doors from all the inpatient wards. When staff arrived Monday morning, all our wards were open. Staff dealt with the new reality by positioning one staff member at the door of each ward, and that worked just fine.

Like other first-year residents, I worked in an inpatient ward, where most patients were classified as psychotic—that is, diagnosed with schizophrenia, bipolar disorder, or severe depression. We were taught to immerse ourselves in the exploration and understanding of whatever the patients had to say. This meant that we heard unbridled expressions of aggression or sexuality directed at family members, significant others, or even at us. One severely ill patient tried to kill me; another attempted suicide. The fact that I brought my own anxieties to this work did not make the experience any easier, but I survived. Along the way, I began to learn what it meant to be a psychiatrist.

At the core, being a psychiatrist meant learning everything you could about your patients, especially about their symptoms, and trying to develop a relationship with them. Out of this process, you created a treatment plan for which you were entirely responsible. While I was learning to care for very sick patients as a first-year resident, John Mack was my principal clinical teacher, and I learned most of these vital lessons directly from him.

The time-honored way for a physician to learn about a new patient was to take a history by asking questions about the present illness. What did the patient complain of? When did it start? Was its course steady or intermittent? Did anything make it better or worse? and so on, with increasing specificity. This was followed by a past medical history, a family history, a social history, and a set of questions reviewing the principal biological functions of the person: vision, hearing, breathing, exercise tolerance, digestion, urination, and so on.

As residents in the 1960s, we were taught to take a medical history called an associative anamnesis, which meant that we encouraged the patient to say whatever came into their mind. We asked an open-ended question, and then we sat back to listen. The idea was that if any history was important, we would hear it when the patient was ready to tell us. They might begin by talking about symptoms that caused distress—for example, delusional fears of being poisoned, or voices saying, "You are a worthless piece of shit." We were taught that these symptoms were not fundamental to understanding the patient's illness. Rather, we listened to them only to find the conflicts that our theory told us lay underneath.

We were expected to see each of our patients twice a week for psychodynamically oriented psychotherapy—therapy based on Freud's theory that the roots of anxiety, depression, and character pathology resulted from early unconscious, anxiety- or guilt-provoking memories. Our work as therapists was to understand how this process developed in patients and to share our understanding with them.

This understanding of the therapeutic process carried implications for how the clinical services were organized. Residents were strictly prohibited from contact with the families of their patients because prevailing theory held that this contact might somehow contaminate or interfere with the developing therapeutic relationship between the doctor and the patient. Instead, families were told that their contact with the hospital would be exclusively through the social worker assigned to the case. In later years, I have experienced firsthand how important it is, both to the family and to me, to exchange information and concerns.

As beginners working on the inpatient service, we were too inexperienced to evaluate the effectiveness of these methods in treating our very sick patients. We had no idea whether these psychoanalytically derived ideas made any sense or not. Essentially, we did what we were told. We could see that medicine was often effective as a treatment for delusions and hallucinations, but we had no clue why medicine worked for some patients and not for others. Similarly, beyond the effects of medicine, we had no clear sense of why patients got better when they did. We could see that we had made a better connection with some patients than with others, and we understood that this connection was important, but, again, we could not say what enabled a connection with some but not with others.

Psychodynamic understanding of neurotic and character problems is valuable, but with hindsight it is clear that the psychodynamic explanation of psychotic symptoms that we were taught was not useful as a basis for treatment. The illnesses our patients suffered were not caused by early intrapsychic conflicts. Our approach to psychotherapy was probably more of a hindrance than a help. We spent many hours with our patients, sometimes over a period of years, trying to make them well with a theory that was irrelevant to understanding the psychoses from which they suffered. When our patients did improve, it was primarily because of their relationship with a committed, caring physician and the medicine we prescribed.

I would have liked to become a psychoanalyst, but in my second year of training, I made a list of my priorities. They were, starting from the top: husband, father, general psychiatrist, research psychiatrist, and psychoanalyst. To be a resident and in analytic training meant a sixty- or seventy-hour work week. These men started before breakfast and often ended after their family had finished dinner. I rarely missed a meal, either with Susan when there were just the two of us, or later after we had children. I could not do everything, so I gave up the idea of becoming an analyst. I have never regretted the choice I made to prioritize family over analytic training. I practiced psychodynamic psychotherapy, and the theory underlying my clinical work was derived from psychoanalysis.

The staff psychiatrists at MMHC were all Harvard Medical School faculty hired to teach and to do research, not to take care of patients. We residents treated the patients. We did different work in each year of residency—evaluating and treating inpatients in the first year, and outpatients in the second, and either doing research or pursuing further training in the third year. Those with schizophrenia were the most challenging. Schizophrenia is the most severe mental illness from which people suffer. People with schizophrenia exhibit severely disorganized behavior as a result of a disease that badly damages their ability to think and relate to other people the way the rest of us do. Delusions and hallucinations, lack of insight, extreme withdrawal, and intellectual deficits are primary symptoms. Psychiatrists and other medical specialists have searched, with varying levels of success, for effective treatments for this terrible disease since it was first recognized in the late nineteenth century.

We also treated patients who suffered from what was then called manic-depressive disease, now renamed bipolar disease. People with bipolar disease experience acute intermittent episodes of mania or depression. Depressive episodes are more common than manic and sometimes include delusions or hallucinations with such negative content that they cause patients to feel worthless or even to think that they should kill themselves. Feelings of hopelessness, poor sleep, loss of appetite, loss of interest in usual activities, low energy, severe guilt, and thoughts of suicide are common during depressive episodes.

Grandiose thoughts, sometimes psychotic—e.g., "I am the son of God"—characterize manic phases. Irritability is another hallmark; a person who is usually even-tempered may get into nasty arguments or fights during a manic episode. Mania is also characterized by distractibility, rapid thoughts, pressured speech, and a greatly decreased need for sleep. Some people report being awake for days. They may have exciting new ideas that can be quite unrealistic or get them into difficulty. For example, they may buy things they cannot afford, make unrealistic business plans, establish problematic sexual liaisons, and generally get themselves into trouble in ways that are highly uncharacteristic in their usual state of health.

Substance abuse often co-occurs with bipolar disease and both complicates the treatment and worsens the prognosis. It also increases the already high risk that someone with bipolar disorder will attempt suicide. Estimates are that between twenty-five to sixty percent of bipolar patients will attempt suicide, and that between four and nineteen percent will die by suicide. Between acute episodes, people who suffer from bipolar disease may return to a baseline level of relatively healthy function.

* * *

As first-year residents, we were responsible for the evaluation and treatment, through both psychotherapy and medication, of the five or six inpatients assigned to us. We could keep patients in the hospital for as long as we thought they needed to be there—either until we judged them well enough to be discharged to the community, or until we gave up and sent them to the state hospital. .

When patients did go home, we arranged outpatient follow-up treatment. Unless there was money for private treatment, we residents provided this follow-up care. It was a great strength of the residency that any patient we treated was our responsibility for as long as we were at the hospital—usually three years. We got to know our patients as individuals with lives, not just as patients with symptoms of mental disorder.

We learned from our patients and also from discussing them with the faculty with whom we met weekly, individually or in pairs. We attended teaching conferences where we presented what we had learned about our patients and our questions about them to our fellow trainees and hospital staff of all disciplines. There was very little reading. Our most revered professor, Elvin Semrad, told us, "The patient is your textbook." Semrad's great skill was his capacity to respond with emotional understanding to acutely psychotic patients. As a result, he was uniquely able to engage patients in meaningful conversations about their experiences. He helped patients acknowledge their pain directly in ways that all of us could appreciate. We saw that this was a skill we could learn, and that if we learned it, we could begin to have these conversations with our own patients. I have always had the sense that I carry Semrad with me. He was a chubby man, and I have imagined him as a small, angelic figure sitting just over my right shoulder. When I've sat with patients, I have felt that I could almost hear his voice suggesting the direction to take.

* * *

Working with psychotic patients is a stressful experience for every new psychiatric resident. For me, the most traumatic event occurred when a new patient with severe schizophrenia tried to kill me. Ahmed was the son of a good friend of one of the senior hospital doctors, and he had become acutely psychotic, delusional, and hallucinatory while living with his parents; he was clearly in need of immediate hospitalization. In order to get the patient into the hospital, his father and his psychiatrist friend lied to him, telling him that he would just be going for an outpatient appointment. When he came to the hospital, security staff laid hands on him and escorted him to the inpatient service, where I was assigned to be his physician. Understandably, he was furious. At our first meeting, he picked up a large standing ashtray set on a heavy base. With this weapon in hand, he began to chase me around the room. If he had caught me, as he clearly intended to do, I think death or permanent severe brain damage would have been the result; fortunately, I escaped.

After that, I only saw him when security was present to ensure that no one would be hurt. I got over my initial terror once he calmed down and accepted his situation. In time, we became comfortable with each other, and I was able to treat him like any other patient. I told him I sympathized with how angry he felt that his father had lied to him, and that the hospital collaborated with his father by hospitalizing him against his will. I said that I could understand how he came to believe that people were trying to harm him. He never acknowledged my interpretation, but I like to think our conversations helped him. Eventually, he became calm enough to be discharged, although he was still psychotic. How much of his newfound calm was due to his relationship with me, and how much to antipsychotic medication, we will never know. Over the almost two years in which I treated him as an inpatient and later as an outpatient, he became quite attached to me, and I to him as well.

One of my other patients was a depressed and suicidal young woman who, unlike my patients with schizophrenia, was able to engage with me as one person to another. Over time, her risk of suicide declined, but she remained in the hospital. I ultimately realized that I was attracted to her, and that made me anxious and guilty. I was afraid to discuss this with my supervisors because I thought I would be criticized as unprofessional. It was not until many years later that I understood this to be one of the experiences every therapist has and must learn to deal with.

Another patient I treated was also a depressed and suicidal young woman. She was evasive in our psychotherapy sessions, and we never established a solid working relationship. After being in the hospital for several months, she almost succeeded in strangling herself. The decreased oxygen to the brain due to her attempt produced conjunctival hemorrhages in both eyes. The medial half of the whites of her eyes (the part between her pupil and her nose) turned a bright red and stayed that way for many weeks. I experienced her hemorrhagic eyes as a reproach and reminder of how inadequate I was as a physician. What somehow made it even worse was that every time I looked at her, she reminded me of "The Scream," the famous painting by Edward Munch.

Although I had difficulty acknowledging this at the time, I was furious at her. Seeing her on rounds every day, and for psychotherapy twice a week, with her ever-present, bright red eyes, I was greatly distressed by this repeated, visible, silent reminder of my failure as her responsible psychiatrist.

As a first-year resident, I experienced the most anxiety and discomfort of my life, clearly related to dealing with psychotic patients. In addition to my general anxiety, I had panic attacks three or four times a week. Most of these occurred at work, but occasionally I would have one at home. I remember multiple instances of sitting in ward rounds, suddenly experiencing wave after wave of severe anxiety, accompanied by a rapid heart rate and sweating. Despite this, I was somehow able to maintain my composure and pay attention to what was going on around me. It always surprised me that no one else seemed to have any idea what was happening to me. I experienced the panic as stretching ahead endlessly and forever: no before or after, just an infinite "now." I had no concept that this experience would ever stop. Of course, it did stop—typically after minutes, not hours, when the attacks ended as mysteriously as they had begun.

The truth is that I thought I was a failure, and for the first ten months of my residency, I was frightened that a senior staff member would come up to me, tap me on the shoulder, and say, "Dr. Beck, we have decided that you are unfit for this profession. You need to plan on finding some other line of work." Not until April of my first year did I think that I knew enough about what

I was doing to belong where I was and to believe that I would become a psychiatrist.

I told Susan little about my emotional difficulties related to my work because I was ashamed of them. To the extent that I shared them, Susan was supportive, but my worries blocked my emotional engagement with her and my performance as a husband. Otherwise, Susan and I had a good life together. We lived in a comfortable, three-room apartment, an easy bicycle commute to work for both of us. Susan had a good job as a research assistant at the Laboratory for Community Psychiatry. We made close friends among our fellow residents who were also married, and we went out to inexpensive restaurants and department parties.

Many of our friends were getting pregnant, and although we were trying, we were not. This was painful for both of us. Susan and I put on brave faces as we congratulated our friends, but it was not easy. That problem resolved when I interrupted my training at the end of second year to go to Washington as a commissioned officer in the public health service. It is no accident that Susan got pregnant within two months after I left the residency.

* * *

At MMHC, we did not rely solely on medication and psychotherapy. Electroconvulsive treatment (ECT), a.k.a. shock therapy, can be dramatically successful for suicidal patients, or for patients with severe major depression who do not respond to medication and psychotherapy. One of my patients suffered from intractable severe depression, called melancholia when it occurs in late life. These patients maintain a sad affect, have no energy, often weep quietly, stop eating, either sleep all the time or have terrible insomnia, feel hopeless, and are convinced that life is not worth living. They are preoccupied with thoughts of suicide or death, typically more acutely in the morning. ECT, now controversial in some quarters, worked well then and still works well for some severely depressed patients. Julia Shaughnessy (not her real name), the aforementioned patient with melancholia, was a seventy-two-year-old grandmother whom we treated with ECT. She improved greatly, and for a change, we knew exactly why. Psychotherapy never touched her, but ECT cured her.

Typically, we would give patients ECT three times a week for twelve or fewer treatments. Following a course of ECT, most patients returned to baseline, and after three or four treatments, Julia began to come back to life. She took an interest in her surroundings; she began to talk and eat and no longer looked so sad. We saw the emergence of a bright, lively woman, engaged with her children and grandchildren, eager to go home and resume her life. To witness the effect of ECT in a patient like Julia was to witness what looked like a miracle.

The good news is that ECT works really well for severely depressed patients like Julia. The bad news is that even now, eighty years after it was introduced, we don't know how or why it works. We only know that in some cases it does, and we are grateful for that. We hope that future research will elucidate the process in the central nervous system that produces this improvement. ECT is also effective for terminating episodes of acute suicidality and episodes of acute delirious mania, but it is not an effective treatment for schizophrenia.

ECT has one common side effect: many patients experience short-term memory deficits during and immediately after a course of ECT. For most, this is reversible, and the ability to learn new information returns quickly. A small percentage of patients experience continuing deficits in long-term memory. The reason for this is unclear but may reflect some other underlying brain pathology. Modifying the treatment technique minimizes both long- and short-term memory deficits. Julia's ECT did not appear to affect her memory.

Repeated citizen campaigns during the 1980s claimed that ECT caused brain damage, including damage in the ability to retrieve memories. There has never been any scientific confirmation of this. Nevertheless, partly as a result of Ken Kesey's book *One Flew Over the Cuckoo's Nest* and the film made from it, ECT became politicized, and many patients who could have benefited never had the opportunity to make the choice. Berkeley, California, passed a city ordinance banning ECT within the city limits, but a judge invalidated the law within a year. Fortunately, this political pressure abated, and ECT is again viewed as a valuable part of the psychiatric armamentarium. It always was, and still is, an effective treatment for melancholia. However, many patients are reluctant to undergo ECT. The risks associated with anesthesia and anxiety about the treatment have dissuaded many from choosing ECT. Regrettably, there is no evidence that treating melancholia with medication instead of ECT is as effective. Nevertheless, many patients prefer to rely on SSRI antidepressants (trade names: Prozac, Zoloft, Paxil, and many others) as their first-line treatment for any depression.

As with any treatment that has the power for good, ECT also has the power to do harm, and we first-year residents had clear evidence of this. In the 1960s, there was a local hospital—now long closed, thankfully—that relied exclusively on ECT as a treatment for everything. One of the patients on our ward at MMHC was a woman in her early twenties who had received more than 300 ECT treatments at this hospital. She had become no better than a zombie. To see her walking around the ward knowing there was nothing we could do for her was one of the saddest experiences of that year. As psychiatrists, we have helped a great many people with very painful illnesses and experiences; but let no reader imagine that psychiatry has not also caused harm.

* * *

Working with outpatients in my second year of residency, I listened to these patients without the anxiety I had experienced with psychotic patients during my first year of training. The outpatients were typically healthier, often with a history of early abuse or neglect. For these patients, psychodynamic psychotherapy was an appropriate, potentially helpful treatment.

I saw each outpatient for a fifty-minute hour, typically once a week. Most were people who could describe their symptoms and give a reasonably clear history. I learned that patients felt helped when I conveyed that I had understood how they felt about their experience. At this early stage in my career, my capacity for empathy was limited. I wasn't always sure how patients felt about what they were telling me. When uncertain, I asked myself: "If I had experienced what this patient has just related, how would I feel?" Figuring that, as two human beings, we were likely to have at least approximately similar emotional responses, I would hazard a response. This usually seemed to work. Later, when I developed more capacity for empathy, I developed a better sense of what the person in front of me was feeling. In my later clinical teaching, I would teach the residents to distinguish this proto-empathy from true empathy. Alcoholics Anonymous teaches, "Fake it till you make it," and this applied well to my process of becoming an empathetic listener.

In the clinic, I saw some patients for whom the psychoanalytic instruction to "say whatever comes into your mind," with my sitting back and listening, made no sense at all. Charles O'Connor, a man in his mid-twenties, was both anxious and depressed. He had lost his job driving a maintenance vehicle at the airport, and as far as he was concerned, that was what brought him to the clinic. In our initial interview, he came across as a person of few words—not at all psychologically minded. Over the next few appointments, we sat looking at each other in almost total silence. I waited for him to talk, and he waited for me to ask questions.

Finally, one day he told me he had lost his job because he had brushed a plane with his vehicle. No apparent damage had been done, but he had committed the one unforgivable airport sin—touching a plane with a vehicle—and he was instantly fired. Then, and only then, was the source of his anxiety and depression clear. We had basically wasted each other's time for weeks! Once I understood why he was symptomatic, I was able to suggest that the source of his distress was not the loss of his job, but it was the guilt and self-reproach he had heaped on himself because of what he had done. With that understanding, his symptoms improved; he returned to baseline and went on his way. I saw that the psychodynamic therapy technique I'd been taught was good for some patients, but not for someone like him, a working-class man who was concrete about his complaints and ideas, and who expected and valued a therapist who could respond in kind.

I also worked with Willy Norton, an African-American man in his forties who was quite depressed. Medicine and a supportive relationship with me appeared to be what he needed. As he got better, he invited me to come to the barbecue restaurant where he cooked so that he could give me lunch. Psychoanalytic theory would have strictly prohibited any such social contact with a patient, but I thought it was important to Willy that I accept. The barbecue was great, and Willy was pleased to cook for me, primarily as a way of thanking me for my help, but also to show me that he too performed socially useful work. This was one of the experiences that taught me that being accessible as a person was an important characteristic of a good therapist—the opposite of psychoanalytic neutrality—especially with patients who were not particularly psychologically minded. This realization changed my understanding and my practice.

Willy taught me a new word that I loved then and love still. Speaking of his two older sisters who treated him like a child, he told me, "They babify me." How much more expressive is 'babify' than 'infantilize!' It's a simple example, but it taught me that one of the pleasures of psychiatry is the unexpected things you learn from patients.

Looking back at my residency, I am both appalled and nostalgic—appalled at how badly we misunderstood psychotic illness, but nostalgic as I remember how naïvely earnest we were in our efforts to help. Fortunately for our patients, our goodwill and commitment to them came through. As first-year residents, the many hours we spent with our patients helped teach us to relate to very sick people with sympathy and understanding. There is no substitute for this—no shortcut that can teach what we learned. Regrettably, twenty-first-century training seldom includes time for the long-term work with patients that helps new psychiatrists build these capabilities.

* * *

I have written this account of my residency as if I had been hermetically sealed in a cocoon, uninfluenced by any outside events. That was true for a time, and then, suddenly, it wasn't. The war in Vietnam changed things for many of us. In October of 1965, when I was a second-year resident, President Lyndon Johnson announced that the government would draft 14,000 doctors for service in the expanding war in Vietnam. Any male between the ages of eighteen and thirty-five, including any physician, was eligible for the draft. The government recognized, however, the value in allowing physicians to complete their postgraduate training before serving in the military, and it offered a deal. A physician who signed up with the government was guaranteed time to finish his postgraduate training. In return, he agreed to serve two years in the military, and the military agreed that he would be assigned as a specialist in his area. Many physicians in training took advantage of this offer and signed. I did not, so I was at risk of being drafted.

From early on, many Americans, myself included, were strongly opposed to the war in Vietnam. Personally and professionally, I wished to avoid service as a general duty medical officer in Vietnam. Fortunately, an alternative existed. The government offered a small number of appointments as commissioned officers in the United States Public Health Service (USPHS) to substitute for military service. These positions were highly desirable and quite competitive. The great advantage of this program to the federal government was that it brought into federal service bright, highly trained physicians who would otherwise not have been interested.

Certain employees at the National Institute of Mental Health (NIMH) and the Job Corps "owned" these commissions, meaning that they could offer a commission to a desirable applicant. I was fortunate to be offered a position at NIMH at a critical moment in the agency's history. For the first time, in 1963, the federal government took some responsibility for mental health services in our country. Until then, only states or smaller governmental units provided public mental health care.

I signed on as a commissioned officer in the USPHS to begin July 1, 1966, after my second year of residency. Susan and I left our Cambridge apartment and the familiar world of Harvard academia to move to Washington, D.C., and a new life, where I began a new job in a new organization. I was excited at the prospect but also quite apprehensive about this new experience. As it developed, my two years at NIMH would be positively life-changing.

#####

PART TWO

A WORKING PSYCHIATRIST

CHAPTER 9

THE FEDERAL GOVERNMENT ACTS

I could not have anticipated the shift in status I experienced immediately upon joining the federal government. On June 30, 1966, I was a second-year psychiatry resident in Cambridge, Massachusetts, occupying one of the lowest rungs on the hospital and academic medical ladder. The next day, at the age of thirty-one, I became Chief of Program Analysis and Evaluation for the mental health services branch of the services division at the National Institute of Mental Health (NIMH). I became both a respected section chief with a staff of three and a commissioned senior surgeon in the United States Public Health Service, equivalent to a lieutenant commander in the U.S. Navy, obligated to serve two years.

I had interviewed the previous October for a position as staff psychiatrist, and Bert Brown, the chief of the branch administering the program, was my last interview of the day. Bert told me he was sorry that I was not eligible to be a staff psychiatrist because I had not completed my residency.

In the course of my day visiting NIMH, I'd learned how the CMHC program was working—and how, in one way, it was not working at all. I'd discovered that the government knew very little about how it was spending the money authorized for this highly visible program. The only aggregate data the government kept was how much money had been awarded in each state. All other information about the funded programs existed as paper records, and these had to be manually searched each time a request for information came in. If, for example, a rural congressman asked how many rural centers had received grants, or if the secretary of Health Education and Welfare asked how many general hospitals had received awards, the entire secretarial staff would be mobilized to review every successful application in order to retrieve the information. While this was going on, almost all other work stopped. These requests came in two or three times a week, with the result that the division did almost no work on its primary task, reviewing new applications in order to decide whether they should be funded.

When Bert told me that I was not eligible for the position, I was momentarily crushed; but then I had a possibly career-saving thought. I could see that the program needed a good database, so I said to Bert, "You don't know what you are spending your money on. I can help you with that." Bert sat straight up and said, "That changes this whole interview." I went on to share my observation of how the division was repeatedly immobilized by their lack of data, and how I could address that. I told him about my experience working on a survey research project during two college summers at the Association of American Medical Colleges, and I explained that I could use my knowledge of the technology to develop a searchable database that his program could use to answer all these requests. Bert immediately offered me a position as a commissioned officer in the United States Public Health Service on the spot, exempting me from military service.

In 1966, when I joined, NIMH was less than twenty years old. The National Mental Health Act of 1946 had called for the establishment of a National Institute of Mental Health, and in 1949 the federal government created NIMH. The NIMH mission was to foster research into the causes of mental illness and to support training for psychiatrists and other mental health professionals. There was no federal mandate at the time for the provision of civilian mental health services; rather, these were provided by the states.

Fourteen years later, in 1963, this changed: Congress passed laws authorizing funding for the construction and staffing of Community Mental Health Centers (CMHCs). This was landmark legislation, representing the first ever federal funding for mental health services for civilians, and NIMH became responsible for monitoring the CMHC program. The CMHCs would provide comprehensive mental health services to the American public. This groundbreaking legislation quickly became the signature program of NIMH, and it was this new program that I joined on July 1, 1966.

The program was firmly grounded in a public health approach to psychiatry, with each CMHC taking responsibility for the mental health needs of the population in a defined "catchment area." Each CMHC was expected to serve people who were severely and persistently mentally ill, rather than the healthier members of the community. Unlike a private practice, in which a psychiatrist can decide to devote their entire professional energy to treating a few relatively healthy patients, public health programs must focus their limited resources on the needs of underserved, severely ill people. This approach was consistent with my own social-political values, and I energetically embraced the program and my role in it.

The program mandated that each community mental health center offer five essential services: inpatient care, outpatient care, emergency care, partial hospital capabilities, and consultation to caregivers in the community, e.g. clergy, social service workers, and others.

In 1966, the federal regulations governing CMHCs required each state, before they could apply for CMHC money, to make an initial plan that divided the state into catchment areas, each with a population of between 75,000 and 250,000 people. After the federal government certified these state plans, health care organizations within any catchment area could apply for CMHC money to construct and/or staff a center. A funding applicant could be one organization or a consortium of as many local organizations as were necessary to provide the five essential services.

In my first month on the job, I was expected to learn what a CMHC was and additionally what a potential applicant needed to do to apply for federal money. Learning this, I became, almost instantly, a national expert on community mental health. Six weeks after joining NIMH, I chaired a national working group on community mental health. Jack Ewalt, my old boss from

Massachusetts Mental Health Center, was a member of that committee. I was more than a little concerned about how Ewalt might take this new relationship, but I might have spared myself the anxiety: Ewalt loved seeing one of his own in this leadership role. I think Ewalt saw himself as inseminating the world with his former residents, and for him, this was just the latest, dramatic example of the process.

Within a few months of arriving at NIMH, I had also set up the proposed database. My staff put all the necessary information onto punch cards that our IBM electromechanical counter could read and count. We had the new information system up and running, and it served its purpose well. With a few instructions to our IBM-based system, we could answer any question put to us, and we were able to provide information quickly to those who needed it. The secretaries could go back to doing their essential secretarial work, and the division could function as it should. I'd come to NIMH to do a particular job, and I'd done it quickly and efficiently. With this service operational, Bert Brown expanded my role to be a staff psychiatrist and a member of the NIMH staff that administered the CMHC program.

I was able to hire my own staff. My first interview was with a woman named Selma Goldblatt, whom I wanted as my senior staff person. She had a relevant work history, and she impressed me as a quietly competent person—modest, even self-effacing—and I thought that I could work with her. I offered her the job, and she accepted, although I almost lost her before she started. Selma needed a job because her physician husband had died recently and suddenly of pancreatic cancer, and Selma was left to raise her son Eli, aged four, alone. As the civil service hiring procedure dragged on, Selma became increasingly anxious. I encouraged her to wait out the bureaucratic delay. Fortunately for both of us, she did.

As we worked together, I grew to appreciate her more and more. She was well organized and had good sense about prioritizing our work. Equally importantly, she was a wonderful ambassador for our small section. She made friends throughout the institute as she negotiated whatever help we needed to fulfill our mission. I could not have done it without her. After I served my two years, Selma stayed on, rising through the ranks to become a senior administrator until she retired many years later.

* * *

The move to the D.C. area was a good one for our family. With our new life in Washington—I worked eight-hour days, and Susan and I shared warm, leisurely nights—Susan became pregnant less than two months after we arrived. As the wife of a commissioned officer in the public health service, Susan was eligible to receive federal health services. She registered for obstetric care at the National Naval Medical Center, an easy walk from our rented, first-ever house in Bethesda, Maryland.

The care was excellent. Susan's doctor, Walter Lonergan, was the chief of the obstetrics service. Taking a history from his new patient, Dr. Lonergan discovered that Susan had been a fourth-grade pupil of his younger brother. For whatever reason, this meant a great deal to him, and we soon saw that Susan had become a special patient. Dr. Lonergan was important to us, but he was also important in the federal health system. He had delivered President Johnson's grandson, and we were excited that he would deliver our child as well. But that almost did not happen because Dr. Lonergan was scheduled to be on leave when Susan was due. To our amazement, he came in from his annual leave in order to deliver our daughter. The delivery went smoothly, and in June 1967, we had a healthy baby girl whom we named Deborah.

Susan shared a double room with another new mother. Visiting hours were liberal, and I came every day. Just about every time I walked into the room I broke into laughter; Susan would join me, but the woman in the next bed could not understand what was so funny. What was so funny was the handwritten message at the foot of each bed. For each new mother, staff recorded religion and feeding. "Jewish breast" spoke to us from a long heritage of Jewish mother jokes. We explained this to the "Protestant breast" woman in the next bed, but she still didn't think it was that funny. Our bill for the entire experience: labor, delivery, and a week in hospital was eight dollars!

Our family life as young parents was idyllic. Susan's time and energy were hers to do with as she wished, and she devoted them to Deborah. She loved being a mother. Our good friends from Cambridge, Roger and Sheila Meyer were in Washington, where Roger was also a commissioned officer in the Public Health Service. Their first child, Tobie, had been born six weeks before Deborah. Susan and Sheila often walked together, pushing their carriages to the park, or to one of Washington's many museums. Other times they just sat together, doing handwork and talking. Our two families developed a close friendship that persists to this day.

When Deborah was old enough to crawl, Susan volunteered for the 1968 presidential campaign of Eugene McCarthy. She was one of a group of women volunteers who sat at a table filling out three-by-five index cards to identify possible supporters of the candidate. In the pre-internet era, this was how candidates developed a database of their supporters. This was Susan's initial volunteer political work, and it was this experience she would draw on four years later in assuming a larger and more responsible role in George McGovern's presidential campaign when we were back in Massachusetts.

As for me, my life felt almost comically easy. A nine-to-five job, using skills I already had, was like a perpetual vacation. I commuted to work three miles down Wisconsin Avenue, riding my bicycle to an anonymous office building on the D.C.-Bethesda line. I made one good friend, Lee, a career civil servant who was my contemporary. As he watched me slowly learn what I needed to know about federal procedures and regulations, he taught me how to negotiate successfully to get things done.

In the 1960s, it was common for people to drink in professional settings more heavily than they would now. Lee and I often went out to lunch, and frequently lunch began with a martini... or occasionally, two martinis. After the two-martini lunches, I would sit zoned out at my desk until it was time to go home. Our favorite lunch was at a local place that made good martinis and excellent pizza. At these alcohol-fueled lunches, Lee provided valuable tutorials that taught me lessons I would remember and apply later in my tenure and beyond.

To a fly on the wall, observing me after one of these two-martini lunches, it would have appeared that I was just putting in time, but that was not the case: I cared deeply about my work. I saw that I was part of a mission to bring integrated, affordable mental health care to people who needed it most, and who had access to little or none. My responsibility to help health care professionals and organizations across the country develop CMHCs gave me a profound sense of accomplishment that carried me over the frustrations that occur in any large organization.

* * *

I was pleased that I did not have to give up clinical practice completely while I was at NIMH. The federal government recognized that doctors need to see patients in order to be happy, so although I was employed as a program analyst and staff psychiatrist, I was permitted one half day a week to do clinical work in a government health care facility of my choice. I chose to spend my clinical time at the National Institutes of Health (NIH) employees' health clinic, a clinic serving an industrial community of 10,000 people.

For four hours a week, I was a psychiatrist in a community clinic, and I saw patients with a broad range of psychiatric problems: patients with headaches, sleeping problems, and mild depression. I saw patients with anxieties related to their soma, their psyche, their social relationships, or all three.

I was on my own, expected to develop my own understanding of my patients and make my own treatment plans. No one asked me to provide psychodynamic formulations of my patients and their problems, which was a welcome change. Instead, I treated my patients as I saw fit. As I'd learned working with Charles and Willy in the outpatient service at Massachusetts Mental Health Clinic (MMHC), there were patients for whom a psychodynamic

113

understanding was not helpful. Here, for most patients, a concrete approach focused on current problems, coupled with appropriate medication, was the treatment of choice.

My clinical work was influenced by the experiences I had on the ground as I consulted at a variety of psychiatric facilities around the country During these visits, I saw psychiatrists with a down-to-earth understanding of treatment providing meaningful services to their patients, in many cases without any knowledge of psychoanalysis. This was a sharp contrast to the exclusively psychoanalytic approach that my supervisors had encouraged at MMHC. This experience taught me the value of starting with a practical approach to problems and helped me to develop my approach to the practice of psychiatry—one that I have retained to this day.

* * *

NIMH staff, myself included, played a critical role in helping community health facilities develop successful applications for federal CMHC money. My colleagues and I traveled through the country meeting potential applicants and helping them understand the clinical services they were required to provide, and we suggested how they might organize their local resources to write a fundable proposal. My background as a physician proved particularly useful when I consulted with potential applicants who were physician-administrators—some doctors really only want to talk to other doctors about medical business.

I had a lot to learn in my new position. First, I had to know about community mental health, but learning that was quick and easy; second, I needed to understand how to function in a large organization, and I had more trouble with that. In addition to the central office in Washington, NIMH had eight regional offices around the country. The regional office staff were responsible for knowing the mental health issues that were important locally, having working relationships with local mental health resources—people, organizations, and activities—and for determining how NIMH should relate to them.

We central office staff were required to coordinate our visits with regional office staff in advance, a policy I viewed initially with disdain. I protested that this was a free country and that I could go anywhere I wanted. "Well, no, you can't," senior staff repeatedly and firmly told me. They finally beat it into my head that for the regional office to do its job, I had to clear my visits with them. Once I learned this, my working relationships with the regional offices improved, and my work consulting with prospective applicants went smoothly. Few visitors are more welcome at a health care facility or an academic department of psychiatry than a federal official with potential access to large amounts of money. I was warmly welcomed everywhere I went.

Early on, I saw the value of community mental health centers as training sites, and I thought that leading psychiatry departments should expand their focus beyond psychoanalysis and apply for CMHC money. I also noticed that relatively few applications were coming in from the Northeast. To address this, I arranged through my contacts in the regional office to consult with academic psychiatry departments in Boston and New York. I made a pitch to them about the value of including community mental health in their training and service mission, and several departments subsequently submitted successful proposals. In later years, these were among the leading academic departments to develop a strong community orientation.

Independent of my efforts, the push to create CMHCs touched MMHC. In the 1960s, MMHC functioned as a referral hospital. Much like a private practice, it could choose whom to admit and whom not, with no responsibility for any sick person it chose to turn away. The Massachusetts Department of Mental Health put pressure on MMHC to become a CMHC. Through the grapevine, I heard that Jack Ewalt had said, "I'll be fucked if I'll serve a catchment area." Ultimately, he accepted this responsibility in the face of new demands for service, and MMHC developed a strong commitment to the community.

The pressures on MMHC were repeated all over the country. After the introduction of Thorazine and other new antipsychotic medications, many state hospital patients became well enough to be discharged. This "deinstitutionalization" meant that state hospitals discharged many patients without any plan for follow-up treatment. Patients were given bus tickets into the city and told, "Go to the local mental health facility." Suddenly, there was an onslaught of new, sick patients in the community. In response, many institutions, including MMHC, applied for CMHC money for the services needed to care for these patients.

In 1964-65, John Mack had been my ward chief during my first year of residency at MMHC, but now, in 1967, he was responsible for organizing psychiatry at Cambridge City Hospital as a Harvard teaching service. By 1967, I knew I wanted to make a career in community psychiatry. Working in a CMHC would offer the possibility of integrating my social and political values

116

about access to health care with my professional work. When John visited Washington for a professional meeting, I asked to meet with him, and we did meet—in his hotel room one evening at 11:00. I proposed that when my two-year tour of duty ended, I would return to finish my residency at MMHC but be assigned full time to Cambridge City Hospital, with the goal of creating a CMHC for Cambridge and Somerville. John was excited by this possibility. He saw it as an important step in establishing a Harvard department of psychiatry at the hospital, and he said yes. (This meant that I was headed for the same Cambridge City Hospital where inadequate care had killed my asthma patient in 1964. By 1967, it had greatly changed for the better.)

After that meeting, I devoted some of my time and energy—not to mention government resources—to learning how to create a successful CMHC. I made several discretionary visits around the country—discretionary in that no superior had requested them—in order to find models that I might adapt to Cambridge. After one such visit, I learned to never again trust a published report of how an organization functioned, but to see for myself whenever possible.

The chief of a new mental health center in the Midwest had written a long article, published in the *Archives of General Psychiatry*, describing his new facility and praising it as an example of a new systematic way to provide mental health services to the severely and persistently mentally ill. Since that was just what I wanted to do, I arranged a visit. One of the strengths of this new organization, he explained, was that staff members were constantly evaluating and re-evaluating their performance in order to render better services to their patients. He invited me into a staff meeting and arranged for me to observe a clinical encounter.

In the staff meeting, I learned that the staff's attitude was quite different from what the article described. Staff explained to me that because what they were doing was so new, outsiders would not understand it. This ideology led them to reject any outside question or concern about their practice. The group had sealed itself off from any possible critical observations. This attitude was bad, but the clinical intervention I witnessed was worse.

A couple, much like the rural people John Steinbeck's *Grapes of Wrath*, had come to the center with their minister in the hope of regaining custody of their child whom the system had removed. The parents presented their request earnestly; the distress at the loss of their child was palpable and, to me, heartrending. Everything about them, from their presentation as suffering parents to their speech as they made their request, seemed fine. There was nothing about these people to suggest that they needed antipsychotic medication.

The clinician with whom they met focused entirely on whether they were taking the medicine the center had prescribed. The couple did not want to discuss medicine—they wanted to talk about their child. As the interview continued, I saw no evidence of psychosis and no obvious need for medicine. As far as I could see, the parents made perfect sense. Their minister appeared to share my view, and he made it clear to the clinician that he was present to support his parishioners. When he tried to intercede on their behalf, the clinician ignored him, and the stalemate continued. The parents' pleas grew more desperate, but this clinician just continued to insist that they take their medicine. Finally, in despair, the minister terminated the interview, and the three walked out. The clinician described this afterwards as just one more example of how outside people did not understand what the center was trying to do. In his view, the patients were the problem. This memory still troubles me. To me, it is Exhibit A for how psychiatry can do harm while believing it is doing good.

I also visited the Harry Solomon CMHC in Lowell, Massachusetts. This center, named after a former Commissioner of Mental Health and later a professor and chair at the Boston Psychopathic Hospital, had received one of the earliest construction grants. This was a state facility, as Massachusetts law at the time required that all matching federal funding go to state facilities. The center, which was less than 100 yards from the local community hospital, had been serving patients for more than a year when I visited in 1968. Staff were justly proud of the work they were doing, and I was impressed.

I also wanted to know how well the center had integrated its own resources with those of the neighboring general hospital. I visited the hospital and learned to my great surprise that no one at the hospital knew anything about the new center. The center might just as well have been on Mars, as far as the local medical community was concerned. Later, I confirmed that center staff had made no effort to communicate with that hospital or, indeed, with any other providers. Looking ahead to my expected return to Cambridge, I vowed that I would write a proposal for the Cambridge-Somerville CMHC that would correct this error. I was determined to deeply embed the proposed new organization in the existing health care structure.

In my last few months at NIMH, I went outside usual professional boundaries in an attempt to change an institution that I cared deeply about. Bert Brown, with whom I'd interviewed in 1965, was now the deputy director of NIMH. The man who replaced him as acting chief of the CMHC program branch was a nice man, but someone I'd come to think of as a "faceless bureaucrat," a long-serving, risk-averse federal employee. To my dismay, I watched as his inherent caution led him to postpone one critical decision after another. I saw the program slowing to a point at which new applicants were not reviewed in a timely fashion or were not reviewed at all. When this wasn't done, no applicant got any money. This meant no new CMHCs. In my view, this was intolerable.

I was and am an activist. When I see something wrong, I try to fix it. By early 1968, I saw that the program was in danger, and I requested an off-the-record meeting with Bert. I went to his office late one afternoon and shared my concerns. Bert asked me to write a memo and send it directly to him, bypassing the usual channels, and I did as he asked. Within several weeks, the acting chief of the CMHC branch was removed, and one of the other young commissioned officer psychiatrists was appointed as branch chief. He proved to be an effective leader.

* * *

Late in my tenure, the civil rights movement had begun to organize the protest movement that included the Poor People's March on Washington. In May 1968, 10,000 poor, mostly black Americans descended on Washington, much to the dismay of the

White House and Congress. The marchers set up a community of 3,000 tents on the National Mall, where they lived for several weeks. During the day, members of the community scattered throughout Washington to lobby members of the government. At the end of the day, they returned to their tent community, which they had named "Resurrection City."

At this time, an informal pipeline existed between Harvard Medical School and NIH, and as a result, quite a few of the young commissioned officer psychiatrists had known each other in Boston. We were mostly politically liberal and supportive of the aims of the march. We came together informally and developed a plan to provide mental health services on the Mall for the residents of Resurrection City while it existed.

I was one of the psychiatrists who were on site duty evenings and weekends. My experience was largely routine, but one encounter escalated dramatically. While the occupants of the tents were away lobbying during the day, an acutely psychotic patient, who appeared to be suffering from schizophrenia, moved into one of the A-frame tents. He told us he had just left St. Elizabeth's, the federal mental hospital. He hung a small, multi-colored ball of yarn high on the tent's wooden frame, announcing that this was his flag, and that he was taking possession of the tent in its name.

My psychiatrist colleague and I engaged the patient in conversation, hoping to help him decide to leave, but we got nowhere. Finally, we called for the police on duty, two of whom came over. The three men engaged in a discussion. The captain was leaning one elbow casually on the horizontal bar of the A-frame. Suddenly, the captain's holster was empty, and the psychotic patient was holding his gun. I told my colleague that this was

121

now a police matter in which psychiatrists had no place, and I left, backpedaling for 100 yards or so until I judged it safe to turn my back. My colleague thought that we continued to have a role, and he stayed to watch the standoff. Ultimately, the police used mace to subdue the patient and return him to the hospital. No one was injured.

Another encounter illustrates differences between social conditions in the late 1960s and the twenty-first century. Only a few weeks had passed since the assassination of Rev. Dr. Martin Luther King, Jr., and Washington had been the scene of a major riot. Parts of the city had burned, and property destruction was widespread. The riot itself was over, but angry citizens still roamed the streets. Guns were not common in the way they are now. People were angry, but they rarely shot each other.

A man came into our health station requesting help for someone in the city, and it sounded serious. An African American nurse wearing a Red Cross armband and I prepared to go. We simply plunged into the city, walking among the milling crowds, to look for our man. It never occurred to me to be frightened. I thought of us as two health care professionals doing our job. We never found our prospective patient, and we returned to the Mall without incident. This story partly reflects the naïve optimism of youth, or at least my youth, but it also reflects real change between then and now.

* * *

I had changed as a result of my two years in the CMHC program, but sadly, American society's commitment to the severely persistent

122

mentally ill had not. Beginning in the 1970s, diminishing federal CMHC grants slowly fell to zero. As available federal funding for CMHCs declined, local governments did not find the resources to keep these centers running, and largely allowed them to close. As a result, many state hospital patients who had been discharged with the expectation of receiving community care were cast adrift. Large numbers of people with severe mental illness became homeless, and many thousands went to jail because society had no other place to send them. But this occurred after my stint working for the federal government was over.

As my own tour of duty was nearing its end, I was satisfied that my two years at NIMH had been well spent. I could leave Washington pleased that I had made a contribution to the nation's health while at the same time finding a new direction for myself professionally. This was a direction that would prove to be profoundly satisfying and that would continue through my professional life.

#####

CHAPTER 10

PUBLIC PSYCHIATRY COMES TO CAMBRIDGE

A 21st-century resident of Cambridge could barely imagine the Cambridge to which I returned in 1968. Then, East Cambridge had large areas of abandoned 19th- and early 20th-century factories and warehouses. These would disappear to be replaced in the 21st century by gleaming high-rise research buildings as the area around MIT morphed into an international center of pharmaceutical and neurobiological research.

Large areas of the city were solid, traditional working-class neighborhoods in which the process of 'flipping' housing and converting it into middle- and upper-class condos had barely begun. As residents died or moved away, putting their properties on the market, these sales would transform the city. The neighboring city of Somerville was much like Cambridge, only with more poverty and fewer resources. No Harvard—no MIT. As Cambridge became increasingly expensive, gentrification would begin here also. Startups would take advantage of the low rents, and Somerville would begin to change.

In Cambridge in 1968, there were no public psychiatry services. This changed as Cambridge City Hospital opened a small, Harvard-affiliated psychiatry service. I had come to join this service, with the hope of developing a community mental health center based at the hospital. This is that story.

* * *

Friday, June 28, 1968: I was discharged from the United States Public Health Service and left Washington, D.C.

Monday, July 1, 7:30 a.m.: I dropped my wife and daughter at our prospective new home in Lexington, Massachusetts, and left them on the front porch to wait for the movers while I bought the house and then a car.

Monday, July 1, 10:30 a.m.: business done, I joined a psychiatry staff meeting at Cambridge City Hospital. I was finishing my third year of residency at the Massachusetts Mental Health Center (MMHC), and at my request I was assigned full time to the new psychiatry service at Cambridge City Hospital.

Cambridge City Hospital had changed radically since the patient I'd treated as an intern died. After the NBC White Paper that drew national attention to the abysmal patient care the hospital provided, the Cambridge City Council approached Harvard's president about the possibility of affiliating with the hospital. In the 1960s, Harvard had a strong sense of its responsibility to the nation—educating presidents and senior government officials—but no real sense of responsibility to the local community. Harvard Medical School saw its mission as training future leaders of the medical profession, not providing health care for local people, and Harvard's president turned down the offer flat.

The city council turned to Tufts University and asked whether its medical school would affiliate with the Cambridge City Hospital. Tufts said yes. Interested third parties then went to the president of Harvard and said, essentially, "It is a disgrace for another university to affiliate with a hospital that is just down the street. Please reconsider." Harvard did reconsider, and in 1965, Cambridge City Hospital became the first primary care hospital with which Harvard affiliated. Until then, all of Harvard's core teaching hospitals were tertiary care institutions.

For reference, primary care hospitals provide general medical care to a community. Secondary care hospitals are regional facilities that provide more specialized care to a wider area. Tertiary care hospitals are more specialized yet, as they provide sub-specialist care to an even larger region. They are often affiliated with a medical school and serve an even larger area, admitting many patients on referral from primary or secondary care providers.

In later years, Cambridge City Hospital morphed into the Cambridge Hospital, and still later into the Cambridge Health Alliance, but the hospital has always remained a primary care community hospital for the people of Cambridge, Somerville, and neighboring communities. The irony of Harvard's reluctant affiliation is that Cambridge Hospital became a unique jewel in the Harvard Medical teaching diadem. The medical school experimented with innovations in clinical teaching at the hospital that were later adopted at the Harvard tertiary care hospitals and eventually across the country, where they are known as the Harvard-Cambridge Integrated Clerkship. Even to this day, when fourth-year medical school students at Harvard apply for internships and residencies, they choose Cambridge more often than any one of the larger, more prestigious tertiary care hospitals affiliated with the medical school.

The new affiliation created opportunities for new psychiatric training. In 1965, MMHC sent its first psychiatry resident, a Harvard Medical School student named Ed Khantzian, to Cambridge City Hospital. Although still a resident, Ed functioned as a consulting psychiatrist, and he proved to be an excellent ambassador from Harvard to the hospital.

I first met Ed when we were both fourth-year medical students. Writing this book, I would learn that Ed was the son of Armenian immigrants. His father, Hovaness, emigrated before the genocide, but his mother, Nuvart, lived through it, surviving the forced marches because a Turkish pasha saw her and made her his slave.

Hovaness and Nuvart eventually met and married in Marseilles. Later, they settled in Haverhill, Massachusetts, where they both worked in a shoe factory, and Americanized their names to John and Rose. After John lost his job because of his union activism, Rose used a small settlement from an auto accident to purchase a neighborhood variety store.

The parents spoke Armenian to each other. Ed spoke English with his father and Armenian with his mother. The whole family worked in the store, which made little money, and the family was poor. John suffered as a storekeeper, developing angina and dying within a year, when Ed was sixteen. He and his mother took over the store.

Ed was bright and ambitious. Through one of his customers he met a local minister, a charismatic man who was trained as a psychotherapist. Ed thought, "I want to do what he does, and I want to make a good living." A local physician, also a customer, advised Ed to go to medical school, and become a psychiatrist if he wanted to be a psychotherapist. Ed was often late to high school because of his morning hours at the store and, after his father's death, he was a marginal student. The principal told Ed, "Either get to school on time or run the store." Somehow Ed did both. After high school, Ed continued his education, attending college in the evening the first three years, while working in the store. He graduated from college and then applied to ten medical schools, but every one rejected him. He got good advice before applying again, and he began Albany Medical School in 1959.

Ed had opted to do an elective psychiatry rotation at MMHC, and he and I did our fourth-year medical school psychiatry together. I remember Ed as a bright, eager student who was clearly anxious about his first venture into the academic big leagues. He felt uncomfortable, imagining that all his fellow students came from circumstances far different from his. Several years later, we trained together as MMHC residents where Ed fit in just fine. Ed has been a good friend and valued colleague ever since.

With the exception of Ed's consulting, the hospital had no psychiatry services when our new team arrived in 1968. When police brought an acutely psychotic patient to the emergency room, the patient received a cursory evaluation from an ill-trained physician who had two choices: discharge the patient to the street, or when in doubt, commit him as an involuntary patient to the state hospital 35 miles away, which in 1968 was where

129

the state Department of Mental Health required Cambridge and Somerville patients to be hospitalized.[3] When I got to know the E.R., I imagined it as a room with a trap door in the middle of the floor. When a psychotic patient was brought in, the staff made a quick assessment, then opened the trap door, dropped the patient in, and sent them, seemingly in an instant, thirty-two miles away to the state hospital. If and when these unfortunates were ever discharged, there would be no public psychiatric services of any kind to help their re-entry into the community. At most, a patient might have a primary care physician who would, often reluctantly, look after them.

At the time, Cambridge was one of the few cities in the United States to have its own city health commissioner. In the three years before we arrived, the commissioner had led the hospital's plans for a new psychiatric service, working closely with John Mack and with me after I arrived. Beginning on July 1, 1968, we provided psychiatric services to the hospital 24 hours per day, 7 days per week, 365 days per year. I was the chief resident for outpatient and community services; my colleague, the one other full time resident, oversaw the inpatient services. In addition to our daytime responsibilities, the inpatient chief resident and I provided night and weekend coverage for our ward and for the hospital emergency room when a mentally ill person came in after hours. We also covered the entire hospital, responding to

---

3   As far as I am aware, no one ever went to a state hospital voluntarily. Massachusetts law required that a physician or a judge find that a person was a danger to himself or others by reason of mental illness as the basis on which to hospitalize a person involuntarily.

the inpatient nursing staff when they were dealing with a patient who was particularly difficult to manage.

We shared a thirty-bed inpatient ward with the "self-care" service, with eighteen beds for them and twelve for us. The inpatient chief resident was comfortable managing as many as eight patients, and so I managed three or four inpatients when the ward was full, in addition to my usual outpatient and community responsibilities. "Self-care" was a euphemism for a service for alcoholic patients who had medical problems that were no longer acute.

Over the first several months, I was pleased with how things were going: we were providing a critical service to our patients and building relationships inside and outside the hospital. Sadly, the tragic suicide of one of our patients brought us up short. He was a depressed and suicidal first-year Harvard law student whom we admitted to our joint psychiatry and self-care ward late on a Friday afternoon. I admitted him when I had another patient waiting at my office, so I took a quick history and did only a cursory mental status exam. The patient was clearly depressed, and he acknowledged that he was thinking of killing himself. I asked him whether he could agree to keep himself safe while he was in the hospital, and he agreed that he could. Although I wasn't sure I believed him, I left him in order to see my outpatient. On Saturday morning, John Mack made rounds with the chief resident for the inpatient service, but they gave this patient scant attention.

This might have been less of a problem if we hadn't been sharing space with the self-care service; but the head nurse on the self-care ward routinely left her diabetes testing kits out where patients had access to them. The psychiatry head nurse had repeatedly requested that she not do that, because the test kit contained a corrosive acid that, if swallowed, would cause severe stomach damage. The self-care nurse ignored those requests, apparently deliberately. On Saturday afternoon, our patient swallowed one of the diabetes testing tablets, then pried open a window and jumped out. We had long before requested that the hospital secure the windows, but the hospital had done a grossly inadequate job, as the windows could still be easily pried open with an ordinary table knife. The patient landed in soft dirt several floors below and sustained leg fractures from the fall. The fall did not kill him; rather, he died several weeks later from damage to his stomach that led to a massive abdominal infection.

At least five errors contributed to his death. I place first my inadequate evaluation. If I had not had a patient waiting, I believe I would have done a more careful assessment. Second was the failure of the Saturday morning team to do its own careful assessment. Third and fourth relate to the hospital failings that had immediate direct impacts: the availability of the corrosive acid he ingested and the inadequate window security. The fifth and last was a more intangible error. At this early stage in our department's development, we thought we could do everything. It never occurred to us that this patient might require a unit more secure than what we could provide. As a result of this avoidable patient death, we rethought whom we should admit and who needed more security than we could provide.

This death led to my first experience with the legal standards for the practice of psychiatry. The standards require that the physician must practice up to the level of competence shown by average practitioners in his field at that time and in that place. The family sued for malpractice, naming as defendants all the doctors involved in their son's care; alleging that we had breached the standard of care required of psychiatrists and that we were therefore legally liable for his death. Ultimately, the lawsuit was settled for an undisclosed amount with no acknowledgment of wrongdoing by the defendants. However, when I read the assessment of my care written by their expert, I was ashamed of myself and resolved never to put myself in that position again. To my knowledge, I never have. Since then, I have not hurried through an assessment of a patient, and I have never lost another patient through negligence. The quality of my work has never again been seriously questioned.

* * *

During my years as a student and intern, events in the outside world had made almost no impression on me. It was not quite true to say that I had existed in an academic bell jar, but almost. Living in Washington, I had re-entered the real world, so when I returned to Cambridge in 1968, I had some understanding of the profound social changes that had taken place in the United States—changes that directly affected me personally and that would affect our new department in ways that neither my colleagues nor I could anticipate.

By 1968, responses to the Vietnam War convulsed America. Americans who held traditional values supported the war, but large numbers of people opposed it. They saw the war as an immoral exercise in which a large, imperial country—the United States—

was seeking, in the name of anticommunism, to impose its will on a small country that had never done the U.S. any harm. Many opponents of the war believed that the President had lied to the country in order to create a pretext for American involvement—an involvement that was creating appalling numbers of American casualties, as well as Vietnamese dead and wounded.

As the war dragged on and casualties mounted, the divisions in the country only deepened. One reason for this was that government policy granted military deferments to all college students until they graduated. Working-class parents whose children did not go to college deeply resented this policy. Their children were at risk, while the children of the privileged were not.

For their part, many of these college students were increasingly enraged by the war and the imperialistic tendencies they thought it stood for. Protesting any involvement of the university with the war effort, Harvard students demanded that Harvard abolish the Reserve Officer Training Corps (ROTC). At the extreme left, Students for a Democratic Society espoused violence as a legitimate political technique—they wanted to blow up the ROTC building. College students at Columbia and at Harvard occupied the offices of their administrations. At Harvard, the university president called in the police to evict the students. This action further turned many students against the police and against the university administration.

This was the political climate when we began at Cambridge City Hospital, and we were very much a part of these events. Our department staff strongly opposed the war, and our political views influenced in important ways how our department functioned and how we engaged with the Cambridge community.

The organization of our inpatient ward reflected the distrust of authority. In a traditional psychiatric ward, the doctor is a virtual dictator who makes every decision involving patient care. They might listen to the nurses, and maybe, if particularly open minded, they would hear from one of the other ward staff before writing an order.

Our almost completely flat ward structure reflected our own distrust of authority. However, to paraphrase George Orwell's *Animal Farm*: all the animals were equal, but some were more equal than others. We considered that the opinions of all staff members were of equal value in reaching decisions about patient care, and our discussions in ward rounds reflected this. In the end, though, the doctor was legally responsible for the care of the patient, so he made the final decision. (Until 1975, our doctors were all men.) By the late 1970s, when the war was over and the country was in the throes of trying to put itself back together, our psychiatry ward administrative structure reverted to tradition: the doctor was in charge.

Until then, however, we continued to protest the war in ways that we saw fit—which were not, admittedly, the most fit. In May of 1970, students at Kent State University in Ohio staged a massive peaceful protest against the war. In response, the governor of Ohio called out the National Guard, and members of the guard shot and killed four students in what became known as the Kent State Massacre. The killing of these students provoked huge outrage on the anti-war left, particularly in universities, and led to further demonstrations in Cambridge. Students for a Democratic Society organized an anti-war rally at Harvard Stadium. We, the staff of our small psychiatry department, were among the outraged, and we resolved to go. We locked our ward and left one intern with no psychiatric experience as the sole physician in charge of our sick patients. This was professionally irresponsible and patently illegal. I am not proud of what we did, but we did it, and it is an example of how strongly the liberal left opposed the war. We walked over to the peaceful protest, participated, and walked back and resumed our professional responsibilities.

* * *

I came to Cambridge in July 1968 planning to finish my residency and expecting to write a proposal for a CMHC. The proposed CMHC would provide the federally mandated five essential mental health services, based out of the Cambridge City Hospital, where the sole existing service was minimal emergency assessment for patients.

From my work in Washington, I knew that federal funding for new centers would end in September of 1968 because the program would run out of money. Any application approved after that date would get a polite letter saying, "Approved but not funded."

Ordinarily, preparation of a CMHC application took between nine and eighteen months. I had just two months to meet the September deadline, but I had a head start since, after two years of reviewing applications, I knew what was required. Nevertheless, meeting this self-imposed deadline as well as caring for patients meant long nights and busy weekends, because knowing the federal requirements would not ensure a successful application.

John Mack and I forged relationships with people representing the five local organizations that were required to sign off on our proposal, if we were to have a successful review at NIMH. These were the Massachusetts Department of Mental Health (DMH), the volunteer community mental health association, the primary care physicians of Cambridge City Hospital, the city government of Cambridge, and, lastly, a bit player, the impoverished city of Somerville. We estimated correctly that Somerville would be grateful for anything we offered.

At that time, every new public mental health position in Massachusetts required DMH approval; in our case, this meant approval by the DMH area office for Cambridge and Somerville. I worked closely with the staff of this office to help them understand what our proposal meant for mental health services in Cambridge and Somerville. For the first time, the ordinary citizens of Cambridge and Somerville would have access to high-quality mental health services.

It was a federal requirement that the local community mental health association must sign off on any proposal. The head of that committee, Lawrence Feloney, was the chief judge of the Cambridge District Court. He was a man with longstanding ties in the community, and he was personally committed to the development of services to combat alcoholism. (Later, when I was the chief of the mental health clinic affiliated with the Cambridge District Court, my respect for Judge Feloney grew when he ruled that a woman who killed her abusive domestic partner should remain in the community with psychiatric treatment as a condition of this disposition, Ch. 14).

Alcohol services posed a particular problem—namely, that we were completely ignorant about how to treat alcohol disorders. The faculty who trained John and me were psychoanalysts who believed that psychiatrists had no business with alcoholics; in their view, alcoholism was *déclassé*.

Our ignorance would have been a serious problem but for the presence of the assistant director of the DMH area office, who was a professional with long experience treating alcoholism. She was able to reassure Judge Feloney that our new mental health center would provide services for alcoholics, and she taught us what we needed to know to provide those services. Under her leadership, we went on to develop a range of alcohol-related services, including a wet shelter that still exists in the twenty-first century.

The local primary care physicians were a more difficult constituency to satisfy. Before we arrived, they had practiced happily, innocent of any contact with psychiatry—and they were not sure they needed or wanted any. They saw our proposed service as another step in Harvard's takeover of patient care in Cambridge.

Since they had been entirely responsible for this care, their fears were justified; but they also recognized the huge unmet needs existed for those who were too sick or too poor to be treated by the psychoanalysts in Harvard Square. This recognition ultimately persuaded them that the new mental health center would be valuable for their patients, as well as for themselves, relieving them of a responsibility for which they were untrained, and which had always made them uncomfortable.

The City Council understood that this new service would ultimately cost the city money, despite our assurances that the federal government and the state DMH would pay the bills.

Like the local physicians, they thought Cambridge had gotten along just fine without psychiatry. They recognized that care at the hospital had improved greatly since Harvard had arrived, but they also represented the longstanding view that the University failed to pay taxes for many city services provided to it. The city health commissioner played the central role in convincing the city government that the new center would provide a valuable service that would be worth the money.

To achieve this consensus took many hours and many meetings. While this was going on, I was also writing our proposal and meeting my clinical responsibilities in the hospital. I managed to get it all done, just barely making the September deadline. To my great relief, we were approved for funding beginning on July 1, 1969. The language of the proposal ensured that, unlike the Lowell center I had visited when I worked at NIMH, our mental health center would be *of* the community, not just *in* the community.

In order to meet its responsibility to provide funding for all new mental health positions, the DMH converted some old state hospital positions to new positions. We were amazed and amused to find that we had inherited a swineherd position that had been created in the nineteenth century, when progressive hospital treatment included meaningful work.

Our CMHC plan called for the federally mandated five essential services to be provided by the Harvard-affiliated psychiatry department based at Cambridge City Hospital, where I was finishing my residency. The center provided inpatient, outpatient, emergency, and consultation and education services at the hospital, and a partial hospital program at the city infirmary. For its part, Somerville would have its own outpatient clinic and a day hospital program in a church basement.

After I finished my training, John Mack offered me the job as chief of community psychiatry at our new CMHC, and I was happy to accept. At thirty-five years old, this was my first negotiated discretionary position. A skeptic might have viewed this as an adolescence prolonged almost indefinitely, but I considered my education and training as time well spent. Still, I was glad that I could finally begin work as a fully functioning adult professional.

The community psychiatry service at the hospital consisted of myself as chief, two nurses, and a mental health worker. Community consultation by mental health professionals was so new and unknown I had to explain ourselves before we could provide any service. The nurses and I did home visits for patients who were either in an acute emergency or were chronically ill and housebound, and we consulted with medical staff in the neighborhood health centers. I worked to establish relationships with community caregivers, including primary care physicians, social service agencies, police, and caseworkers in the local welfare department, with whom I developed a strong relationship as we navigated issues with clients who appeared to be mentally ill. I also began a consultation with clergy, including a group of Christian clergy—but that ended after a few meetings, when they told me they wanted a consultant who was a Christian.

* * *

Community psychiatrists develop relationships with organizations, as well as with individuals within those organizations. The Cambridge Police Department was the most important of the organizations with which I built a relationship. The Vietnam War and its resulting turmoil was a major source of stress for the police, as was dealing with Harvard's takeover of the Cambridge City Hospital which had changed the experience of the police at the hospital.

Why this stress and tension? In the 1960s, "town versus gown" friction between Harvard and the city was a fact of life, and Cambridge City Hospital was very much a "town" institution. Almost all the nurses were the wives and sisters of the police and firemen who brought in many patients. When these men brought patients to the E.R., they had a comfortable social experience with these women while they dealt with the town physicians whom they also knew. After the Harvard takeover, they had to deal with a constantly changing group of young Harvard doctors, some of whom could be arrogant. As a group, the Harvard doctors failed to recognize the importance of the police to the hospital and to the community at large.

The police-hospital relationship ultimately improved, thanks in large part to a community contact named Jack Collins, who had grown up in a Somerville family that included many police officers. Jack had always wanted to be a police officer, but at five feet four, he was too short. He dealt with this loss by developing an informal role as liaison between the community and the police, who viewed him as one of their own. When Jack saw the deteriorating relationship between the police and the hospital, he suggested to me that we form a discussion group to address

141

the problem. The group consisted of Sheila, the head nurse in the emergency room; her longtime Cambridge police officer boyfriend; several members of the police department command structure; and Jack and me serving as co-leaders.

The captain and the lieutenant in the group were Irish Catholic men with strong traditional values. They had a great respect for Harvard and for the students they saw as the privileged, future leaders of the community. Before the Vietnam War generated adversarial relations, the Cambridge police had an easy tolerance for the foibles of the Harvard youth. Back when I was a medical student, a classmate and I were driving in his classic English sports car, top down, with an open beer between us. We were on our way to a Harvard football game when we were stopped by traffic alongside a Cambridge police officer, who looked down directly at us. We thought we were in trouble, but in a cheerful, pleasant way, he waved us on.

That cheerful, tolerant relationship changed when students staged anti-war demonstrations in Harvard Square. When the police confronted them in an effort to maintain order, the students spit on them, threw bricks, and verbally abused them. One of the officers, a sergeant, was hit by a brick, which severed some tendons on the back of his hand. As part of my consultative work, I interviewed him and several other patients who were admitted with injuries, including a young female protester whom I saw after I had seen the sergeant. When I told her how frightened the sergeant had been during the confrontation, she was dismissive and could not believe my account, an illustration of how divided and at odds relations had become.

From a clinical perspective, I saw the student behavior toward the police, and the student strike of 1970 that shut down Harvard for five days, as examples of the psychological defense mechanism of displacement. The students were furious at the President of the United States, whom they could not reach for his conduct of the war, so they displaced their rage and took out their frustration on the authority they *could* reach—that is, the leaders of the university and the police.

In our hospital discussion group, the police voiced their distress at what was happening, and I used that forum to give them my understanding of what these demonstrations represented. My explanation appeared to comfort the police—not because my explanation was convincing, but rather because it demonstrated that I took their complaints seriously and that I, representing Harvard through the hospital, respected them.

In the early days of this group, the police largely kept their distance from me, and that contributed to the difficulty I experienced. I took the brunt of their criticism, much of it legitimate, about how the Harvard doctors were treating them. Sheila was able to provide an independent report on how the Harvard doctors in the emergency room disrespected the police, failing to understand their value as members of the community and as providers of information about the patients whom they brought to the hospital. Not surprisingly, this behavior riled the police.

Jack played an important role, interpreting the hospital to the police in the group. My role in the group was largely to be the listening pincushion they could jab as needed. Slowly, over time, trusting relationships developed, and the group became a safe place for the police to discuss their concerns about the new role of Harvard in the hospital and what was happening between the students and the police. Outside the group, I consulted with the chief of medicine to help him understand how the attitudes of some of his residents were damaging to the hospital, and in the end, to patient care. Over time, the police saw the improved quality of Harvard-based medical care. Relations improved over eighteen months to the point that we were able to end the group.

Through this experience, I developed some informal relationships with police, which were at least as educational for me as for them. I learned that among themselves, they called a man who groped women's breasts a "tit puller," while a man who exposed himself was a "flag waver." One cop once asked me, "Doc, I just arrested a tit puller. What would make somebody do that?" The throwaway line was too good to pass up: I told him, "He probably hates his mother." Later, I saw the officer and he told me, "Geez, Doc. You were right! I went back and asked him, and he does hate his mother." So my reputation grew with the Cambridge Police Department.

Over time, the police chief started to refer me a few officers for my professional services. Dealing with these referrals was a new experience that led me to change my practice. These referrals were not preceded by any phone call from the department or from the officer. Instead, I learned about them directly when I opened the door of my office, and the officer was standing there waiting patiently. He would tell me, "The lieutenant told me to come and see you."

Being responsive to these men meant a different model of practice than I was used to. I learned to invite them in on the spot, regardless of whether I had another patient waiting, and to spend fifteen or twenty minutes with the officer right then, before giving him an appointment at a later time. This practice clearly satisfied my new patients, and it helped me redefine what I offered to patients. Not everyone needed or wanted a fifty-minute hour. For many patients, twenty or twenty-five minutes made more sense. I learned to distinguish what I had been taught by my psychoanalyst supervisors from what made sense in the real world of Cambridge. These referrals typically involved men who were drinking too much and were depressed amidst marital problems, and I treated these men with a combination of an antidepressant and brief psychotherapy, counseled them about alcohol, and referred them to AA.

* * *

Our role as a community health facility took a dramatic turn in 1970, when the heroin epidemic struck Cambridge full force. The city council asked psychiatry and medicine at large to respond, and we did. Trained at MMHC in the 1960s, we had learned nothing about drug and alcohol abuse. If faculty members knew anything about these problems, they never let on, and they certainly never suggested these were problems a psychiatrist should know about or treat. When John Mack asked consulting psychiatrist Ed Khantzian to develop our approach to the heroin epidemic, Ed was just as ignorant as the rest of us. He had the good sense to realize it and made it his business to go to New York in order to learn about methadone as a treatment for heroin addiction. Ed played a critical role in developing our methadone-based drug treatment service in Cambridge.

Methadone is a long-acting, synthetic opioid that acts on the brain like heroin, morphine, or any other opioid pain medication. In appropriate doses, methadone blocks the euphoric effects of heroin. A person who takes methadone can give up the illegal opioid addiction, but he or she will become dependent on methadone. This is better for the patients and for society: when your drug connection is the city hospital, you don't have to resort to illegal means in order to raise the money that a street dealer charges. A patient attending a methadone clinic can live a normal life apart from required visits to the clinic, which in the 1970s were twice daily. A good substance abuse clinic would offer more than methadone; it would also offer psychotherapy, which we did, often as group therapy that focused directly on problems of addiction and maintaining sobriety.

We set up our clinic in one of the old buildings at the hospital, where our patients lined up outside twice daily to get their oral methadone. This is where the law enforcement approach to illegal drug use collided head-on with the medical approach to addiction. Duncan McNeil, the chief of the narcotics squad, was a hard-bitten, old-line detective. Ed used to joke that Duncan made the detective in the 1971 classic film "The French Connection" look like Mr. Rogers. One day, Duncan McNeil showed up in a squad car in the hospital parking lot with a state police officer and a file of "wanted" mugshots to match up against our patients. Ed stood up to Duncan McNeil, telling him straight out that this was unacceptable—it would close our clinic. McNeil did not back down until Ed and John Mack had a desk-pounding session with the city manager.

The conflict quieted down after a city council member learned that one of his adolescent children was a heroin addict. We treated him successfully, and this cemented our position in the city political structure. With time, we developed a good working relationship with Duncan McNeil, and the clinic flourished. The police and the mental health center came together with a joint approach to the problems of drug addiction in Cambridge.

During this time, I had a few private patients, but my clinical practice consisted largely of patients in our outpatient clinic where I learned the value of long-term supportive psychotherapy and the value of patience. One of my patients was a depressed alcoholic woman who continued to drink despite all interventions. Discouraged, I was ready to terminate her treatment when I presented her to one of my colleagues, who urged a little patience. "Why don't you give her a few more weeks and see how she does?" he said.

I gave her the suggested few weeks, and I watched from the sidelines as she got sober with the help of AA. This time, she stayed sober, and I saw her as an outpatient for the next forty years, making home visits after she was housebound, and finally visiting at her terminal nursing home placement.

Over the years, I got to know her daughter well, and through the daughter, I heard about the third and fourth generations. She, the daughter, was sober and hard working. After several bad choices, she found a good man. Her daughter, my patient's granddaughter, got pregnant early; that child, my patient's great-grandson, ran wild and had bad substance abuse problems. Over these forty years, I learned about the struggles of ordinary people through the lifespan and across generations, something I could not have learned in any other way.

* * *

In 1969, as my colleagues and I were building a psychiatry department and a CMHC, my own family was expanding with the birth of our daughter Emily. Susan filled the role expected of women in the 1960s. She was wife and mother, while continuing the volunteer political work she had begun in Washington. She proved to be an adept political operative and led successful campaigns in Lexington for candidates for national office.

Susan waited to make her next career move until both children were in elementary school. She started law school in 1975, when the children were eight and six. She was accepted at Northeastern University, Boston University, and Harvard. She chose Harvard, not least because it was closest to home, so she could get home quickly if one of the children got sick.

Supporting her political work had required very little of me beyond enthusiasm, but law school required more. I had enough control over my own time that I could arrange to be home two afternoons a week when the children came home from school. I enjoyed that time with them, making snacks, getting them to after-school activities, and just spending time together. We had a wonderful teenage babysitter two afternoons a week, and Susan came home on Friday afternoons.

Susan graduated with honors in 1978 and went on to a distinguished legal career in the public sector, appointed in 1996 as an Associate Justice of the Massachusetts Court of Appeals, serving until her untimely illness in 2006, and death in 2009, Ch 17.

* * *

In the early years of the Cambridge-Somerville CMHC, Cambridge patients were sent to a state hospital thirty-two miles away when they needed [involuntary] hospitalization. We sent staff there to help prepare discharged patients for transition to the community. After several years, the Massachusetts DMH closed this hospital and moved our patients to a unit at the Metropolitan State Hospital, just a few miles distant. We could provide significantly more service to these patients, and we immediately increased our staff presence in the hospital to create the Ambulatory Community Service (ACS) as a separate unit dedicated to providing follow-up services to our most chronically and severely ill patients. Recent college graduates who wanted experience in mental health provided the core case management.

* * *

Our psychiatry department at Cambridge City Hospital was an integral part of the services provided by the CMHC, but through our Harvard connection, we provided training as well as service. Beginning in 1968, we trained residents from MMHC who rotated part-time to Cambridge, and we went on to become an independent department of psychiatry affiliated with Harvard Medical School, enrolling our own first residency class in 1970.

The residents from MMHC who rotated through our department at Cambridge City Hospital profited from this unique training experience. Unlike their patients at MMHC, the patients in our hospital often had both medical and psychiatric problems, so the residents had to call on different areas of knowledge in order to fully and effectively treat these patients. More importantly, they learned how to consult with the primary care physicians who referred patients to them.

Our training program embraced a dual approach: training in public health psychiatry and in psychodynamic psychotherapy. We looked for young physicians who shared our commitment to treating the sick and poor people in Cambridge and Somerville—those whom the private sector failed to reach—and who wanted to learn psychodynamic psychotherapy in the process. We never altered our belief that understanding psychodynamics was an important part of working with any patient. To this day, Cambridge City Hospital—now as Cambridge Health Alliance—continues to attract residency applicants who share the belief that social justice requires good medical care for everyone, and that a psychodynamic understanding and treatment of patients is a core competency for psychiatrists.

One of the MMHC residents who rotated with us, David Spiegel, remembered years later, "For me, Cambridge [City Hospital] represented a breath of fresh air. I loved Mass. Mental for the intensity of the clinical experience and for the intellect of most of our supervisors, but the orientation was still heavily psychoanalytic. Cambridge was a community-embedded hospital, with a more practical and open approach to patient care. The psychiatrists at Cambridge set a tone of open-mindedness and taught us to help patients however we could. Cambridge led me to undertake a fellowship at the Laboratory of Community Psychiatry. Cambridge provided me with an alternative and liberating model that did not replace Mass. Mental, but gave me a sense of humor about it." Dave later did important work on trauma and dissociation and on group therapy for cancer patients. He is now a distinguished professor at Stanford University.

Nina Marlowe was the first of many residents I trained in community psychiatry. As a medical student at Mt. Sinai Hospital in New York she thought she would go on in pediatrics, but in talking with a patient with a serious medical illness she realized, "I liked listening to him," and she decided to go on in psychiatry.

Later, she realized that her experience growing up in the San Francisco area with a mentally ill grandmother played a role in her choice. Nina described her grandmother, who suffered from recurrent psychotic depression, as a delightful woman when she was healthy. She and Nina played cards together and her grandmother was also a wonderful cook. But when she became ill, she needed hospitalization, and this was a trauma for the whole family.

In the 1960s, California law required that a family member sign a petition for a mentally ill person to be involuntarily committed to a mental hospital. Nina remembered this as a very painful task for her mother, and an even more painful experience for her grandmother who was given ECT (shock therapy) without anesthesia. Later, Nina came to believe that part of her motivation for choosing psychiatry was the unfulfilled wish that she could have helped her grandmother. She thought, "I couldn't help her but now at least I can try to help others."

After her medical training Nina became interested in community psychiatry. She applied to Cambridge and was accepted. Cambridge Hospital became a community mental health center site in 1969, and when our mental health center was in operation, the state hospital began to discharge patients to Cambridge some of whom had been there for 10 years or longer. The mental health center provided care for these patients beginning in 1970.

As we began to develop community treatment options for these patients, Nina was one of our first psychiatrists to work at the state hospital thirty-five miles away where Cambridge patients were sent until the late 1970s. After working there for three years, Nina joined the new Ambulatory Community Service (ACS) that worked with these patients.

The ACS had no facilities of its own. We used church basements, we made home visits, we borrowed space where we could. ACS case managers worked with our patients, supervised by the nurses and by Nina and our other psychiatrists. Many of these newly discharged patients were totally unprepared to live in the community. We helped them find housing, often shared with other patients, and if there were interpersonal conflicts we helped with those. We talked with the patients about what they might expect; we told them about the treatment resources available through ACS, and also how to apply for disability so that they would have an income. We followed up with patients who missed medication appointments, and we worked hard to help patients stay on their medicine, because we knew that medicine was an essential part of their treatment. A few years later, when that state hospital closed and our patients were moved to Met State, ACS staff were able to make contact with them in the hospital in order to help them prepare for re-entry into the community.

One of the things ACS did not do was help patients look for competitive employment. Our department failed to develop a supported employment service, which we could have done. But if we failed to do that ourselves, we did train the resident who would go on to become a national leader in creating programs to help patients obtain competitive employment. That is a story for another chapter.

More recently, as the federal government has provided incentives for mental health care and primary care to integrate, the ACS has begun to work with primary care providers to provide integrated health and mental health services. Consistent with this, the ACS has become the Health Integration Program (HIP).

From the beginning, the ACS was a training site for our residents, psychology interns and others. We taught them their own role in a community-based service, and they saw with their own eyes the valuable work that the case managers were doing as the core members of the ACS team. Many years later, a day center opened in Cambridge where these patients could gather and socialize. It was a smoke-filled room but the patients loved it. In the 21st century, the ACS has continued to provide meaningful clinical service for the sick poor of Cambridge and Somerville, using increasingly scarce resources to do the best it can.

Nina came without any particular interest in dynamic psychiatry but she did a rotation at one of the other, more traditional Harvard psychiatry departments, and she saw that psychodynamic psychotherapy helped many patients. Later, she trained as a psychoanalyst.

I was happy in my work training residents and administering the community psychiatry service, but troubling events in the Cambridge City Hospital's psychiatry department led me to make a major professional change in 1980. One member of the department made the front pages of the *New York Post* for prescribing opiates to maintain the addiction of a celebrity patient. Two other faculty initiated an extensive and highly inappropriate social relationship with a patient.

My colleagues' behavior raised serious ethical questions, not only for me but also for other senior faculty. Two of these men left the department altogether, but I was too committed to our mission to leave entirely. Happily, a position opened at Metropolitan State Hospital for a medical director of the unit serving Cambridge and Somerville patients. In that position I could continue my affiliation, but elsewhere, and so in 1980, I returned to Met State for the third time in my career. I had first been a volunteer, and later a research assistant. Now I would be the medical director of the state hospital unit that served Cambridge and Somerville. Many of the hospital's patients were diagnosed with schizophrenia.

#####

CHAPTER 11

UNDERSTANDING AND TREATING SCHIZOPHRENIA

Schizophrenia is the most damaging disease psychiatrists treat. It attacks young people, is often chronic, and causes more psychological damage than any other mental disease. Worse yet, our medicines have limited effectiveness: they can quiet the delusions and hallucinations that mark this disease, but they rarely help the emotional flattening and disabling cognitive problems that make these patients difficult to engage and treat.

These are the patients who need us most, and for whom we are able to do the least. It was the combination of their need and our inadequacy that led me to devote a major part of my professional efforts to these patients.

My first experience treating people with schizophrenia came in 1964 during my first year as a resident at the MMHC, and it was stressful. My first patient with schizophrenia was a woman who was always severely agitated and whose speech made absolutely no sense. She was never assaultive or threatening, but attempting to engage her was a strange and fruitless experience that left me deeply unsettled. Ahmed, the patient who tried to kill me also carried a diagnosis of schizophrenia. This was not the easiest introduction to the disease or those who suffered from it, and I would not have thought then that I would spend a significant portion of my working life treating and advocating for very similar patients.

My commitment to understanding and treating patients with schizophrenia came well after I finished my residency. I had finished residency with a firm grounding in the psychodynamic understanding of patients, but after my two years in the clinic at NIH I knew this was not the only, or even the best, way to understand many patients. Interestingly, it was my psychology training, with its emphasis on rigorous observation, that would lead me in a new direction in understanding schizophrenia.

During my first year of residency at the MMHC, my supervisor, John Mack, had advanced the hypothesis that acute episodes of schizophrenia occurred after the patient had suffered some romantic disappointment, or what John called "heterosexual impasse".[4] Years later, when I took up my position as chief of community psychiatry and research at Cambridge City Hospital's new department of psychiatry, I resolved to test John's hypothesis by interviewing patients on our inpatient service. This was before the federal government required that research on human subjects be approved by a committee specifically charged to protect the

---

4   Note that homosexual impasse was not even a possible construct for a psychiatrist in 1964

rights of human subjects, and I simply interviewed patients who had presented with a psychotic diagnosis.

To test John's hypothesis, I first had to develop a method for deciding which of these psychotic patients had schizophrenia, but nothing I had been taught provided any guidance for this task. Fortunately, I had learned something about British descriptive psychiatry in preparation for my visit to the Maudsley Hospital several years earlier. Under the leadership of Professor John Wing, British psychiatrists had spent years developing an interview, the Present State Exam (PSE), that asked patients concretely and specifically about their experience—that is, about their symptoms of mental disorder.

Unlike the psychodynamic approach I had been taught in residency, answers to the PSE provided a basis on which one could make a diagnosis, and begin to understand the person's experience as well. Later, with the publication of DSM-III, American psychiatry developed a similar interview, the Structured Clinical Interview for DSM Disorders (SCID), which was suitable for research but far too detailed for clinical practice. Later still, I adapted that interview, along with some questions from the PSE, to my clinical interviewing and teaching. A copy of that interview, along with a discussion of how to use it, is attached as an appendix to this chapter.

This interview does much more than provide a basis for a formal diagnosis. It provides a basis to understand the patient's experience. The irony is that this descriptive approach, antithetical to what I was taught in residency, achieves what the psychodynamic approach did not: an understanding of the patient's experience— precisely what the psychiatrist is tasked to do.

This experience was professionally liberating as I began to better understand the experience of my psychotic patients. My new interview was particularly useful when dealing with patients with schizophrenia, given how difficult their experience was to understand—both because it was more obscure, and because the patients had more difficulty in communicating it.

Schizophrenia affects relatively few people—about one percent of the population. In America, that still means there are over three million people with schizophrenia [3], and for many, the disease is disabling. Relationships with a schizophrenic family member or friend can be troubling, confusing, and occasionally frightening.

The disease is more common and more disabling in men than in women. Five or six percent of people with schizophrenia will die by suicide, and people with schizophrenia die on the average fifteen to twenty years younger than others, typically from co-occurring medical illnesses [4, 5]. Effective treatment programs exist, but they are available to relatively few people because society has failed to spend the necessary money to fund them. Where available, these can help people with schizophrenia manage their illness and live more productive and satisfying lives. Some people with schizophrenia learn to adapt to their symptoms and are able to function at a high level, but this is unusual.

Until the 1950s, we cared for many people with schizophrenia in state hospitals. They were among the 558,000 state hospital patients at peak census in the mid-1950s [6]. The introduction of chlorpromazine, trade name 'Thorazine' after its commercial development, made it possible to discharge many chronic patients, and by the 1990s, ninety percent of patients had been discharged into the community, leading to the closure of many state hospitals.

Sadly, we failed as a society to provide an adequate replacement for those institutions. In 2010, there were 43,000 psychiatric beds available in this country to serve more than 500,000 patients who had been discharged from state hospitals [6], as well as new patients with acute psychiatric problems. The paucity of treatment resources has meant that many people with schizophrenia are homeless or in prisons and jails. Roughly 2.2 million people with chronic severe mental disorders receive no treatment, and about 200,000 of these people are homeless. More than 300,000 are in jails or prisons. This is a national disgrace [7]. If comparable inadequacies existed for severe medical disease, such as cancer, we would consider this a public health emergency. It is unfortunately true that, as journalist and author Ron Powers writes, "No one cares about crazy people [8]."

* * *

The history of schizophrenia illustrates how the understanding and treatment of a disease can change radically over time. At the end of the nineteenth century, German psychiatrist Emil Kraepelin [9] made a fundamental contribution to our understanding of mental illness when he differentiated what he called dementia praecox— what we would later call schizophrenia—from what he called manic depression and we would later call bipolar disease. He did this through careful observations of his hospitalized patients over many years, noting that one group of psychotic patients appeared to remain ill indefinitely, with no prospect of recovery. He called

159

this "dementia" because he thought it was a brain disease similar to other dementias, and "praecox" because it began in the second or third decade of life, unlike other dementias that developed late in life. He thought dementia praecox was a brain disease—and he was right.

Swiss psychiatrist Eugen Bleuler made the next contribution to our understanding. In 1908, he renamed dementia praecox as schizophrenia to call attention to what he saw as the primary psychopathology: the splitting of affect and intellect [10]. Bleuler knew and admired Freud's work, and he believed that mental processes could be unconscious. He identified problems with associations, affect, and ambivalence as fundamental. The contributions of these two men have value for us more than 100 years later: Kraepelin taught us to carefully observe the signs and symptoms of psychosis, while Bleuler taught us to understand the mental experience of these patients.

In the 1920s, there were no treatments that specifically targeted symptoms of schizophrenia or other psychotic disorders. We had medicines that affected the whole brain, like barbiturates, and we had physical treatments, such as high colonic irrigation, that we imagined might be helpful. Cleanliness may be next to godliness, but a clean colon did not improve the symptoms of schizophrenia. Hydrotherapy, which involved placing patients in a tub of water at body temperature, where a leather skirt attached to the rim of the tub with a hole for the patient's head secured the patient, was another approach. Patients who continued to act out of control or violent despite these treatments were placed in physical restraints or isolation.

European psychiatrists led the search for new physical treatments. Later in the 1920s, they developed insulin coma therapy, and in the 1930s, electroconvulsive therapy (ECT) and psychosurgery (prefrontal lobotomy). As these treatments became available, they were widely used in psychiatric hospitals in the United States and in Europe. For decades, psychiatrists believed that these were effective treatments for schizophrenia. Later research showed they were not.

ECT carried out without anesthesia or muscle relaxants can be painful: the convulsions can break bones, and consciously experienced convulsions can be terrifying. Without anesthesia, musculoskeletal damage was fairly common, occurring in as many as forty percent of cases [11]. Patients might experience nausea and headache. In the 1950s, clinicians began using anesthesia and muscle relaxants with ECT [11, 12], and this quickly became standard practice. Although ECT can be an effective treatment for severe depression, there is no good evidence that ECT helps people with schizophrenia—but nor is there evidence that it does lasting harm.

* * *

In 1961, during medical school, I returned to Metropolitan State Hospital (Met State) as a research assistant, five years after my undergraduate volunteer experience there. Sadly, the hospital had changed very little. Antipsychotic medication was the only therapy in daily use at this traditional state hospital, with one major exception: insulin coma treatment on a specialized ward.

My work during this time brought me into contact with Dr. Karl Theo Dussik (1908-1968), one of the world experts on insulin coma therapy.

Dr. Dussik was a model state hospital psychiatrist. His concern for his patients was palpable, and he devoted his best professional efforts to helping them get better. Based on his many years of clinical experience with insulin, he believed passionately that insulin coma therapy was an effective treatment for schizophrenia.

The use of insulin coma therapy dates back to Manfred Sakel [13], a Viennese psychiatrist who developed it in 1927. From anecdotal clinical observations, Sakel and others believed that patients with epilepsy seldom developed schizophrenia. That was not true, but Sakel drew from this belief the idea that inducing coma in patients with schizophrenia could be therapeutic.

Insulin coma therapy involved giving the patient sufficient insulin to lower blood sugar to the point that the patient became unconscious or comatose, typically for hours. A patient in coma required careful vital sign monitoring, as hypoglycemia (low blood sugar) can result in death. Safe use of insulin required a ward staffed by specially trained nurses and led by a physician with insulin coma experience. Even with these safeguards, mortality was as high as one percent, and obesity was a common side effect. Some patients spontaneously experienced new episodes of coma after treatment, at times with convulsions during which they were partially conscious.

Despite these troubling side effects, psychiatry greeted initial positive reports of insulin coma treatment of schizophrenia with enthusiasm, partly because at that time there were no effective alternatives. Evidence later emerged suggesting that the improvement rates were a result of patient selection, optimistic estimates of improvement, and other confounding variables. Still, insulin coma therapy remained in relatively wide use through the 1950s. When it became clear that a new medication—chlorpromazine —was an effective treatment with far fewer side effects, insulin coma therapy fell out of favor [14]. Yet true believers persisted into the 1960s. Dr. Dussik, who had trained with Dr. Sakel before the Second World War, was one of them. With thirty years' experience administering insulin to patients with schizophrenia, he had developed a unique expertise in its management.

It was a privilege to know Dr. Dussik and observe his administration of insulin coma treatment, and it was an opportunity for me to participate in a living part of psychiatric history. When he told me that he was sufficiently comfortable with insulin coma treatment that he could do it safely while the patient was sleeping, I saw an opportunity for a potentially valuable piece of research. If an insulin coma could be induced during sleep, patients under treatment would be indistinguishable from patients who were asleep without insulin. That meant it would be possible to design a double-blind, random-assignment study of the efficacy of insulin coma treatment for schizophrenia.

In a double-blind study, neither the person being treated nor the person administering the treatment knows whether the patient has received the treatment or a placebo. Random assignment means that whether a subject gets the active treatment or a placebo is decided by the equivalent of a coin flip. If we can create these conditions, and if we also have a good measure of treatment outcome, then we can be reasonably confident that a positive result is not a function of the wish by either the patient or the practitioner for the treatment to be effective.

When I proposed that such a double-blind study of insulin coma therapy might be possible, Dr. Dussik was excited. But I had a problem: I'd reviewed the literature and knew that the broad consensus in American psychiatry was that insulin coma therapy was ineffective. I believed that assessment to be accurate, and that the improvement Dr. Dussik observed in his patients was real, but more likely a result of the kindly, interested treatment patients received from him and his staff than from insulin. If this were true, the result of my proposed research would show no difference between the insulin coma patients and the placebo patients.

I presented my concerns to Dr. Dussik, suggesting that perhaps his patients got better not because of insulin but because of his good care. I asked if he would be able to accept such an outcome. He said that he would think about it. I waited, but he never mentioned the project again. He continued to provide insulin coma therapy on his ward until he retired a few years later, and, regardless of the reason why, his patients benefited from his kindly care.

The story of Dr. Dussik and his insulin ward is a paradigmatic example of how the history of medicine has developed. Throughout history, sick people have turned to physicians, and caring physicians have applied their skills using the understanding current in their time. R.I.P., Carl Theo Dussik. You had a good heart and the best intentions.

* * *

When physicians have no understanding of what causes a disease, they will find a treatment that appears to help, rather than do nothing. The history of medicine and science provides many instances of incorrect theories and harmful practices that were continued in the face of strong evidence that they were wrong. Not until some positive alternative exists—a new medication or a new theory—are old practices and theories recognized as wrong, and ultimately abandoned. The history of psychosurgery is a dramatic example of how a desire to help went terribly wrong.

Egon Moniz, a distinguished neurologist, developed psychosurgery, more commonly called "lobotomy" or "prefrontal lobotomy," in Portugal in 1935 [15]. He reported strongly positive results for patients with schizophrenia and other severe psychotic conditions. The surgery was relatively simple: it involved severing the connection between the prefrontal cortex and other brain structures. Moniz was awarded a Nobel Prize in 1949 for his work on psychosurgery and for his earlier work on developing radiologic studies of the blood vessels of the brain. From early on, though, some independent observers questioned Moniz's reported results.

American psychiatrist Walter Freeman was an early proponent of lobotomy. Freeman thought that if the operation could be simplified, then lobotomy would be a possible treatment for chronically ill state hospital patients. To that end, Freeman, along with neurosurgeon James Watts, developed a technique that could be carried out in a mental hospital without the need for an operating room [16]. Freeman and others recommended this procedure for any severely, chronically ill patient with uncontrolled violent behavior and/or agitation. His procedure "managed" undesirable behaviors, helping out-of-control patients regain control, and contributed to a more peaceful ward.

As a medical student and resident, I had no experience with lobotomy. I never worked with a patient who had undergone psychosurgery, and no doctor I knew performed this procedure. I did not learn the extent and duration of lobotomy practice in this country until I did research for this book, and what I learned appalled me.

The prefrontal cortex of the brain provides the ability to think things through, assess likely future outcomes, choose between conflicting choices, and understand the social consequences of behavior. Destroying the connection between it and the remainder of the brain severely damages the personality as well as intellectual capacities. As a result, lobotomy patients could no longer think, reason, or have meaningful social interactions. Complications of prefrontal lobotomy included epilepsy and occasionally death, usually from brain hemorrhage.

In spite of these consequences, early anecdotal reports of success led to great enthusiasm. Thirty thousand patients were lobotomized before studies raised serious doubts about earlier claims of success. Rosemary Kennedy, President John F. Kennedy's oldest sister, was one of the thirty thousand. Her lobotomy in 1941 left her severely damaged, and her parents hid her away in institutions for twenty years. Many years later, her siblings responded by advocating for people with disabilities and mental illness. In 1962, President Kennedy, in what he called "a bold new approach" [17], signed legislation creating community mental health centers. In 1968, Rosemary's sister, Eunice Kennedy Shriver, founded the Special Olympics.

As a result of the many patients damaged by lobotomy, a strong ethical backlash developed, and these procedures fell out of favor in the 1950s. The introduction of chlorpromazine (Thorazine) in 1954 sounded the death knell for lobotomy [18], as the drug could control the symptoms of psychotic disorders without lobotomy's horrible damage. By 1960, very few hospitals were still doing these procedures; by 1970, there were none.

To dismiss lobotomy as a heinous crime perpetrated by uncaring psychiatrists is to miss an important part of this story. Most of Freeman's patients were considered hopeless cases for whom all other treatments had failed. These were chronic patients who were often behaviorally out of control, aggressive, and a danger to themselves and others. For these patients, it was lobotomy or nothing.

Freeman and Watts were strongly motivated to believe that what they were doing was helpful, and Freeman enthusiastically promoted lobotomy, traveling the country in a VW microbus with "lobotomobile" painted on the sides in large letters. Freeman cared deeply about his patients. He wrote to their families, in some cases for years after the lobotomy, wanting to know how his patient was doing. He wrote personal letters expressing concern, and the families of his patients greatly valued their relationship with him. Not only would they write back on the current status of the patient, but some would also ask for advice about unrelated personal problems. Families would express gratitude for Freeman's work even when describing a former patient who was in manifestly terrible condition.

* * *

The real breakthrough in the treatment of schizophrenia and other major psychotic diseases came about almost by accident. In the 1950s, with the introduction of chlorpromazine (U.S. trade name Thorazine), psychiatrists could for the first time effectively treat the crippling delusions and hallucinations that characterize schizophrenia and other psychotic disorders. The World Health Organization (WHO) immediately recognized the importance of chlorpromazine for the treatment of psychosis [19], designating it as an essential medication, noting that chlorpromazine is as important for the treatment of mental illness as penicillin is for infectious disease.

Originally synthesized in France in 1951, chlorpromazine was developed as an antihistamine, used for cooling patients during surgery. Surgeons hoped that by cooling the body, they would induce a state of artificial hibernation so that the patient would be less susceptible to surgical shock. In 1952, Henri Laborit, a surgeon and physiologist in the French army, noticed the calming effect this medication had on postoperative patients. Sensing how valuable this could be for his nation's severely mentally ill, Laborit convinced colleagues at the neuropsychiatric service of Val de Grace, the military hospital in Paris, to try chlorpromazine in the treatment of one patient [20]. They tried the drug on Jacques Lh., a severely manic twenty-four-year-old patient. After twenty days of treatment and 855 milligrams of chlorpromazine, Jacques was able "to resume normal life." With further investigation, the findings were undeniable. By 1953, the drug had crossed the Atlantic, and by 1954 Thorazine was in wide use for the treatment of psychotic patients in the United States [18].

Thorazine was effective in treating the most pronounced symptoms of major mental illness, blunting the delusional fears that led patients to act in ways that seemed bizarre and could be dangerous. With this medication, these delusions and hallucinations lost much of their emotional power, making some patients more accessible and receptive to other forms of treatment. Further, the bizarre behavior that made it difficult, and sometimes impossible, for these patients to remain in the community declined. While Thorazine did not treat negative symptoms or cognitive difficulties, these were not the cause of the disruptive behavior then led patients to be hospitalized. The new medications represented an extraordinary medical advance. They made it possible to discharge these patients and to prevent the hospitalization of many.

The pharmaceutical industry has introduced many new antipsychotic drugs since the mid-1950s, all claiming to have some form of advantage over the existing drugs. Research largely fails to confirm those claims. Only one antipsychotic drug—Clozapine—has proven to be effective in patients with chronic schizophrenia who have failed to respond to treatment with other antipsychotic medication [21]. A large, well-designed study comparing antipsychotic drugs found little difference in effectiveness in the primary outcome between any of the drugs [22]. The first-generation drug did just as well as the second-generation drugs and, in the prescribed doses, did not produce more disfiguring involuntary movements (tardive dyskinesia) than the others.

All antipsychotics except clozapine act primarily on the neurotransmitter dopamine. Clozapine, which the FDA approved in 1989, acts on serotonin receptors in addition to dopamine

169

receptors. We do not understand why or how these differences relate to what we observe clinically, but research has repeatedly documented that clozapine decreases the risk of suicide in patients with schizophrenia [23, 24], and it is effective in patients with chronic, treatment-resistant schizophrenia.

Many people with schizophrenia do not understand that they are ill, but in my experience, patients who take clozapine do often understand that they have a mental illness. The change in patients I saw in Cambridge City Hospital was so dramatic that I have referred to it informally as a "clozapine cure." These patients had been admitted after being acutely psychotic and disruptive in the community, refusing all help or engagement with mental health professionals. With this medication, they came to understand that they were ill, and they recognized that they had had problems as a result of their illness. They seemed more like "normal" people in how they engaged with me.

Despite clozapine's unique advantages, psychiatrists are reluctant to use it, even in chronic patients who fail to improve, because it requires weekly blood draws during the first several months of treatment, and it has serious side effects, such as a fall in circulating white blood cells, and more rarely, damage to the heart. For patients who do not improve on one antipsychotic, psychiatrists were more likely to add a different antipsychotic than switch to clozapine.

Antipsychotics are only effective if patients take them. Regrettably, many patients stop taking their medication, because they do not believe they are ill, so why should they take medicine? In other cases, they don't like how the medicines make them feel, or they are too disorganized, or they run out of money. Fortunately, better treatment is now available for such patients. Newer injectable formulations of antipsychotic medication are effective for thirty days or longer. Patients who receive one shot each month show greater medication compliance and significantly fewer episodes of relapse requiring hospitalization. Injectables represent a meaningful improvement in our ability to treat schizophrenia.

* * *

In the 1920s, as psychiatrists became familiar with Freud's work, they increasingly recognized psychoanalysis as an effective treatment for neurosis. Observing this, they began to hope—or, more accurately, wish—that psychoanalysis could also provide effective treatment for severe mental disorders like schizophrenia. If schizophrenia could be understood as a reaction to life events—specifically pathogenic early life experiences—rather than as a biologically determined illness, then successful psychological treatment, like psychoanalysis or a modified analytic technique, was possible.

From those observations, it was a short step for psychiatrists to conclude that there was a direct relationship between the severity of adult illness and the age at which pathogenic life events occurred. Severe adult psychological illness, including schizophrenia, could be understood as a direct result of parental failure that began in the oral stage, when the mother was nursing or otherwise feeding the new infant—in other words, bad mothering caused severe illness.

Beginning in the 1940s, the concept of the mother who caused schizophrenia—the schizophrenogenic mother—grew out of these beliefs and wishes [25]. Analysts explicitly linked mothers with schizophrenia, and these ideas continued to hold well into the 1970s and, for diehard believers, into the 1980s. The intellectual history of these ideas is best understood as part of psychiatry's relationship with women (Ch.15). Here, I focus on their treatment implications.

When I began training at MMHC in the 1960s, social workers, not doctors, were responsible for meeting with patients' families. One focus of these weekly meetings was on how to help the mother understand how her behavior had led to her son or daughter becoming schizophrenic. These mothers were already burdened with the pain and difficulty of having a son or daughter with schizophrenia, and on top of that, they were accused of causing the illness. It is painful to contemplate the mothers' experience in this "therapy."

Since we residents were forbidden to make any formal contact with family members, I could not assess the mothers of patients with schizophrenia, and I accepted that bad mothering caused the illness. Later, as a working psychiatrist, I knew better.

As compelling evidence developed that schizophrenia is primarily an organic, brain-based disease with a strong genetic component, most psychiatrists abandoned the schizophrenogenic mother theory. Over the next few decades, cognitive neuroscience began to document, with increasing specificity, just what was wrong in the brains and minds of people with schizophrenia.

People who developed schizophrenia were much more likely than other people to have a close biological relative who also had schizophrenia. This was true even when the identified patient had been adopted away in infancy and raised in a "normal" family. With twenty-first century advances in genetics, we now know that more than half the risk for schizophrenia is based on genetic factors [26]. In other words, a big part of the risk for schizophrenia is inherited.

Unfortunately, this finding has no implication for treatment. Schizophrenia is unlike sickle cell anemia, where the genetic risk is a result of one modification in a single gene, giving rise to the realistic hope that we can modify that gene and cure that disease. The genetic risk for schizophrenia is related to modifications in many genes that add together. For schizophrenia, it seems highly unlikely that we will ever be able to change the genetic risk.

Environmental factors also play a role. We know that adverse life events can adversely affect the brains of genetically vulnerable people. Clinically observable schizophrenia is more likely to appear when the vulnerable person experiences pathogenic life events. These include prenatal maternal hunger, especially in the first trimester [27], maternal flu [28], childhood severe infection [29] or trauma [30], migration [31], or urban residence, at least in northern Europe. Heredity and life experience combine to determine whether a vulnerable person will develop clinically apparent illness. Schizophrenia appears to be less severe in third world countries, and we think this is because these societies offer social roles that people with schizophrenia can adequately fill.

* * *

As ideas about the cause of schizophrenia changed, ideas about assessment also changed. American psychiatry came around to the view of those few psychiatrists who had maintained a focus on signs and symptoms for decades. They knew that accurate diagnosis and scientifically respectable research on mental disorders would be based on the careful collection of these data [32, 33]. In the 1980s, as the belief in the role of unconscious conflict as a cause for schizophrenia declined, their approach to assessment came to dominate American psychiatric thinking.

As these changes were occurring nationally, I integrated my clinical experience with what I had absorbed about the importance of evidence during my psychology training, and I came to understand that psychiatric assessment required an integration of the descriptive and the dynamic. For the patient, symptoms represent a salient and troubling aspect of experience, not only the basis for a formal diagnosis. This meant in order to understand my patient's experience and convey that understanding to the patient I had to learn about and accurately describe their symptoms. As I understood this, it became the core of my clinical practice and clinical teaching. With this information in hand, accurate diagnosis followed. In some cases, as I gathered more information, I thought I could understand a relationship between the current symptoms and memories of past experiences, a connection of which they may or may not have been aware.

You may know from your own experience as a patient how often you have come out of the doctor's office annoyed with yourself because you forgot to mention something you thought was important. This illustrates that if the doctor wants to know something about their patient's experience, they must ask; you cannot rely on the patient to tell you, especially with psychotic patients, because their thoughts may be fragmented and their memory impaired.

To learn about the experience of psychotic patients, there is no substitute for the kind of concrete inquiry described in the appendix to this chapter.[5] Asking these questions takes time. The psychiatrist cannot ask them all in one interview, but they can ask the most important ones and come back to the others later. Regrettably, as described in the last section of this book, managed care under which most psychiatrists practice does not pay for the time required. This is a key factor in understanding the damage that has been done to the profession of psychiatry.

As I became comfortable in my clinical judgment, I had an increasing sense that I knew what I was doing, and that I could teach residents how to understand and treat their patients. Teaching my descriptive interview to the residents helped them understand the experience of their patients with schizophrenia, and so I made this basic to my teaching about how to approach psychotic patients.

* * *

Near the end of the twentieth century, we came to better appreciate that cognitive deficits are also present in schizophrenia and that these deficits are responsible for much of the limited capacity these patients possess to engage with the world. Multiple

---

5   The interview as presented in the appendix is an exact copy of the document
    I hand out to new residents at the beginning of our teaching relationship.

domains of cognition—including executive function, attention and vigilance, working memory, verbal fluency, visuospatial skills, processing speed, and social cognition—are affected in patients with schizophrenia.

Functional magnetic resonance imaging (fMRI), which tracks brain activity, has revealed abnormal brain functioning when a person with schizophrenia is asked to carry out relatively simple tasks requiring executive function. The cerebral cortex—especially its frontal lobes—is critically important in all aspects of thinking, and fMRI shows damage to this region in patients with schizophrenia [34]. The frontal lobes are active when a person engages in any activity requiring sequential thinking. Observational studies have shown that patients make many errors and are quite inefficient in cooking even a simple meal.

Schizophrenia may not be the only cause of deficits in patients' cognitive function. Antipsychotic medication, especially in the large doses that were once common, also interferes with cognitive functioning [35]. Current practice has greatly reduced recommended doses of antipsychotic medication.

There is now substantial work assessing the cognitive function, genetics, and brain activity in first-degree relatives of patients with schizophrenia, as well as in the patients themselves. This work is exciting for our future understanding and treatment of schizophrenia. For now, we are just beginning to grasp how the brains of people with schizophrenia differ from the brains of everyone else. So far, this has not made a contribution to our ability to treat patients. Our treatment advances have all developed empirically, or, in other words, by trial and error.

* * *

In treating patients with schizophrenia, I wanted to know what was helpful and what was not. I knew that medication had ameliorated symptoms in my patients, but the evidence on the efficacy of psychotherapy was mixed; so, in 1977, I designed and carried out a small study on psychodynamic-based psychotherapy with my patients who had schizophrenia.

Patients reported that they liked having someone to talk to, and some individuals reported functional gains, e.g. "could balance my checkbook", or "held a part-time job," but overall, we found no evidence that psychotherapy was associated with improved social function [36]. This research suggested that a supportive social relationship is a good experience for patients with schizophrenia, but that psychodynamic psychotherapy cannot be expected to accomplish much beyond that.

The recent development of cognitive behavioral therapy as a treatment for psychosis offers the possibility of achieving more substantial gains with these patients. In the 1960s, Aaron T. "Tim" Beck (no relation), a psychoanalyst who was distressed by the interminable nature of psychoanalytic treatment, developed cognitive behavioral therapy (CBT)—a problem-solving, short-term therapy that focuses on the present. CBT seeks to help patients identify distorted beliefs in order to change behaviors [37]. For many years, CBT was offered to people with depression or anxiety, not psychosis.

Late in the twentieth century, psychologists and some psychiatrists in the U.K. adapted CBT for the treatment of psychosis [38], including the psychosis experienced by people with schizophrenia. Known as CBTp—"p" for psychosis—this treatment is based on the recovery model: the patient is in charge. The patient defines the problems and chooses the treatment, and the treating professional accepts the patient's agenda. CBTp is far more available in the U.K. than it is in this country, and early work suggests that it has great promise for the treatment of psychotic patients who are distressed by the symptoms of their psychosis.

The big change in the treatment of schizophrenia in the late twentieth century has come from the change in our understanding of the relationship between the person and the disease. Earlier psychiatric literature talks about "schizophrenics." In the last quarter of the twentieth century, we began to write about "people with schizophrenia." This reflected our new understanding that we were dealing with people who had a disease, not dealing just with a disease.

Important advances in psychosocial treatment came when psychiatrists began to listen to patients and their advocates and looked at patients' strengths, not just the weaknesses their disease created. The National Alliance on Mental Illness (NAMI) was founded in 1979, and the recovery movement began in the 1980s, when individuals with a history of major mental illness, including schizophrenia, went public with their (often noxious) experience as patients. They insisted on being recognized as individuals with strengths, and they demanded that society recognize them as autonomous individuals and no longer stigmatize them as psychiatric casualties.

Daniel Fisher, MD, PhD, co-founder of the National Empowerment Project and a current leader in the recovery movement, was one of the first people to go public about his mental illness [39]. He was hospitalized three times with a diagnosis of schizophrenia when he was in his twenties and working as a researcher at the National Institute of Mental Health. He was appalled by how he had been treated, and he resolved to work to change how society treated people who were hospitalized after a psychotic break. He went to Harvard Medical School and then trained as a psychiatrist in our department at Cambridge Hospital, completing his training in 1979.

In 1994, Dan wrote that the attitudes of many professionals and the hospital environment are major barriers to recovery [40]. He added that the treaters must recognize the patient as a person and acknowledge their strengths. He stressed, as does the recovery movement generally, that patients must have some choice in how they are to be treated, as well as some control over how they are actually treated. Dan and others wrote that, given the opportunity, a person with a disability could be self-determining, able to independently plan for and lead their own life.

Even before that, research done in the 1980s, much of it by psychologists, led to a new interest in patient strengths. Resiliency is considered to be a significant factor in recovery. Resiliency (or resilience) is loosely defined as the inner strength that helps a person cope with life's stresses. Resilience develops from a combination of the individual's assets—e.g., capacity for executive function, a stable identity, and a future orientation— and external social supports. These social resources include parents or parent equivalents and communities that provide safe streets, public recreational facilities, and decent schools for all. Resiliency research has also raised the question of whether society could help develop resilience in individuals, especially children and adolescents, through appropriate interventions, and there is evidence to suggest that we can increase resilience at least marginally in some vulnerable individuals.

As psychiatrists became aware of this, we began to ask: if resilience can protect against social stress, can it also protect against the development of psychosis, including schizophrenia? Work to date suggests that differences in resilience do make a difference in the future course for young adults who have risk factors for developing psychosis [41], but research on treatment to increase resiliency has not shown convincing evidence of effectiveness. It represents largely a hope.

* * *

One of the bright spots in treatment history is a highly successful program developed to help severely mentally ill patients become gainfully employed. When patients can be employed in a competitive workplace, they report improvement in their mental state, as well as decreased symptoms and a better level of function. This new treatment program grew directly out of research designed to evaluate current treatments for severely and persistently mentally ill patients [42].

This program is the life's work of Robert Drake MD, PhD, now a professor of psychiatry at Dartmouth College and one of the best residents we trained at Cambridge City Hospital. Bob is a man of medium height, medium build, and a quiet, unassuming manner, with sandy hair when we trained him, now turning gray. He is thoughtful, attentive, and an easy, comfortable person to talk with. He grew up in rural Florida. He had a good friend in high school who became severely mentally ill, whom he visited often in the hospital.

"I was predestined to be in mental illness without knowing it," he said when I interviewed him in the course of writing this book. "I had a good friend who was a lovely guy with a serious mental illness, so I have a natural liking for people who have a psychotic illness. It's easy for me to talk with them—I have done that my whole life."

Bob went to college and graduate school at Duke, earning a PhD in developmental psychology. He received his MD from Harvard Medical School and went on to do his psychiatric residency at Cambridge where I was one of his supervisors. He then became director of research at the New Hampshire Department of Mental Health. There, he started a pioneering program demonstrating that, with the right treatment and support, severely mentally ill patients can be gainfully employed in the larger society, rather than being confined to a sheltered workshop.

The inspiration for the program came when Bob learned what happened to patients after the state closed a clubhouse social program for chronic mental patients. Bob wondered what happened to them, and he compared these patients with others who had remained in a comparable clubhouse program in another city. He followed the patients in these two programs and, to his surprise, found that the people in the open clubhouse program were unchanged at the end of the year, while those whose program had closed down improved significantly.

When Bob looked into this result more closely, he found that a vocational specialist at the closed program had worked with the patients to help them find jobs, and sixty percent of those people were employed. "I never would have believed that sixty percent could work," Bob said. "And there were no negative outcomes. We re-interviewed these patients, and they all said, 'our lives are better.' I did a lot of those interviews myself, and that is when I realized these [clubhouse] centers were socializing people into disability."

That experience led Bob and colleagues to create Individual Placement and Support (IPS) programs [42]. IPS programs always include employment assistance professionals who, optimally, are integrated with clinical treatment program staff. IPS is available to any patient who says they would like to work, regardless of diagnosis or how sick or impaired that patient appears to be.

Rehabilitation services generally, and IPS in particular, grew out of a strength-based approach to helping the mentally ill. The theory of psychiatric rehabilitation dictates that finding or creating supportive environments and improving the individual's abilities can enhance a person's self-esteem. IPS programs have eight empirically derived principles:

1. Rehabilitation is considered an integral part of mental health treatment.
2. The goal is competitive employment and integrated work settings, rather than prevocational sheltered or segregated work.
3. People with severe mental illness can obtain and succeed in competitive jobs directly, without pre-employment training.
4. Work performance assessment is continuous and based on competitive work experience.

5. Support for the individual is tailored to what they need, rather than terminating at a set point.

6. The employee determines what they want in the way of job finding, disclosure, and job support. This, not the provider's judgment, determines the plan.

7. Services are provided in the community.

8. A multidisciplinary team approach is key.

Any client who expresses interest in competitive employment is helped to find it. This is a "place/train" model, which means that employment experts engage with clients to find jobs in the community (placement), even if only for a few hours a week or for a limited time. Then they continue a supportive relationship to help the client succeed (train). The key is finding a real job, not make-work, that matches the client's interests, skills, and unique qualities, rather than trying to change the client. IPS maintains a relationship with the new employer, as well as with the client. With this support, many employers are happy to continue participating in the program, hiring a new client after the original placement has moved on.

Treatment systems like IPS can promote recovery by shifting the focus from segregated or institutional settings into integrated, ordinary settings in the community. Integrated services where the IPS is part of a multidisciplinary team that includes clinicians are always superior to services that are separated.

Bob has consistently evaluated IPS [43, 44], repeatedly designing and carrying out controlled trials in which IPS has been randomly assigned to one of two similar programs. The other program continued with treatment as usual. Where a randomized controlled trial was impractical, IPS programs were compared with other similar programs in the same area. The evidence of this solid research is that IPS is consistently more effective than traditional, sheltered workshop programs in helping patients obtain and keep employment. Furthermore, patients who are employed in a competitive workplace report improvement in their mental state, including decreased symptoms and a better overall level of function.

Research on resilience confirms and supports this approach. The essence of these ideas is that disability is a conferred status and not an inherent part of illness. Rather, disability is a secondary problem created largely by how society—individuals and institutions—respond to people with mental illnesses. People who suffer an illness can easily be isolated, devalued, persecuted, and socialized into thinking of themselves as defective. When opportunities for healing, recovery, growth, and success are available, they work strongly against these pernicious changes. Not every patient in IPS is a success, and work for these people does not necessarily mean full-time, permanent employment, but it does often mean an improved, less disabled status with a corresponding improvement in self-esteem.

In 2001, Bob and his group received a grant of $15 million—$1 million a year for fifteen years—to develop these programs. Since 2001, Bob and his group have received almost $300 million in grants from government agencies and private foundations. They have passed this money on to the states to help them develop IPS programs. As of 2018, twenty states are using IPS as a core part of their service system for the severely and persistently mentally ill: Alabama, Alaska, Arizona, California,

Colorado, Connecticut, District of Columbia, Florida, Kansas, Kentucky, Maryland, Mississippi, Montana, North Carolina, Ohio, Oregon, Minnesota, Montana, South Carolina, Tennessee, Utah, Vermont, Washington, and Wisconsin. It is rare for an individual physician to make a contribution to the health of an entire country, but Bob, with his group, has done just that.

These new developments in psychosocial treatment of schizophrenia are heartening. First and most important, patients who receive these treatments will do better than those who do not. Second, it is gratifying to see the profession develop an understanding of schizophrenia and its treatment consistent with what we tried to teach at Cambridge City Hospital—that the person who has the disease should be respected and treated as an equal member of the treatment team, with the doctor and patient working together.

* * *

This chapter presents a summary of the intellectual history of schizophrenia—but intellectual history is only half the story. At least as important as what we know is what society does with our knowledge. Here, America fails. We know how to help people with schizophrenia, but we do not allocate the resources to do it.

Programs that effectively help stabilize the lives of people with schizophrenia require more than antipsychotic medication to succeed. Medication enables patients to leave the hospital, but it does not address what they need in order to live in the community. They need case management to help address issues with activities of daily living—personal hygiene, financial management, and help

185

in continuing to take their essential medication. They need stable housing, which is not available or is not within their reach in most places, so many people with schizophrenia end up homeless. They need expert assistance if they are to return to work after an episode of acute illness. Almost nowhere in this country are the full range of these needed services. The result is that these patients frequently stop their medication, become acutely ill again, and require re-hospitalization in beds that are no longer available.

The predictable result is that society forcibly removes these acutely ill patients from the community. Today, more people with schizophrenia and other severe persistent mental disorders are housed in jails and prisons than are treated in the mental health system [6]. Of the 300,000 incarcerated mentally ill, as many as 50,000 are estimated to be people with schizophrenia. This is a national disgrace, and as of 2020, no change is in sight.

####

Chapter 11 – Appendix

Descriptive Interview Outline

Introduction. This represents a summary of basic questions that can serve as an outline for doing a careful descriptive psychiatric assessment. Some of these questions are drawn from the SCID Structured Clinical Interview for DSM Disorders, some from the comparable UK interview, the PSE (Present State Exam). I like to get this information beginning in the initial interview. The interview contains sections on depression, mania, substance abuse, psychosis and anxiety disorders.

Note: This is not a complete initial assessment. It does not cover history. It is not a thorough risk assessment for self-harm, and not a risk assessment at all for potential violence.

General comments:

- Ask the q.s in the order that makes sense. If the patient's chief complaint is about anxiety, begin there; if about depression, begin there, and so on.

- <u>Do</u> feel free to ask questions about anything else (e.g., personal relationships, life events) that the patient raises, e.g. if the patient says, 'it started after I broke up with my boyfriend (girlfriend), do ask about what happened.

- <u>Do</u> complete as much or as little of the modules as makes sense at any one sitting. Sicker patients may not be able to do it at all. Healthier patients may have enough to say about their experience that you can't get through much in one session.

- <u>Don't</u> try to do this when it's obvious the patient is not in shape to provide meaningful answers.

- When you get a positive response to a q. do go on to ask as much as you need to in order to learn what the experience was like for the patient. Q.s on **d**uration, **i**ntensity, **r**elation to life events, **w**hat makes it better or worse. **(Dur; intens; life events, better/worse; is it impairing and in what way?)**

- For inpts ask about the month before admission. For outpts: the month before you are seeing them.

- For patients from another culture, some place in the interview where it makes sense, ask
  - ¤ What is the understanding of mental illness in your culture? (or similar q.)
  - ¤ What is the attitude toward suicide?

<u>The interview.</u> To begin with I would like to get an idea of the sort of problems that have been troubling you during the past month. What have been the main difficulties?

Depression. What has your mood been like in the past month (month before adm)? Have you been depressed? If yes, **Duration and Intensity, e.g.** most of the day, nearly every day? How bad has it been?

What are your interests?
How long since you've done …?
Did you lose interest in …?

If yes to either depr or loss of interests, ask the SIGECAPS[6] q.s (If no to both, go on to next topic)

Sleep (early, middle or late sleep difficulties)
Interests (Already asked)
Guilt (Have you felt guilty about something you've done or said?)
Energy: How has your energy been?
Concentration: How about your concentration?
Appetite: How has your appetite been? any weight change?
Psychomotor retardation or agitation: Fidgety/restless or slowed down?

---

6   Sleep, Interests, Guilt, Energy, Concentration, Appetite, Psychomotor, Suicide

Thoughts of self/harm; death. **This does not purport to be a guide to a good evaluation of self-harm.**

Functional impairment: Has this made it hard for you to work, take care of home/children, get along with other people?

Rule out or in: recent medical illness, substance abuse (s/a), med changes, death of a significant other.

(When I am seeing a pt for the first time I like to focus on what brought the pt here now, so I ask first about present depression. I do ask about past major depression or chronic low-grade depression (dysthymia) where it seems to make sense clinically.)

Mania. In the past month were you feeling so good or high or excited or hyper that people thought you were not your normal self, or you got into trouble?

If yes: what was that like, **(Dur; intens; life events, better/ worse)**

If no, what about being irritable, shouting at people, losing your temper, starting fights or arguments, (even w. people you didn't know). If yes **(Dur; intens; life events, better/ worse)**

If No to both, go on to the next topic. I may ask past manic here if the pt presents w. any significant symptoms of affective disorder.
If Yes, Follow-up q.s on self esteem grandiosity
How much Sleep per night?
Observe speech and thought: -racing, pressured, tangential
Distractibility

How spend time? Level of activity? Always on the go?

Anything that could have gotten you into trouble?

Problems in work or social relations during this episode?

R/O or In: recent medical illness, s/a, med changes,

If any indication that pt is irritable or angry, ask here

Are you angry at anyone?

If yes, Are you thinking about hurting them?

If no, Have you ever hurt anyone seriously?

If yes to either, do a risk assessment interview. **Again, this outline does not cover risk assessment for potential violence.** If you are unsure how to do this, either read or seek out someone who can teach you.

Ref: Webster, Christopher D. et al: HCR –20: Assessing Risk for Violence (Version 2).

www.sfu.ca/psychology/groups/mhlpi/hrc-20.htm

Dysthymic Disorder: For the past few years, have you been depressed most of the time, more days than not? (need 2 yrs for a dx in adults)

If no, go on to the next topic.

If yes, re-ask the SIGECAPS q.s above.

Psychotic Symptoms

Can you think clearly or is there any interference with your thoughts?

: If any evidence of thought disorder:

Are you in full control of your thoughts?

191

Are you concerned that people can read your mind?

Have you had the feeling recently that things around you were unreal? (as though everything was an imitation of reality, like a movie, with people acting instead of being themselves)

Have you yourself felt unreal, as if you were not a person?
(Or that you were outside yourself, looking at yourself)

Is something odd going on that you can't explain?
Have other people been talking about you, or taking special notice of you?
Is this just an idea or is it really happening?

Are you concerned that anyone is trying to harm you in any way?
(either physically, psychologically, financially or in their personal relationships?)
Are you special in any way? (Do you have any special powers?)
Have you had any unusual religious experiences?
Is there anything wrong with your body?
Have you felt like you have done something terrible for which you should be punished?
Are you concerned that someone may be controlling your thoughts or behavior in some way?
Have you heard what seem to be voices when no one else is present?
(awake? real or imagination? inside or outside head? Who? Saying what? Affective tone?)

Have you ever had visions or seen things that other people didn't? (specifics as w. auditory;

Awake? Who? Saying, doing what? Affective tone?)

What about strange sensations in your body?

Strange Smells or tastes?

If any of the above are positive, ask the usual q.s (duration, intensity) to explicate.

If pt endorses any of these psychotic experiences so that you are convinced pt has positive sx, ask "have you thought about doing anything or done anything about x?

Substance abuse

How much do you drink? Ever been a problem? If yes: or if concerned: blackouts, seizures, DTs, morning drinking or the CAGE q.s as well as duration, etc.)

CAGE: **C**oncerned to cut down? Others **A**ngry? **G**uilty about your drinking? Ever take an **E**ye opener?

Repeat for drug abuse—either street or prescription drugs?

Anxiety Disorders

Have you ever had a panic attack when you suddenly felt frightened or anxious or had a lot of physical symptoms? If yes, out of the blue? Or related to something? (number, duration, intensity, etc.)

Worried you might die or are going crazy? Worry about having another one? Not go out for fear of having one and not being able to get home? (segue into agoraphobia)

Ask about autonomic sx: heart racing, pounding? Sweat? SOB (short of breath)? Choking? Chest pain/pressure?
Nausea, might vomit or have diarrheas? Dizzy? Feel faint? Tingling/numbness? Hot flashes/chills?

R/o med changes, phys illness.

Frightened about having a panic attack in some situation? In a crowd? Away from home? Closed place? Heights?
  If yes to any, do you avoid?

OCD

Are there thoughts that come into your mind against your will? If pt unsure, 'like hurting someone? Or worrying about germs or contamination?
  If yes, Probe for how often? Duration, how dysphoric?
  What can you do to help?

Is there anything you have to do over and over even though it doesn't make any sense?
  Oven off? Door locked? Cleaning? Or rituals: step over cracks? Clothes laid out?
  Why do you think you do that?

PTSD

In your life have you ever had any experiences that were very frightening or awful,
and in the past month

You have had nightmares or thought about it when you did not want to?

Tried hard not to think about it or to avoid anything that reminded you of it?

Were constantly on guard, watchful or easily startled?

Felt numb or detached from other people, activities or your surroundings.

If you get a 'yes' to any of these, explore duration, intensity, etc. and go back to your DSM to see what else to ask.

Social Phobia or Anxiety

Are you a person who gets uncomfortable when you have to do something in public? Like make a speech? Or eating or using a public restroom?

If yes, Do you refuse to do … in public because you get too anxious?

Generalized Anxiety Disorder

In the last six months have you been particularly nervous or anxious?

Do you worry about terrible things that might happen? What? Is that realistic?

Would you say that you worry most of the time? Or more days than not?

If yes, run the same list of symptoms as for panic.

Somatization

Do you worry about your physical health?

How often do you go to the doctor? Do the doctors find anything wrong?

(Consult DSM[7] for further questions on hypochondriasis?

Anorexia

I want to ask you about your eating habits and weight.

Have you ever weighed much less than other people thought you should? (When? Duration, lowest wt? etc.)

Were you afraid you were too fat? (Missed periods?)

Bulimia

Have you ever had eating binges? Was your eating out of control? (freq. Duration, etc.)

Did you purge? Vomit? Take laxatives?

Were you especially concerned about your weight or your shape or how you looked?

---

7   Diagnostic and Statistical Manual of the American Psychiatric Association

CHAPTER 12

METROPOLITAN STATE
HOSPITAL: I SERVE AGAIN

Twelve years out of residency, I had enough experience that I enjoyed caring for very sick patients, and I was pleased to accept the Met State job. The Cambridge-Somerville unit, where I was medical director, occupied a building of its own with 160 patients on three wards—two in general psychiatry and one in dual diagnosis for patients with mental disorders and substance abuse. My office was just outside one of the general psychiatry wards, so that I was easily available to staff and patients. Amazingly, the directorship was considered a half-time job—off the charts, even for the public sector. (I also had a half-time job at the Cambridge Court Clinic; see Ch. 14)

In addition to our patients, Met State cared for 320 other patients in separate buildings, all housed on a sprawling campus that hugged the towns of Waltham, Belmont, and Lexington. It was built in the late 1920s at the edge of all three communities, because none of them wanted the hospital.

The living conditions at Met State had changed little since my days as a volunteer more than twenty years earlier. Our building was old and tired; the heating system barely functioned. There was no privacy, even in the bathrooms— the toilets had no seats, and the stalls had no doors. Occasionally, patients could be found having sex in a toilet stall. The food was edible, but not much more. The inadequate conditions troubled me, but the care we offered was significantly better than what I'd witnessed as a college volunteer, and I was happy to lead a service that provided active treatment for the patients.

Our Met State unit was an integral part of our Harvard-affiliated psychiatry department in Cambridge. We had twenty-five clinical staff, including psychiatrists, psychologists, social workers, trainees, and nurses. We were both a clinical and a teaching service. Psychiatry residents did a six-month rotation, long enough to learn how to evaluate and treat patients too sick to be treated on the open psychiatry ward at Cambridge City Hospital (renamed around this time to Cambridge Hospital).

For our patients, the route to Met State led through the psychiatry emergency service at Cambridge Hospital, where our psychiatry residents did the initial evaluation. They took a history, performed the mental status and physical exams, and wrote the admission orders. When new patients arrived on our ward at Met State, the staff had only to make sure they could be safely managed—usually, but not always, a straightforward task—and help them settle in.

Teaching at Met State was more informal than it was on the psychiatry ward at Cambridge Hospital, where we made rounds on every patient every day. In a state hospital, there were too many patients for that. Many had been in the hospital for months or years and were quite stable, so our rounds focused on the new admissions and on any of the long-stay patients for whom we had immediate concerns.

Teaching for residents and other clinicians occurred during these rounds. We discussed the symptoms and likely diagnoses of all new admissions, using information we gained from their admission notes and medical status from the nurse practitioner. This would lead to a discussion of what we might want to learn about the patient's social situation and to the development of a treatment plan. Psychiatrists could provide medication, and we had staff psychologists and social workers, as well as residents, who could provide psychotherapy when appropriate. This was a full academic state hospital service in which we were able to do biopsychosocial assessment and treatment.

One of these residents, Bruce Gage, later commented on his experience at Cambridge and at Met State: "My time at Cambridge was the most important time in my life professionally. My first assignment was Metropolitan State Hospital. One of my supervisors was an old Viennese analyst, a woman in her mid-seventies, slightly demented but a wonderful supervisor. After we got to know each other, she said to me, 'When are you going to stop being a doctor and start being a psychiatrist?' I saw immediately what she meant, and I began to embrace the psychological way of relating to patients."

The one formal teaching exercise we had every month was a session with an invited faculty member, often the expert psychopharmacologist Bessel van der Kolk. Bessel was also a trauma expert. We presented our most difficult cases to him—patients who were severely agitated, often with florid delusions, suffering greatly and not getting better despite our best efforts. These discussions were a great resource in helping us understand these patients. To our great surprise, these most difficult patients were almost always women, and they almost all had incest histories. With this information, we could reformulate our treatment plan to include psychotherapy related to these issues. Bessel and I published these findings in the *American Journal of Psychiatry*. The paper we published was limited to a description of the patients and did not comment on whether their new psychotherapy was helpful.

* * *

I made two important changes soon after I arrived as medical director. When I arrived, the entrenched senior ward physician, Gerhardt Duda, a European-trained German psychiatrist, struck me as somewhat rigid in that he was doing his job the way he did it, and resisted any discussion with his new chief.

Dr. Duda defined his role in an unusual way. Typically, psychiatrists on an inpatient unit make rounds in the morning, see any new patients, address problems or patient requests, and then spend the rest of the day in their offices. Not this man—he spent the entire day sitting out on the ward, chatting informally with patients. I was positively impressed with this, but I soon learned that another aspect of his work was problematic.

Many patients who had been transferred in when the state created our unit had lived on this unit for months or years, and sometimes for their entire adult life. Whenever a patient became too loud, violent, or otherwise disruptive, a nurse would come to Dr. Duda and say, "He needs more medicine." And Dr. Duda would write an order for more medicine. In a state mental hospital, behavioral upsets are frequent, and Dr. Duda wrote correspondingly often for "more medicine." That was all well and good, except that after the patient's acute problem resolved, Dr. Duda never lowered the medicine back to a more appropriate chronic-dose level.

When I first took the job, I reviewed the chart of every patient and was appalled to discover that some patients were on astronomical doses of antipsychotic medication—as much as four grams of Thorazine a day, when the maximum recommended dose is one gram. Inquiring from the nurses how this was possible, I got the story of, "He needs more medicine," and the absence of any subsequent reduction.

These antipsychotic medications all have serious side effects. The most serious of these—tardive dyskinesia—is irreversible and dose-related. Slow, involuntary movements of various muscle groups, most often and most noticeably rhythmic movements of the tongue and lips, characterize tardive dyskinesia. In more severe cases, movements of the trunk, arms, and legs occur. Restless legs are also a common side effect—less disabling, but very troubling for patients. Appalled by these high doses, I began to reduce these levels of medication as fast as I safely could. Dr. Duda quit six weeks after I arrived, which was a good thing for both of us and, in my opinion, an especially good thing for patients. He took a new job as head of a mental health day care center in Cambridge, which was an important resource for our chronic patients. The day center patients were chronically mentally ill, but behaviorally stable and not as acutely ill as the hospitalized patients, so "he needs more medicine" would have been, I hoped, only an occasional issue.

The second change I made concerned the medical care. The hospital relied on part-time medical specialists to address any medical problems that were beyond what the psychiatrists could handle. The specialists were each paid for four hours per week, and it was clear that they had no continuing sense of responsibility for our patients. They came when called, assessed the problem in front of them, made a recommendation, and left.

I persuaded our unit administrator to terminate all these contracts. With the money we saved, I hired a full-time medical nurse practitioner. She loved the work, and she practiced as an almost completely independent professional, taking on responsibility for the total medical care of our patients. These were her patients, and she knew every one of them personally; care improved enormously as a result.

* * *

In these days, for better or for worse, we were able to keep patients in our facility for as long as we thought we might possibly help them further. Clarence was one of our difficult patients. He was a highly intelligent, appealing young man diagnosed with bipolar, or possibly schizoaffective, disorder, whom we had been treating as an outpatient in Cambridge until he went on an angry rampage and almost destroyed his therapist's office. That got him committed to Met State, where over the next few months he improved enough to be discharged. However, a social worker who was his psychotherapist felt that more progress would be possible if she and Clarence could continue their psychotherapy. On that basis, we kept Clarence in the hospital for two more years. These additional years of psychotherapy appeared to make no difference, and we finally discharged him. In hindsight, it is clear that our treatment of Clarence should have raised a moral issue for us, but to be honest, it didn't. By the standards of the day, we were doing what we thought was best for our patient.

I followed Clarence as an outpatient over the next few years, and he continued to struggle, living a marginal life as a chronic mental patient, until I lost the connection. Many years later, I walked into a law office in downtown Boston, and to my great surprise, the receptionist who greeted me was Clarence. But it was not the Clarence I remembered—this was a poised, professional man. I was happy to see him, and he to see me. I was delighted to see these changes in him. How did this happen? I wanted to know. He was happy to tell me: Clozapine, a medication that the FDA approved in 2004, was responsible for this dramatic change. Clozapine didn't cure Clarence, but it did give him back his life.

Our facility treated patients with a range of diagnoses. Some of our patients carried a diagnosis of borderline personality disorder (BPD), a disorder characterized by extreme emotional dysregulation. These patients were typically admitted after they had become despondent and threatened to kill themselves. Some had become so disorganized in their thinking and behavior that they appeared psychotic, and we were concerned that they could be a danger to themselves.

Robin was a twenty-three-year-old woman who came to the emergency room crying and intoxicated. She had cut her forearms, but not deeply enough to require stitches. She told us she was thinking of killing herself, but when asked why, she could only shake her head and sob harder. Even after several hours in the emergency room, she was unable to give us a history, and the resident decided to admit her.

My experience with these patients was that initially they were too disorganized to give a good history, but that small doses of antipsychotic medication would make a huge difference in how accessible they would become. Once the patient could engage with me, I could begin to try to find out what had gone wrong. Initially, Robin could only shake her head when asked if she had any idea what was troubling her. The image I had of Robin and patients like her was that they were blindfolded in a big, dark, empty room, where they were being pummeled by boxing gloves they could not see and were helpless to avoid—helpless to deal with their situation and their misery. With time and a little help, Robin and other patients could begin to understand that their sufferings were connected to events in their lives. The experience of being buffeted randomly into misery would abate, and these patients would begin to calm down.

Because we kept patients in the hospital far longer than is possible today, I could then go on to try to help the patient learn to look for some connection between disappointments and episodes of acute distress. These disappointments appeared to precipitate the self-harmful behavior, severe psychological disorganization, and possibly psychosis which typically characterized these patients on admission. Some BPD patients did begin to understand how life events related to their symptoms and self-harmful behavior, and they could begin to manage their distress better. We could discharge them and refer them for psychotherapy that might help them manage their lives better and begin to address the childhood trauma or neglect that was so commonly present. Robin did learn to make these connections, and we discharged her to the community with a referral for psychotherapy. She appeared to have returned to her baseline—a troubled woman functioning with difficulty in the community, but with some new awareness of how she had repeatedly gotten into difficulties in the past.

We were also able to discharge an occasional long-stay patient by adjusting medications that in some cases had not been reviewed in many years. With such adjustments, these patients "woke up" and were able to participate in the social life of the ward. We could then refer these patients to the Ambulatory Care Service that had the expertise and experience to help the patient get ready for discharge, and then to manage life in the community.

I was happy in the job, feeling that I was contributing to and even improving the lives of people who had been ignored and neglected for years, and for whom our efforts made a difference. The work with the patients was always satisfying; dealing with the administration of the hospital was another story. It was a difficult place to work, in significant part because of the intransigence of the bureaucracy responsible for administration. I could see a problem and a way to fix it, but when I requested a change, nothing would happen. After a few experiences like this, I learned that there was no point in imagining that I could get this system to change. I accepted these conditions for four years, but it got to be too much for me emotionally, and I moved on.

In 1980, I joined the staff of the Cambridge Court Clinic, becoming medical director in 1985. This position fit nicely with the part-time private practice of forensic psychiatry that I also began in 1980 and have maintained throughout my working life. The next chapter is about my involvement with the law.

#####

CHAPTER 13

PSYCHIATRY AND THE LAW

I was driving alone in a rented car through the sparsely populated piney woods of southern Alabama. It was midsummer of 1994 and blindingly hot. When I stopped for coffee at a roadside restaurant, I had a strong sense of isolation, and I wondered what the few people in the restaurant would have thought had they known my business: trying to help save a Black man on death row from execution.

I arrived at the prison and stood in the middle of a barren, dusty parking lot. I could see the guard in the watchtower holding a long gun and looking out. I felt like I was in the middle of a 1940s gangster movie, and I thought to myself, "What is a nice Jewish boy like you doing in a place like this?"

Alabama death row is a long way from Cambridge Hospital, but my career had taken a meaningful turn in 1980, when I began working half time at the Cambridge Court Clinic, a job that led me to become an expert in forensic psychiatry—the practice of

207

psychiatry in a legal context. As part of this work, I lectured and demonstrated how to be an expert witness at Harvard Law School, where a young man named Bryan Stevenson was a student. It was thanks to Bryan that I had come to Alabama.

Bryan graduated from law school in 1985, and he began his lifelong career as a civil rights attorney in the South. In 1994, he started the Equal Justice Initiative (EJI) of Alabama, a nonprofit organization that provides representation for defendants who have been sentenced to death. Since then, Bryan, who won a MacArthur "Genius" Grant in 1995, has become a nationally known advocate for social justice who has argued before the Supreme Court on death penalty cases. He is the author of the bestselling book *Just Mercy: A Story of Justice and Redemption.*

In the 1990s, when Bryan needed a psychiatrist to assist in the defense of a client, he reached out to me. I flew to Montgomery, Alabama, and met with Bryan at the office of the EJI. To find it, you had to know what you were looking for: like a speakeasy or secret club, there was no sign on the building. Once inside, the office was a bare set of rooms furnished with secondhand wooden desks and tired-looking chairs. A handful of lawyers and student interns were studiously working. Bryan and most of the staff wore blue jeans, although I saw hanging on a clothes rack in the corner a dark blue suit that was clearly for court appearances. I had the strong impression that this was a guerrilla operation—a small band of partisans operating behind the lines in enemy territory. I felt even more strongly that I wanted to help if I could.

My task was to evaluate Reggie F., a twenty-nine-year-old single African American man, who had been on death row in

Holman Prison for eight years for allegedly killing and raping his then-girlfriend's three-year old son Damian. At trial, Reggie testified to what he had done and stated that the death was unintentional, and he denied that he had ever raped the child. He was glad to see me and expressed the hope that I might be able to help his attorney on appeal. I was impressed that he appeared to be an open and direct person.

Reggie had grown up in an intact family, did well in school, had friends, played sports, and generally enjoyed a productive, normal life; until the eleventh grade, when he began hanging out with an older crowd that smoked marijuana and drank. He started cutting classes, drinking, smoking, and selling drugs. After flunking the eleventh grade, he dropped out of school. With no employment history to speak of and two drug convictions, Reggie had moved away from his earlier, more responsible years.

Reggie told me he had become sexually active at age fourteen and had a number of relationships, typically with women slightly older than himself. Prior to his arrest, he was in a stable relationship with his current girlfriend, JoAnn, living with her and her three-year-old son, Damian. The evening of the crime, JoAnn had gone out, leaving Damian home with Reggie. The two fell asleep, but around 1:00 in the morning, Damian woke up crying. To quiet him down, Reggie hit him a few times. Damian did settle for a time, but later he woke up crying again, and Reggie hit him repeatedly with such force that Damian fell and hit his head against the wall. After that Damian was quiet. When JoAnn came home Damian was not breathing. She and Reggie took Damian to the hospital, where the child was pronounced dead.

At trial, there was testimony that Damian had been raped and that he died as a result of repeated blows to the head. Reggie was convicted of rape and murder. The jury recommended a sentence of life in prison, but the judge overruled the jury and recommended death. The attorneys, who had been working to keep him alive since his death sentence, asked me to evaluate him, which I did over two successive days. I found him to be a pleasant, polite young man with no evidence of mental disorder despite his act of violence. He was adamant that he did not rape Damian, and his counsel told me that the state's evidence on this point was badly flawed.

When I asked Reggie about his sexual history, he said that he was "old-fashioned," meaning that he liked sexual intercourse with adult women. He admitted to hitting Damian but could not understand why he hit him so hard or so often. He told me that he loved Damian and got along well with him and with JoAnn. He said he was very sorry for what he had done and that he could not understand how it had happened.

I was sympathetic to Reggie. I thought he told the truth about how he had killed Damian— that he had been almost entirely asleep and had done something he would not have done when awake. I thought his remorse was genuine.

His attorney told me that the physical evidence of rape presented at trial had been badly flawed. Accepting that, and believing Reggie's story, I thought he had been wrongly convicted and sentenced to death. To me, this sounded like a case of involuntary homicide, and I looked forward to presenting my findings to the prosecution.

After the interview, I spoke on the phone with the assistant attorney general who was prosecuting the case, and I said that Reggie had no mental disorder. His background provided no clue as to why he might have committed this crime, but he had continued to insist that he did not rape the child. I said also that his sexual history was inconsistent with the rape of a child. The attorney appeared to be surprised, and he asked quizzically, "Mr. F. wasn't psychotic or anything like that?" I answered, "Nothing like it."

The same judge who had overruled the jury's recommendation for life in prison reheard the case on appeal. Reggie's defense attorneys argued that the state's evidence of rape was badly flawed. Both the state's psychiatrist and I agreed that Reggie was mentally healthy. Apparently, this testimony and testimony about the physical evidence helped the judge to question whether there had, in fact, been a rape, and he ordered a new trial. The defense attorney told me he believed that the fact that two independent psychiatrists presented a history inconsistent with child rape had led the judge to conclude that the original verdict had been flawed. Reggie was removed from death row while he was awaiting a new trial. At the retrial, he got life in prison with opportunity for parole in 2021.

* * *

After I began working in forensic psychiatry at the Cambridge Court Clinic in 1980, I faced many questions and misconceptions about what forensic psychiatry was. People often assumed that my work had something to do with dead bodies, and I would then explain that forensic *pathology* is the medical specialty that deals with bodies. The word 'forensic,' from the Latin word *forum* (the place where Romans made their laws), simply means 'pertaining to the law.' Forensic psychiatry, then, is the application of psychiatric expertise in a legal context.

A forensic psychiatrist may be called on in a wide variety of legal cases, including both civil and criminal matters. Civil cases include questions of competency to make a decision, for example to refuse antipsychotic medication or to execute a contract or a will. Other civil cases can involve allegations of malpractice by a mental health professional or institution, or questions of psychological harm, for example, following an auto accident or a home invasion. Questions in criminal cases include competency to stand trial and criminal responsibility.

Rather than going to trial, many legal cases are settled by negotiation between the attorneys who represent the contending parties. This is true in civil matters, where the contending parties will agree on a compromise monetary settlement, and in criminal cases, where a plea bargain will be negotiated, rather than having the matter proceed to trial. In these negotiations, the forensic psychiatrist will serve as a consultant to the attorney who hired him, [or, in a minority of cases, her]. For the cases that end up in court, the forensic psychiatrist has the status of an expert in matters within their field. This means that they are allowed to give their opinions, as opposed to fact witnesses, who must have first-hand knowledge of the facts at issue and do not need any special expertise, but are not allowed to offer an opinion.

The forensic psychiatrist may be asked to evaluate an individual's capacity to make a decision. To demonstrate capacity, a person must show that they understand the need to make a decision and have a rational as well as a factual understanding of the choices involved. Determining factual understanding is usually straightforward; rational understanding is not so easy, as it requires that the person have an understanding of the consequences for making (or not making) either choice. I have been asked to evaluate capacity in both civil and criminal cases. On the civil side, I have evaluated capacity to refuse antipsychotic medication and capacity to make a will. On the criminal side, I have evaluated capacity to stand trial.

Competence is a legal construct decided only by judges. In American law, every person is presumed to be competent to make a decision until a judge rules that they are not. In ruling on whether a person is competent, the judge may rely on the definition of capacity explained above.

In one case on which I advised, an inpatient psychiatry service in Massachusetts asked me to assist them in petitioning the court to require a patient on their ward to take a recommended antipsychotic medication. The attending psychiatrist told me that the patient, whom I will call Suzanne, was refusing medication that the psychiatrists strongly believed she needed, and they wanted my opinion on whether she had the capacity to make a competent decision.

I reviewed the case with the attending psychiatrist and then met with Suzanne in a quiet, private room. I introduced myself, explaining who had hired me and what they were asking me to evaluate. I informed her of the limits on confidentiality—what I would disclose under what conditions, and what I would keep confidential. I told her she had the right to refuse to answer any particular question and even to decline to participate in the interview. I made clear that I was not her doctor and she was not my patient; we were here for the specific purpose of evaluating how well she understood what she was being asked to decide.

This last point is very important, because when people talk to a doctor, they fall naturally into thinking of the doctor as *their* doctor. The forensic psychiatrist emphatically is not *their* doctor. We are solely the agents of the attorney who hired us, or the court that appointed us.

Suzanne told me that she understood my explanation, and she agreed to go forward. If I'd had any question about whether she understood, I would have asked her to tell me in her own words what I'd just told her. If she appeared so cognitively impaired that she could not repeat the sense of what I told her, then I would decide that she lacked the capacity to give informed consent. In Suzanne's case, I had no reason to doubt that she understood. She was pleasant and cooperative throughout the interview and eager to tell her story. She told me she believed that the interview would help to keep her safe from the people she feared were trying to kill her. Suzanne had many delusional beliefs, such as her assertion that there were five messages on her cell phone saying, "You will be killed." She said that although the messages were hidden, an expert hacker could retrieve them. During the interview, she took out her cell phone and asked some app to provide the name of the best hacker in the United States.

On account of her fears, Suzanne had purchased a handgun to protect herself from possible attack. In response to my specific question, she stated clearly that she was no longer concerned that people were trying to harm her because the interview created a public record that would protect her. Nonetheless, it was clear that she continued to be very fearful. She told me that, if discharged, she would leave the hospital by the back door so that potential assailants would not know where she was, and she planned to obtain a bulletproof vest. Throughout the interview, Suzanne insisted that everything she told me was absolutely true and that there was nothing mentally wrong with her. The following is an excerpt from our conversation:

Me: "Do you believe there is anything wrong with you? Not what the doctors think, but your own opinion."

Suzanne: "There is nothing wrong with me besides overwork, distress, and overweight."

Me: "Why did the doctors give you Zyprexa (an antipsychotic medication)?"

Suzanne: "They told me I needed that stuff because my muscles did not work, and I had blood clots. They concluded nothing else was wrong, but they said, 'Let's give her that so that she can't have sex and she can't run away.'" And much more along the same line.

I concluded that Suzanne lacked the capacity to decide whether to accept or refuse antipsychotic medication. Believing there was nothing wrong with her, she not unreasonably refused to take medication. Unfortunately, her belief was wrong; she was clearly suffering from a psychotic mental illness, best diagnosed, in my opinion, as a paranoid psychosis.

Suzanne and her psychiatrists continue to disagree about whether she should take medication, so a judicial ruling became necessary to determine whether Suzanne would be required to take medication against her will or not.

I agreed with her psychiatrists and recommended to the court that Suzanne be ordered to take antipsychotic medication. The judge found her incompetent to make this decision, but not so dangerous as to be involuntarily medicated.

Suzanne's story illustrates the complexity of the law on involuntary treatment. At the time of my consultation. Suzanne was a voluntary inpatient, refusing medication. Absent an emergency, her psychiatrist could not medicate her involuntarily without a judicial finding that she was mentally ill and sufficiently dangerous to be medicated against her will. There was no question that Suzanne was mentally ill, but the judge did not order her to be medicated against her will. The court hearing itself had a salutary effect: the patient decided after the court hearing to voluntarily remain in the hospital and take medication, which she did until she was discharged a few days later.

Issues pertaining to involuntary treatment arise in other ways as well. Forty-seven states have laws governing involuntary outpatient commitment (Massachusetts is one of three that does not). In these 47 states, if a court rules that a person is mentally ill, a danger to himself or others, unlikely to survive safely in the community, and unlikely to take medication, then it can mandate involuntary outpatient medication or hospitalization if they refuse. In a triumph of bureaucratic euphemism, the New York state law is called 'assisted outpatient treatment' [45] The state provided additional money to treat patients who are adjudicated AOT, and by report, the program is working well.

In 1994, when Massachusetts was considering involuntary outpatient commitment, I chose to spend several months as a visiting psychiatrist in Manchester, England, in order to observe how the National Health Service (NHS) was providing involuntary treatment. The NHS had an integrated service system for involuntary patients that included regional secure hospitals and specialized community residences for treatment of these patients after discharge. Nurses visited patients for their monthly injections of antipsychotic medication, but they also spent time with these patients, reviewing personal matters and providing support. If patients needed additional psychosocial services, these were available.

From this experience, I drew the lesson that involuntary outpatient commitment should represent a social contract: if society requires a patient to take medicine whether he wants to or not, then society should provide in return an adequate system of mental health services. Our psychiatry department in Cambridge adopted this approach and continues to make substantial efforts to fulfill this commitment.

In the three states without involuntary outpatient commitment, when a patient in the community refuses to take medication but does not meet standards for involuntary hospitalization, the state has no legal basis to compel the patient to take the medicine.

Competency can also be an issue when a will is challenged. The legal standard for competency to make a will (technically referred to as testimonial capacity) is specific and minimal: it requires that the person know that they are executing a document that will determine who will inherit what from their estate, how much their estate is worth, and the identity of the "natural objects of their bounty"—that is, the people who would normally be beneficiaries. Attorneys consult forensic clinicians in testimonial capacity matters either, in anticipation of their client's will being challenged after their death, or after the client has already died and the will is being challenged on the grounds that the decedent lacked testamentary capacity.

The testamentary capacity cases on which I consulted all suffered from the same problem: the only evidence relating to capacity was in the medical record. Had the lawyers obtained an assessment of capacity at the time the will was drawn, the issue would have been clear; the lawyers would not have needed me, and it would have been more difficult to successfully challenge the will.

The most unusual competency evaluation I ever performed was in a criminal case and showed the court's determination to provide a fair trial, and the strength of the resources the court was able to marshal to support that effort. An ordinary evaluation involves just two people: the person to be evaluated, and the professional doing the evaluation. Occasionally in my work at the court clinic, I was asked to evaluate a defendant who spoke no English, in which case the court would provide an interpreter. The evaluation in question here required a chain of four people, with the defendant at one end and I at the other. The defendant was a profoundly hearing-impaired Hispanic man who communicated only in Spanish Sign Language. The interpreter who communicated with him was also hearing impaired, and she was bilingual in Spanish Sign Language and American Sign Language. She communicated with the defendant in Spanish Sign Language, then passed on the message to the third person in the chain using American Sign Language, who then communicated with me in spoken English. This sounds daunting, but I was surprised to find that communicating through this chain was relatively straightforward. I concluded that the defendant could communicate with his attorney using a similar chain, and as I thought he was competent to go forward, I left him and his attorney to do their work. In this case, the court went to remarkable lengths to ensure that this defendant would have a fair trial.

* * *

I got into forensic psychiatry almost as a matter of chance in 1980, when child psychologists at the Cambridge Court Clinic asked for my help on a research project. Many juveniles whom they evaluated displayed serious cognitive difficulties despite having a normal IQ. They wanted to better understand their cognitive functioning, but they had no research backgrounds—which is where, they hoped, I could help.

Drawing on my psychology training, I helped them design their research. I became interested in the project, and when a half-time position for a psychiatrist opened at this clinic, I applied and was accepted. In 1985, I became the director of the clinic, the oldest and largest court clinic in Massachusetts. The clinic psychiatrists commonly assessed capacity in order to assist the court in ruling on competency. In other cases we assessed criminal responsibility, presence of mental disorder, or dangerousness. We had a separate adolescent consultation service, as well as a group of clinicians specifically available for evaluations of troubled families appearing in the probate court, usually in contentious divorce cases.

The clinic was a placement for psychiatry residents and other mental health trainees at the Cambridge Hospital, and I taught them about how the law related to their clinical practice and how the court as an institution functioned. Bruce Gage, one of these residents, went on to a career in forensic psychiatry. Recently, he told me what the experience had meant to him: "The forensic training from you and your colleagues at the court clinic was as good as a fellowship. In a forensic context, you are not caring for the patient, but you can be decent to people and be helpful along the way. You never sacrificed the person to get what you needed to know."

Bruce became the Program Director and Lead Psychiatrist at the Center for ForensicI Services (named for Bruce when he retired, the "Dr. Bruce Gage Center for Forensic Services) and later Chief of Psychiatry for the Washington State Department of Corrections. He was also the founder and Program Director of the University of Washington Forensic Fellowship and a Clinical Associate Professor in that Department, and the psychiatric consultant to the federal government in their suit to require the Los Angeles County Jail to provide adequate clinical services for the inmates.

* * *

Even though treatment was not a standard practice at the court clinic, long-term quasi-therapeutic relationships with repeat, re-arrested offenders were sometimes possible. Ralph, a well-known Cambridge character in his mid-forties who often hung out in Central Square, the hub of working-class Cambridge, was one of these. He was a walking provocation, often seen wearing a harlequin suit festooned with homemade signs bearing messages like, "Oppose police brutality," and "Abortion is a woman's right." Not surprisingly, he got into altercations with passersby, and these repeatedly led to his arrest.

Ralph experienced episodes of both mania and depression. He recognized the depression, but not the mania. He thought his "community activism" was perfectly fine and rejected any suggestion that he take medication that might affect it. I saw him intermittently as often as he was arrested, or occasionally when he came voluntarily to the court clinic.

He had had his first manic episode in his early twenties. At that time, he was a brilliant graduate student in linguistics at MIT. He never became completely well after that first break, but he continued to cherish the belief that he would one day be well enough to return to graduate school. Sadly, this never happened, but Ralph often brought it up when we met.

He came in one day to tell me he had read a newspaper article about a man named John Boswell, a distinguished medieval historian at Yale. As an openly gay scholar, Boswell had made fundamental contributions to our understanding of gay men in the medieval church. Boswell knew many languages, and he was widely admired for how he learned them. Every year on January 1, he would begin to read the New Testament in a language he did not know, looking up words as necessary until he could read fluently, thus adding another language to the many he already knew. Newspaper articles routinely described his accomplishment.

Ralph was very focused on this story. He admired the man and his work and compared Boswell's situation with his own. His sense that he would never achieve what he hoped for himself or anything like what Boswell had accomplished was palpable. A week later, I learned that he had thrown himself out a high window and been found dead. Of all the precipitants that lead men to such deep depression, I would guess that this one is unique. Profound existential despair led him to suicide, despondent that he would never reach his goals.

* * *

After several years at the court clinic, I began a private practice in forensic psychiatry, which was almost exclusively civil rather than criminal. While I was still working for the state at the court clinic, I declined to work privately for defendants in Massachusetts criminal cases because I considered that to be, if not unethical, then at least disloyal to my employer. Attorneys hired me to review cases involving allegations of psychological harm caused by noxious events: motor vehicle accidents, dog bites, workplace accidents, or malpractice committed by mental health professionals or institutions. Approximately two dozen of these were cases brought by female psychotherapy patients who had had sex with their therapist [see chapter on women]. The cases that follow are from my private practice.

My experience with the Cambridge police department provided the basis for a subspecialty I developed in evaluating police officers for fitness for duty. These cases often involved a claim of injury on duty, with the question focusing on whether the injury caused PTSD or depression, and if it did, whether the officer was entitled to retire on a work-related disability. I reviewed half a dozen cases after another psychiatrist had found the candidates psychologically unfit to become police officers. The attorney who represented a number of these rejected men and women sent her clients to me for a second evaluation. I consistently found that this psychiatrist had based recommendations entirely on personal opinions during an interview and typically found that the subject was "distant, uncooperative, or evasive." There was no evidence that this board-certified forensic psychiatrist considered the person's work record, including supervisors' reports, citizen complaints, or letters praising the officer for something she had done in a particularly difficult situation. ("she" because it seemed to me that this psychiatrist had rejected a disproportionate number of women.) More than once, the record in question contained laudatory letters. On the basis of my review of these cases, the initial verdict was almost always overturned, and after a new evaluation, the officer candidates were able to pursue their chosen career. These cases were particularly troubling to me because they represented injustice perpetrated by a psychiatrist on an innocent person. These applicants had been nearly thwarted in their life choices by one subjective, and possibly sexist, viewpoint. This once again illustrates that psychiatrists can do harm when they believe they are doing good.

My private practice had rewards different from those I experienced working at the court clinic. When I served as a plaintiff's expert in cases of psychological harm, I met people from all walks of life and all social classes. Often, these people were high functioning before they had been injured in an accident of some kind. They were quite different from the criminal defendants I met at court and from the patients I saw at Cambridge Hospital. Malpractice cases in particular interested me because they had a detective story aspect—first, discovering what happened, and then, if things had gone wrong, why they did and who was responsible. In cases of severe injury or death that I have worked on, juries have awarded the plaintiffs millions of dollars.

The law on malpractice dates back to 1700 B.C. and the code of Hammurabi. In ancient Babylon, damages were awarded based on the social position of the patient. The code states, "If a physician performed a major operation on a seignior with a bronze Lancet and has caused the Seignior's death, or he opened the eye socket of a seignior and has destroyed the seignior's eye, they shall cut off his hand. . . . If the physician kills a person who is only a slave, he shall make good slave for slave. If he destroyed the slave's eye, he shall pay one half his value in silver."

Thankfully, the law has evolved. People of different social classes receive compensation for similar injuries, and we have developed a system of representation in which a person with limited resources can compete on a level playing field for claims against an insurance company or other large, powerful corporation with essentially unlimited resources. To address this inequality, plaintiffs' attorneys typically work on a contingency fee basis. They agree to represent the plaintiff for no charge, but if they win the case, they receive thirty-three to forty percent of the sum awarded for the damage. In contrast, the psychiatrist is a consultant paid a fixed fee agreed on in advance. It is unethical for a forensic consultant to have a financial interest in the outcome of a case in which he is an expert.

Many of my cases involved allegations of malpractice against mental health professionals or institutions. The standard for medical malpractice or negligence is clear: if a physician functions as well as the average practitioner in their specialty at that time and place, then the physician's practice meets the standard of care. If the physician fails to do so, this is evidence of malpractice. A patient injured as a direct result of physician or of other health care malpractice is legally entitled to recover damages.

In one particularly distressing malpractice case on which I advised, the plaintiff claimed that a local hospital had committed malpractice in the treatment of a psychiatric patient. This long-divorced patient had a history of severe, recurrent depression, and he came to the hospital after taking an almost lethal overdose. The hospital did an emergency evaluation and admitted him. After a few days in the hospital, the patient requested that he be allowed to go home to change his clothes. A staff member agreed to this plan after a cursory evaluation and the man left the hospital—but he did not return. Instead, he drove to the local elementary school where his ex-wife's second husband was waiting to pick up their children. The patient shot and killed the man in the presence of his two children. He then shot himself in the head and chest in a serious, but ultimately unsuccessful, attempt to kill himself.

The newly widowed mother sued the hospital, and her attorney hired me to review the record in order to determine whether the hospital's treatment of the patient met or fell below the required standard of care. The record documented the patient's suicide attempt, as well as his long depression and earlier attempts. It also revealed that he had killed his brother some years earlier in circumstances that were unclear. His emotional problems appeared to have either begun or have gotten much worse after this earlier killing.

I concluded that the hospital staff had committed malpractice, first by failing to obtain a known history of lethal violence and then by allowing this visibly depressed patient with a known history of attempted suicide to leave the hospital after an inadequate evaluation. Additionally, I found that the two children had suffered severe emotional trauma and were badly damaged psychologically as a result of witnessing this tragedy.

The case went to trial, and I testified to my findings. The jury found that malpractice had occurred and that as a direct result of this malpractice, the children's father had died, and the two children had been severely traumatized by witnessing his murder. The jury awarded a total of $9.3 million to the mother and the two children.

Years later, I served as an expert for the same attorney in another tragic case after one client at a local drug treatment program had caused the death of three other clients and the severe injury of a fourth. The drug treatment facility—the defendant— was part of a national network of for-profit facilities. Testimony by the director and staff revealed an appalling ignorance of the fundamental clinical policies that should govern the treatment of their clients, and as a result, the staff failed to enact simple precautions that would have prevented this tragedy. I wrote a scathing report and was equally scathing in my testimony at deposition; ultimately, the case settled.

In personal injury cases, plaintiffs can potentially be awarded monetary damages to compensate them for physical injuries, lost earnings, lost value of household services, medical expenses, and emotional distress. In my private practice involving civil cases, I was usually asked to evaluate emotional distress; psychological rather than physical injury. Traumatic events produce psychological harm that can lead, in a vulnerable person, to post-traumatic stress disorder (PTSD). PTSD is a one of many types of emotional distress for which people can recover monetary damages. That does not mean that all such claims were true or guaranteed to prevail, and I did not always find that claims of PTSD were supported by the facts. I was hired by the defense in a case in which a man who was hit by a car while riding his bicycle alleged that he had PTSD as a result and sued the driver. One of the cardinal symptoms of PTSD is that the person suffering from it avoids anything that reminds them of the situation that caused the symptoms. This man was back riding his bicycle within a month of the accident. This fact alone was enough for me to question his claim of serious psychological injury as a result of this accident.

In another, far more serious case, I worked with an attorney who was representing a trauma nurse named Tom. Tom was allegedly suffering from PTSD following the 2013 bombings at the Boston Marathon. His anxiety as he worked on resultant injuries prevented him from working effectively, and ultimately prevented him from working at all. His repeated absence resulted in termination and he sued his employer, claiming his experience at the job produced the anxiety that led to his impaired function at work.

At the time of the marathon bombing, Tom, who was in his forties, was working as a trauma nurse at a Boston hospital. On the day of the bombing, as the casualties rolled in, Tom began a marathon of his own, scrubbing in and assisting on one trauma case after another. One man he was working on died during the surgery; another had severe damage to both legs, and after the amputations, staff threw his legs into the trash. He worked on that man through the night, picking pieces of bone and shrapnel out of the patient's body. In the weeks that followed, he assisted on other surgeries with this man. He also scrubbed in on many other operations involving post-bombing surgical trauma—amputations, shrapnel extractions, and burn repairs.

Tom, who had fourteen years of experience as a trauma nurse at the time of the bombing, told me he'd had no anxiety symptoms prior to these surgeries. But after working on the victims, he experienced anxiety so intense that he would have to pull over while driving, unable to operate the vehicle. While his longtime partner knew about these episodes, he never told colleagues at work what was happening to him because he did not want anyone to think he could not do his job.

Although Tom had used recreational drugs during late adolescence and early adulthood, he told me he had taken no drugs for years before April of 2013. He always worked out and stayed in shape. After the bombing, he sought relief, using cocaine for the first time in his life. His cocaine use got so heavy that he was unable to work. He took a month of medical leave and began seeing a psychotherapist, but his anxiety and cocaine use continued. He asked for a second month of leave without saying why, but the hospital denied his request. He then missed two more days of work, and the hospital offered him a choice: resign or be fired. Tom resigned, and his life deteriorated. He went on long cocaine binges, spending all his money and pawning everything he owned to maintain his habit.

His symptoms included severe sleep disruption with nightmares and night sweats, restless thrashing and kicking, flashbacks to the operating room, and dreams that did not make sense. His partner told him that he talked in his sleep and yelled profanely. He could no longer share a bed with her because he was so violent. Instead, he slept on an air mattress in the living room. He told me he'd had no loving feelings for a long time, and his partner confirmed that he appeared numb to her. When I first saw him two years after the bombing, he reported that he had been clean for six months, but he was still not working and was unsure whether he would ever be able to work again as a trauma nurse. He went on one job interview and had to excuse himself because he was sweating so badly.

In my opinion, Tom suffered from a severe case of PTSD resulting from his work in the operating room after the bombing. Using my report, Tom's attorney argued in court that the hospital was wrong in forcing Tom to resign because his failure to function at work was a result of trauma he had experienced on the job. The court agreed and awarded Tom $105,000.

This case puts into perspective the limitations on what the law and forensic psychiatry can do in a case of psychological damage. The law refers to monetary compensation as "making the person whole." This addresses monetary loss, but money does not make the person psychologically whole. The settlement of $105,000 did not touch the fundamental problem: Tom remained symptomatic and damaged. Tom's partner called me eighteen months after the court case to report that Tom had spent the $105,000 on cocaine, and not long after, that he was arrested for getting into a bad fight and sent to the hospital for the criminally insane, where he hanged himself.

* * *

In the course of my career as a working and teaching forensic psychiatrist, I have researched and written many papers and book chapters, as well as a monograph. The book I edited—and wrote a substantial portion of—won the Guttmacher Award from the American Psychiatric Association [APA] as the best work in forensic psychiatry in 1990. Much of what I wrote was about the duty of therapists to protect third parties foreseeably endangered by a patient, resulting from a 1974 court case and its follow-up in 1976, *Tarasoff v. Regents of the University of California.* [46, 47]

This case created a stir in the mental health professions because it articulated a new duty for psychotherapists: it said that therapists had to warn potential victims if they learned a patient intended violent harm. In the case, a California man who was disappointed in love became depressed and sought psychotherapy. He told his therapist he was thinking of killing the woman who dumped him, and ultimately, he did just that. Her parents sued the therapist, claiming that the therapist's relationship with his patient created a duty to the victim.

The court agreed, writing in 1974 that in situations such as this one, the therapist has a duty to warn the potential victim. In their second opinion in 1976, the court expanded the duty of the therapist, stating that the therapist "incurs an obligation to use reasonable care to protect the intended victim against such danger."[46, 47]

Courts in other states often follow California decisions, so it was expected that many others across the country would adopt this opinion. Accordingly, there was a great outcry from the profession, particularly from its leaders, claiming that this duty would severely damage the therapeutic contract that promises the patient confidentiality, and that this damage would be enough to deter people in need from seeking psychotherapy. Various authors noted that this controversy persisted independent of any empirical study.

The new duty hit psychiatrists in a particularly vulnerable place—the pocketbook. This 'duty to protect' meant that anyone who claimed to be damaged by a patient could sue the patient's therapist for malpractice, alleging the therapist's failure to use 'reasonable care' to prevent the damage. Prior to *Tarasoff*, only patients could sue a doctor for damages. This new duty meant that potentially anyone in the world could sue the psychotherapist of the person who injured them, which terrified psychiatry and the other psychotherapeutic professions.

In preparation for a talk I had agreed to give on this subject—a subject on which I knew nothing at the time—I contacted thirty-eight psychiatrists whom I knew well enough to ask about their experience with the duty to warn or protect. Sixteen of these psychiatrists had warned a victim when they were concerned about potential violence. Within this subset, I found that if the therapists told patients that they proposed to warn the victim, then the warning had either a positive effect on the therapy or no effect at all. In every case in which the therapist had gone ahead with a warning without telling the patient, the therapeutic relationship had been damaged. I wrote that preventing violence had value for the patient as well as for the victim, and that engaging patients in this discussion was in their interest. The question of whether a therapist owes a duty to protect unnamed third parties remains controversial in the profession more than forty years later.

* * *

As I became more comfortable in my role as a forensic psychiatrist, I began working with Charles Ogletree, a faculty member at Harvard Law School, to demonstrate the role of an expert witness. Ogletree thought that it would be a useful exercise for his students to have the opportunity to examine and cross-examine authentic experts, rather than having other students in the class play the role of an expert in a field of which they knew little. This in turn presented an opportunity for psychiatry residents at Cambridge Hospital to learn about appearing in court.

Doctors are typically terrified of going into court, and if they can possibly avoid the experience, they will. I wanted our residents to have the experience of being examined and cross-examined by attorneys, hoping that this experience would be enough to encourage them to testify later if a patient needed them.

We wrote a sample case that required expert testimony by a psychiatrist. Our residents learned the case and presented themselves at the law school as experts to opposing counsel, who were played by the law students. I also played the role of expert, and was examined and cross-examined by law school faculty, countless times over the course of twenty-five years before I ultimately retired from the exercise.

Eighteen years after retiring, I decided to return because I was curious to see how the program had progressed over time. The small exercise Ogletree and I had started had gone national. Ogletree had retired, but his successor told me that "Introduction to Advocacy" was the most popular course in the law school, with the week of trial advocacy serving as one of its biggest draws. Judges and attorneys now came from all over the country to serve as faculty. Psychiatry residents from several programs participated, and trainees from programs in psychology and social work appeared as experts as well.

It is remarkable to consider that I entered forensic psychiatry knowing next to nothing about the law, and by the close of this chapter of my career, I had co-developed a well-regarded module in one of the most popular courses at Harvard Law School. As of this writing, the "Trial Advocacy Workshop" is in such demand that it is given twice a year, and there are mental health trainees available in sufficient numbers to support two sessions. This history suggests that both professions have evaluated this exercise as worthwhile.

* * *

By 2000, I was looking to leave Cambridge, and I made a safe landing at the Law & Psychiatry Service at Massachusetts General Hospital where Ronald Schouten, MD, JD was the director. Ron knew my work as a forensic psychiatrist: we had a long personal–professional relationship and he was glad to hire me as his associate chief. I served for one year in 2000 and again for eight years from 2002–2010.

Forensic psychiatry had by this time become a recognized subspecialty of psychiatry. By 2000, certification as a forensic psychiatrist required the completion of a one-year fellowship after residency and passage of a specialized exam. The MGH fellows were going through this process, and this meant that I could do what I loved best: teach. I supervised forensic psychiatry fellows on their cases, and I taught forensic psychiatry to the fellows and to MGH psychiatry residents.

I was always fundamentally a teacher, first at Cambridge and then at MGH, but the business arrangements between the two hospitals and I were very different. At Cambridge, I was paid for my work. MGH (referred to locally and somewhat caustically as Man's Greatest Hospital), on the other hand, took full advantage of its reputation not to pay me. MGH is a private, nonprofit institution, and unlike the publicly funded Cambridge Health Alliance, MGH runs a tight financial ship. When I arrived, the administrator of the Law and Psychiatry Service explained to me, "You eat what you kill." By this, she meant that I would be paid entirely on the basis of clients I evaluated who had been referred through the MGH program, and MGH would take 30% of what I billed. For the privilege of being a Harvard Faculty member at MGH, I was expected to teach on a volunteer basis.

Many years after I left MGH, I asked Ron to comment on my teaching and he said: "Jim was a mentor for me, and in the personal and professional lives of many others. Jim has always delighted in taking junior colleagues, not to mention undergraduates, medical students, and trainees, under his wing and showing them the world that he knew and enjoyed. Jim has taught those of us fortunate to know and work with him about life, and he did it with the grace and style that mark good teachers." Through the forty years that we have known each other, our relationship has deepened into a profoundly close friendship. I am as likely to consult him, as he is to consult me. These are the relationships that provide meaning in my life.

* * *

I end this chapter with cases of attempted murder, and murder.

Occasionally, I was asked to assess whether a defendant was criminally responsible or whether he might plead 'not guilty by reason of insanity' (NGRI). The defendant's plea of NGRI bears directly on the question of guilt or innocence. Under American law, to be guilty of a crime, the court must find that the defendant did the criminal act, that he knew what he was doing when he did it, and that he knew that what he did was wrong. An NGRI plea is an affirmative defense—that is, the defendant acknowledges that he did the criminal act but maintains that he did not know what he was doing or did not know it was wrong. It is available in all but a few states. Defendants whom the court finds NGRI are typically severely mentally ill and dangerous enough to meet standards for involuntary commitment to a mental hospital, where they will remain until a court finds that they are no longer mentally ill and dangerous. This is usually a matter of years, not months. In my work at the court clinic, I occasionally consulted on cases in which I assessed whether a defendant was criminally responsible or whether he met the standards for the NGRI plea, which had direct bearing on the question of guilt or innocence.

The NGRI plea has been the target of acrimonious claims that it is used as a scam by criminals to avoid punishment, but the facts are otherwise.[48] When a defendant offers the NGRI defense and the prosecutor opposes it, the NGRI plea is successful for less than one case in 10,000. One study by a colleague whom I particularly respect found that in more than 80% of successful insanity defense pleas in Oregon, the prosecutor and the defense attorney agreed that the defendant was not criminally responsible and recommend that the judge make a finding of NGRI.[49]

The standards to meet the NGRI plea are stringent, and I did my best to evaluate fairly and present my findings clearly, but one can never discount the sway of a jury in the outcome of a trial. In one particularly remarkable case of criminal responsibility the jury ignored my recommendation and did what they thought was right. The defendant, Phan Loc (not his real name), had been an officer in the Vietnamese army decades earlier during the war in Vietnam. He had been captured by the Viet Cong, who tortured him—he had the crooked fingers and missing nails to support his story. He had gotten to the U.S., where he was living with a Protestant minister and his family. At trial, the minister testified that the defendant's character was exemplary, that he was a much beloved member of the family, and that he made valuable contributions as a volunteer in the community.

The act that led to his arrest, though, was clearly criminal. He learned that the North Vietnamese defense minister had been invited to speak at Harvard Law School. Believing that this man was a war criminal, he felt it his duty to prevent the minister from speaking. Phan Loc learned how to construct a Molotov cocktail and resolved to throw one at the invited speaker, which he did as the man was being driven to the law school. He had not lit the wick, so the bottle struck the car and fell harmlessly. Phan Loc was apprehended and charged with assault with a deadly weapon and assault with intent to murder.

This was a jury trial in which the defense attorney offered the NGRI defense, and the judge asked me to evaluate the defendant for criminal responsibility. After doing so, I found that the defendant understood exactly what he was doing, carried out a deliberate plan, and he was very clear that it was criminal under U.S. law. Nevertheless, he stood by his actions.

I testified in court in front of the jury that there was no evidence to support a finding of NGRI—he was not mentally ill, he knew what he was doing, clearly able to decide to do or not to do this, and he knew it was wrong under the law, but he did it anyway. Neither prosecution nor defense contested my testimony. As is customary, I left the courtroom after I testified. Later that day, I saw one of the jurors in the courthouse lobby, and I asked her what the jury had decided. "Not guilty by reason of insanity," she said brightly.

To me, this illustrates the strength of trial by jury. Going against clear expert testimony, they had found a basis to excuse the defendant's conduct. The judge, finding no indication that the defendant was mentally ill or a danger to anyone by reason of mental illness, had no basis on which to order involuntary psychiatric treatment. Instead, he sentenced the defendant to "continued without a finding," meaning that if Phan Loc did not break the law for a year, the charges would be dropped. I was as sympathetic to the defendant as the jury clearly had been, and I was pleased with their verdict, despite contradicting my testimony.

This case illustrates that forensic psychiatrists and psychologists must be scrupulously honest in reporting what they find, no matter what their personal values may be. I was deeply sympathetic to this defendant and I would have loved to find evidence that he was NGRI, but it simply wasn't there so I told the truth as I saw it. This posture is what gives forensics psychiatry and psychology credibility in the eyes of the law.

My final story, in which NGRI was also an issue, shows the power of the people to find a path toward justice as they understand it. Alan was a twenty-nine-year-old single white male, living in Alabama, who shot and killed two police officers. He was awaiting trial when his court-appointed attorneys requested that I evaluate his mental status. Did Alan know what he was doing on the day he shot and killed these two young men? Did he know it was wrong? Did he have sufficient mental capacity to stand trial on these charges, and did he appear to meet standards for not guilty by reason of insanity (NGRI)? If he qualified, Alan's attorneys would need psychiatric testimony to support his plea.

I interviewed Alan for four hours over two days, three years after he killed the two men. Alan had been given antipsychotic medication while incarcerated, so we were able to have a reasonable discussion. He did not volunteer information, but he readily answered my questions, providing additional facts as I asked for them. The most dramatic aspect of these interviews was his total absence of emotion as he described what he had done. Someone listening who could hear the tone but not the content of what he said might easily have concluded that Alan was discussing a trip to the supermarket, rather than the unprovoked killing of two young men.

I also interviewed Alan's mother and one brother, who were deeply troubled by what Alan had done. The interview with the mother was what you might expect: a woman distraught over her son's alleged acts, saddened by the death of the two young men, and more than a little convinced that perhaps this tragedy could have been averted if Alan had received more consistent and effective treatment. The brother was equally distressed and regretful about the whole episode.

Alan had been well-known to their mental health system prior to this killing, and he had been repeatedly hospitalized, and repeatedly discharged. Soon after discharge he would stop his antipsychotic medication, and eventually do something that led to his involuntary rehospitalization. In addition to a psychotic disorder, variously diagnosed as schizophrenia or schizoaffective disorder, he also had a very serious substance-abuse problem, and this complicated the diagnostic question and the treatment options.

My opinion was that at the time of the murders, he suffered from schizoaffective disorder, a close relative of schizophrenia. He had a prior history of serious drug and alcohol abuse, but he told me he had not used drugs during the three years since the killings that he had been incarcerated, and I believed he was giving an accurate account as far as he was able. In prison, he had been given medication for his mental disorder so that his psychosis appeared to have greatly improved. I concluded that at the time of our interviews, he was generally in good contact with reality and was able to follow the substance of a trial and collaborate with an attorney. In short, he had sufficient capacity to defend himself, and I believed a judge would find him competent to stand trial.

Alan's troubles had begun at fifteen, when he began to use marijuana daily and drink heavily. He went on to heavy use of crack, opiates, LSD, mushrooms, and ecstasy, and he was hospitalized repeatedly for drug and alcohol problems. During his twenties, he became increasingly paranoid and psychotic and began to experience frightening hallucinations. The psychiatrists who saw him during repeated involuntary hospitalizations consistently diagnosed him with polysubstance abuse and schizophrenia, usually chronic paranoid schizophrenia.

He told me that he might have told his mother that he might have to kill someone in order to get off the planet, but he added that he was probably drinking when he made that statement. In the weeks before the shooting, he bought a gun, using $100 his family had given him to buy Christmas presents. Alan told me he had no plan to buy a gun, but he went to a gun show with his brother, and since the gun cost exactly the amount of money he had and seemed to be in good shape, he bought it. He used it for target practice on several occasions, and he told me that he was quite accurate.

During the weeks before he killed the two officers, he believed that hostile forces were sending him messages through his dental fillings and that there were people shooting microwaves into his brain. To protect himself, he took the lining out of his microwave oven and walked around wearing it on his head in order to deflect the feared microwave radiation. Additionally, he believed he was caught up in a new war, telling me directly, "I thought that the terrorism war was my fault. I thought I was Osama Bin Laden

and the voices went along with that. They said, 'It's your fault.'"
At different times, he called the Army, the FBI, the Federal
Communications Commission, and the police to ask for help
because someone was burning his head. Alan explained to me,
"I thought that they were reading my medulla oblongata, and I
would take the remote from the television and point it at the back
of my head to mess them up."

On the day of the shooting, Alan told me, he drank all the
vodka left in a half- gallon bottle he found at his mother's house,
all while continuing to hear voices. Eventually, he explained, "The
voices hit a high and I was suffering intensely. The TV was reading
my mind. I called the FBI and the line was busy. I called them
for my life." He called 911, and the dispatcher told him they
were sending a policeman. "I thought everything was a conspiracy
against me, and I went and got my gun. I saw people walking in
the yard and I thought they were demons or gangsters. They were
glowing. I thought they were hyped up on radiation. I shot at
them, and they were gone. The police pulled up just then, and I
thought they were bad guys coming at me. I shot at their heads.
They fell to the ground. Then I thought, 'Oh shit, I really shot,'
and I put my gun down and went out into the yard."

Using my opinion that Alan suffered with schizoaffective
disorder as the basis for his argument, Alan's defense attorney
negotiated with the district attorney, and she agreed that
she would not ask for the death sentence. Instead, Alan had
the opportunity to plead guilty and receive a sentence of life
without parole.

Following a summer trial, he was sent to the state prison,
where there was no air conditioning and the temperature in the

cells sometimes rose to 107 degrees. A prisoner might or might not have access to water. Within forty-eight hours, Alan was found unconscious in his cell with substantial bruises on his body. He was transferred to a local hospital, where he never regained consciousness. A week later, his family agreed to withdraw life support, and Alan died. Later investigation was unable to attribute the cause of death to any particular event or circumstance, but the bruises were consistent with physical assault, and independent observers concluded that Alan's death appeared to have been the result of deliberate neglect and possible physical assault.

Like the case of Phan Loc, this case illustrates that individual ideas of right and wrong can be more important than the legal process in determining what happens to the defendant. These cases also illustrate the limitations of the forensic psychiatrist. In each case, I performed a careful forensic evaluation. In neither case were my findings or my conclusions challenged. But in Massachusetts, the legal system found a way to excuse the defendant's criminal conduct despite my testimony; in Alabama, society arranged for a man sentenced to life in prison to die even more quickly than if he had been found guilty and sentenced to death. If these cases taught me nothing else, they taught me some humility.

#####

CHAPTER 14

ACADEMIC PSYCHIATRY

In 1996, our psychiatry department at the hospital called me back from the court clinic to be the associate chair. This was a new role for me; one I was glad to take on.

The popular image of a psychiatrist is a man, or perhaps now a woman, sitting in an office with a single patient. This is accurate, but we work in other situations as well. In this chapter, I have tried to convey some idea of the responsibilities of a psychiatrist in a teaching hospital. An academic physician serves two masters: the hospital or clinic where they work, which determines work responsibilities, and the medical school or university that determines academic status.

I have been fortunate in my professional life to have had the freedom and latitude to move when I needed to move. In some cases, I moved because I wanted to; in others, because my situation became intolerable. I have always worked in a Harvard-affiliated hospital, and I continued to teach while serving in different leadership positions.

Harvard Medical School owns no hospitals, but it has formal affiliation agreements with sixteen hospitals and medical institutions, including the Cambridge City Hospital, now Cambridge Health Alliance. Twelve thousand physicians are employed at these institutions, many of whom have faculty appointments at Harvard Medical School. I am one of these twelve thousand: I climbed the academic ladder, becoming an assistant professor in 1972, an associate professor in 1988, and a full professor in 1999. I taught residents part-time at the Cambridge Health Alliance until 2018.

I assumed new, greater responsibilities when I became associate chair of the psychiatry department in 1996, as new fiscal demands were affecting clinical practice. My explicit mandate at the hospital was to help the staff adjust to the new fiscal realities. They resisted proposed changes that required change in clinical practice as we faced these new financial realities. The no-show rate for our patients was between thirty-five and forty percent—not unusual in a clinic serving low-income patients. We did not get paid unless we saw the patient, so I suggested we double schedule to meet our revenue goals. I understood that, on occasion, both patients would show up, but I thought we could deal with this on a case-by-case basis. Staff, however, thought this was unfair both to the patients who would occasionally have shorter appointments and to the clinicians who would have to work harder when two patients showed up, so they rejected this proposal. Similarly, I suggested to one of our outpatient therapists that perhaps she could see her patients for forty-five minutes instead of fifty minutes. "Oh no," she said, "I couldn't possibly do that," and nothing changed until years later, when more stringent fiscal realities forced the department administrator to impose changes.

My administrative responsibilities varied, but teaching was a constant. Teaching, especially teaching residents is what I have always loved best. I have always been primarily a clinical teacher. Clinical teaching involves listening as residents tell me about their work with patients, or, even better, interviewing patients jointly with these residents. At Cambridge, each resident had four hours per week of individual supervision, one hour each with four different staff members. I would meet each resident I supervised once a week over the course of a year. The resident would present the cases they had been working on, and I would draw on my experience as we discussed them together.

The foundation of my teaching is: approach all patients, no matter how bizarre their behavior or their language, with respect and compassion, while you try to understand them. I teach that a good evaluation focuses on the patient as an individual, not as a receptacle for signs and symptoms. I also emphasize careful attention to each patient's symptoms, as these are a salient and troubling aspect of the experience of mentally ill people. Good descriptive psychiatry requires a careful description of signs and symptoms, and good dynamic psychiatry involves understanding the meaning of these symptoms as they relate to life events. When we evaluate symptoms descriptively and dynamically, understanding the person and a diagnosis naturally follow.

After teaching how to assess patients, I teach how to treat them, with this as the guiding idea: "You should always treat the patient as a person, not simply as a vessel holding disease.

No matter how sick, the patient's opinion matters." Too often, the clinical encounter is structured as a relationship between a powerful doctor and a powerless patient—one in which the doctor tells the patient, "This is what is wrong with you, and this is what you should do about it." That is not constructive. Clinicians should work with a patient to reach an agreement on how to go forward. This is especially important with psychotic patients, many of whom don't like taking medicine and stop taking it within a relatively short time. When they are told to do something they don't like, patients, like most of us, avoid doing it. In my experience, things go better if the patient helps develop the plan.

Unfortunately, psychiatry has changed, and much current practice has become mechanistic, consisting of fifteen- or twenty-minute interviews in which the doctor focuses largely on medicine. That change hasn't stopped me from teaching my trainees how to do the kind of person-focused evaluation and treatment planning that characterizes good practice—not just for psychiatrists, but for all clinicians. I am passionate about my teaching, and I want to be sure that the residents I teach have heard my message.

As a supervisor, I have tried to take on a mentorship role, engaging residents on personal issues, such as choosing a professional path consistent with their personal goals. Almost all the residents I have worked with are interested in pursuing public psychiatry. This choice creates a realistic problem for anyone who wants to support a middle-class family, as most physicians do. Balancing these issues typically meant figuring out how to combine work in the public sector with some other source of income, such as a subspecialty in child psychiatry or a private practice. In part, I think, due to my active interest in their lives,

I remain friends with many of my former residents. I tell some stories of the capable young people whom I have been fortunate to teach.

The psychiatry department at Cambridge differed from the usual hierarchically structured academic department in that we did not restrict our teaching to physicians and other professional trainees. We psychiatrists offered supervision to our mental health workers if we thought they would benefit from it. One of these was Fran Arnold, a recent college graduate, with whom I worked early in my career. Fran took a first job as a mental health worker while trying to decide her next career steps. She thought she might be a doctor or maybe a clinical psychologist, but she wasn't sure.

I was a supervisor on the inpatient service when I met her, and she often came to me with concerns or questions about patients. Her judgment about patients was excellent. After about a year, I invited her to be a co-therapist with me for a couple who came to our outpatient service. I have never made a similar offer to another trainee or staff member. After a relatively few sessions, the couple got what they came for and stopped therapy. Fran went on to graduate school, earned a PhD in clinical psychology and practiced as a psychotherapist. Later she became a psychoanalyst and a faculty member and supervising psychoanalyst at the Boston Psychoanalytic Institute.

Fran wrote this about her years working with me, "It was a great, life-changing first job. You did not treat supervision as a top-down experience, but rather as a forum where you would exchange ideas and be as curious about my impressions as you were about your own. Supervision was more about wanting help with containing and understanding the big feelings and fears (both the patient's and mine) that come up in clinical work. I remember a lot of the supervision being about watching you interview patients, seeing how you talk to them and think with them, and then discussing all that with me. You wanted to know firsthand what was most important or most troubling to patients, without judgment or preformed ideas. You encouraged an atmosphere where various reactions to patients could be expressed and considered as something important and telling about the clinical situation. You accepted fear and anger as basic reactions to patients that could be worked with and found meaningful."

By the late 1990s, I had the reputation at Cambridge of being a supervisor who would not just address clinical issues but would also help residents consider how their professional choices might relate to their larger lives. This appealed to a young resident named Kevin Mack, and he asked to be one of my supervisees.

I don't remember what I taught Kevin or what he may have learned from me; but I remember what I got from Kevin, which was a deep friendship that lasted as long as his tragically short life. I remember his remarkable intellectual prowess and his energy—he thought clearly and incisively on a wide range of topics, and his enthusiasm about all of them was contagious. He was open to sharing his experiences and to learning about mine, with the result that we got to know each other well over the year that I supervised him.

A fit, handsome, openly gay man with an easy laugh and an intense sense of engagement, Kevin came to psychiatry as a fourth career. After high school, he had spent eighteen months as a lay brother in a monastery in Italy but ultimately decided that a religious career was not for him. He then went to college, concentrating in physics. He worked in physics before going on to graduate work in psychology at the University of Hawaii. His interest in psychology led him toward medicine, which then brought him to psychiatry. After finishing residency with us, Kevin moved with his partner to San Francisco, where he became the staff psychiatrist on a medical ward at San Francisco General Hospital. He also worked half time with a small experimental program at the University of California Medical School, where it was his responsibility to shape the curriculum. He abolished all lectures and created a program where students learned in small groups and in laboratories, totally without exams. His students performed well on the national exams all medical students take, demonstrating that it was possible to teach medicine in collaborative groups that students enjoyed. Kevin's approach became a model that other medical schools, including Harvard, adapted for their own use some years later.

Kevin knew enough about information technology that CHA hired him to be chief of clinical informatics after he finished residency, and in that role, he flew back to Cambridge three or four times a year. He and I maintained our friendship through those visits, and through trips I made to San Francisco.

He and his partner built a family through the process of artificial insemination of women who were willing to carry their children. They first had a daughter, and five years later a son. Kevin was the breadwinner; Naoki stayed home with the children.

Naoki was away at a meeting when I was a guest at their home for the last time. Kevin worked as usual, so I functioned in Naoki's role helping the children get ready for school. Their daughter was

249

nine and went to school on her own, and I walked their four-year-old son to a Japanese-American school in the neighborhood.

On my last visit to them, Kevin and I were sitting in his car when it was time for me to leave. As we said goodbye, he leaned over and kissed me on the cheek, an experience with a man that was new for me and touched me deeply. A few weeks later, when Kevin was taking a small shuttle bus to the hospital at 6:30 a.m., a semi-trailer truck struck the shuttle. Kevin was killed instantly, the only fatality. I still miss him. I will never erase his name from my address book.

* * *

In 1999, the chair of the psychiatry department at Cambridge died unexpectedly, and I was appointed chief of the search committee for the new chair. I recommended the man who was ultimately hired. He was then the head of a department in the South, and his references from there were excellent. He turned out to be a mixed bag—good ideas but limited interpersonal skills. In hindsight, I realized that we should have checked references from earlier jobs, as he might have received good references from his most recent position because they wanted to see him go.

When he arrived, he discussed his ideas about direction for the department with senior staff and faculty. I was eager to work with him on the projects he outlined, but I soon found that his idea of working together was to ask for facts and then tell his subordinates what they were to do. He wanted servants, not colleagues.

Early in his tenure, I said something that in retrospect illustrated how different the two of us were. For Jews, Yom Kippur is the holiest day of the year. If we are observant at all, we fast, and we spend a good part of the day at services. An important tradition is that we say to family, friends, and even work associates, "If I have offended you during the past year, please forgive me." I explained this tradition to our new chief and then I said to him, "If I have offended you during the past year, please forgive me." He looked at me like I was from another planet and said nothing. I was stunned that he reacted in that way even after I had explained this part of my culture to him. After I had more experience with him, I thought he was right: we *were* from different planets.

Clearly, it was time for me to move on, and my forensic experience led directly to my next position. I became associate chief of the Massachusetts General Hospital (MGH) law and psychiatry service, but I left in 2001 when I was unexpectedly offered the position of acting chair of the Harvard psychiatry department at the MMHC. I was honored to be offered the job and thrilled to accept. "Acting," I decided, was an adjective; I was the chair, and I would act the part.

As I began my new job, I thought about how important MMHC had been in my family. My father had trained there in the 1930s when it was still the Boston Psychopathic Hospital, "The Psycho" to everyone who worked there. My mother remembered those years as a happy time in her life. In 1936, when our family left, my mother took a table knife from the hospital dining room. It was an ordinary state hospital table knife, but it maintained a surprisingly good edge through all its years in our kitchen. It was a favorite of my mother's, who always referred to it as the "Psycho knife." It had been part of my life for as long as I could remember.

251

When I arrived, the staff were naturally apprehensive about what kind of leader I might be, so I began by telling the Psycho knife story at our first formal staff meeting. It showed the staff that I cared about MMHC and that I would care about them. I behaved as a department chair as I had done earlier as an associate chair and as a chief of service. I got to know the people in my department, and I encouraged them where I could. I am proud that two people I recommended to Harvard Medical School for promotion from associate professor to professor were both promoted. One was a psychologist and one was a woman, neither of whom would be an obvious choice in a psychiatry department in 2002.

At MMHC, I continued to supervise residents just as I had done at Cambridge, and I tried to encourage and mentor young faculty. One of them was José Hidalgo, a solidly built man, soft spoken but with a direct manner. José had a heavy financial burden, and I helped him make some better financial choices. I later urged him to consider a subspecialty in forensic psychiatry. He subsequently completed a forensic fellowship at MGH and found a niche as the psychiatrist in a local jail, where he sees inmate-patients and teaches a successful rotation for MGH psychiatry residents.

A child of immigrants from Ecuador, José graduated from Fordham and NYU Medical School, and then did a psychiatric residency at Boston University. When I knew him at MMHC, he was working to develop a program to provide mental health assistance to victims of human trafficking, especially unaccompanied adolescents who came into this country illegally across the Mexican border. These children, some of whom were as young as eight years old, were all at risk of deportation. They were defendants in Immigration and Customs Enforcement Agency (ICE) courts, where the government's default position was that the children were here illegally and should be deported. While awaiting adjudication, the children were placed in detention centers that were run more as jails than as social service facilities. Many of the children had histories of trauma, and they suffered with trauma-related symptoms. The uncertainty of their legal status contributed to their anxiety and behavioral problems. As of 2019, there are many more of these children, and their situation is even more uncertain as the institutions designed to process them have become overwhelmed by their numbers.

With encouragement from the federal government, José applied for and received a grant of $1.9 million to develop trauma-related training for the staff of these centers. The goal was to help the detention centers shift from a criminal justice perspective to a therapeutic orientation. Before then, staff dealt with acting out by physical control and punishment. José and his staff developed a more psychologically oriented approach to difficult behavior. They tried to help staff understand that this behavior could be symptomatic of post-traumatic stress anxiety rather than of nastiness.

José had no experience that prepared him to administer a large grant, and he came to me to request a few hours of consultation. The first advice I gave him was possibly the most important. He had been planning to have this grant administered through Boston Children's Hospital, which would have taken an indirect cost rate of eighty-seven percent. José had not understood that this indirect cost rate would be deducted from his $1.9 million and take much of the money needed to implement his proposed training program. José had an affiliation with the Latino Health Institute of Boston, and I suggested that he might strike a better deal with them. That agreement began a constructive relationship between his program and that organization.

José understood trauma and trafficking and had good ideas about the training program he proposed to offer, but he was naïve about administrative issues, an area where I had experience. Even though I spoke no Spanish and would be of limited value in the hands-on teaching, José brought me on as a part-time staff member. We worked together on this project for four years. José has since called me his brother in the trenches along with his mentor.

The training we developed was a play-based approach designed to teach the staff of these institutions how to help these children and adolescents develop better behavioral control. We made site visits to these facilities, most of which were in the Southwest. Over the next several years, we saw the facilities begin to shift from a custodial- and criminal justice-based approach to a more psychologically informed social service orientation. The federal government agency that oversaw our work was pleased, and we published papers on this play-based therapy. It gave me considerable satisfaction to be able to aid these disenfranchised children and adolescents; and I was proud to help a young member of my department pursue this work as well. It is, I believe, at the heart of what we as public sector psychiatrists can and should do.

In 2016, José wrote a note describing our relationship. "I learned from Jim by being his friend, as much, if not more, than by being his supervisee, I met Jim for the first time at Massachusetts

Mental Health Center, where he served as the chairman. Still wearing his bicycle-riding pants, Jim led me to the opposite side of the office suite where he kept his cappuccino machine. He made me an excellent cappuccino. This kind of gesture was typical. Jim has always been generous with his time, attention and wisdom. He is a very intense person, almost impatient. As I got to know him, it became clear to me that his intensity reflected devotion to the people and the things he cares about. In everything he does, in the way he walks, thinks, and talks, there is a surety in him and clarity of purpose. If Jim, for example, decides to take on a project, he is fully committed, and has a clear methodical plan of how to achieve his goals. Jim would always say to me, 'The most precious resource is time.' With Jim I learned to appreciate time as a tangible resource not to be wasted. Before initiating a new program direction Jim would say, 'We need to do the thinking first. That's the most important part and the part most people don't do.' We would spend as much time as was necessary thinking through what it was that we were intending to do. Step by step we turned lofty goals into a concrete program; we developed a play-based intervention and helped the facilities we trained to be less punitive and more loving.

"One of the things that I treasure most about Jim is his direct approach to problems. For example, he would say, 'If you want to know the answer to a question, ask it.' He would add, 'You don't necessarily have to believe the answer, but you can learn a lot that way.' This was one of the biggest lessons I learned from Jim: To name things that needed to be named in the kindest way possible and not to turn away from reality. He could be forceful without being overwhelming. Like a true friend, he had the fierceness to tell you things as they are without making you feel bad."

* * *

Being an academic psychiatrist means being responsive and adaptable to change, as universities strive to stay abreast of the latest technology. Sometimes, this requires difficult choices and sad farewells. In 2003, the building housing the MMHC was old, tired, and increasingly expensive to maintain. The Massachusetts Department of Mental Health decided to close it. At the same time, Harvard Medical School decided to abolish MMHC as one of its departments of psychiatry, because the dean was concerned that MMHC did not have the stature needed to attract new research funding.

It was unclear what would happen to the department, and everyone, from the senior staff through our administrative and secretarial people, was badly demoralized. I knew what would happen to me when the medical school abolished the department: no department, no department chair—I would be out of a job. In the end, the department became a division of the Beth Israel Department of Psychiatry at Harvard. The rest of the staff kept their jobs, and I stayed on for a year to supervise residents.

I resolved to do what I could to help people through this transition. I knew how important ceremony and ritual are in difficult times, and I decided that we would mark this sad and disruptive event clearly and dramatically. We contacted a performance artist, Anna Schuleit, who, three years earlier, had created a dramatic piece to mark the closing of the state mental hospital in Northampton, Massachusetts. There, she had arranged for a panoply of high-tech audio speakers to be arranged around the outside of the hospital. One cold January day, they all played the Bach "Magnificat."

At Northampton State Hospital, Anna had been struck by the absence of flowers. "Usually, when people are sick in the hospital, everyone brings flowers," she said. "When people are in a state hospital, there are no flowers at all." Anna suggested we use flowers to mark the closing of our drab, ninety-year-old building. The twenty-nine-year-old Anna, who later received a MacArthur fellowship, proposed to fill the halls at MMHC with flowers, and on her own, she raised the $50,000 necessary to achieve her vision.

She filled the hallways of our closed building with 28,000 potted flowers. The results were stunning, especially an array of violets in the long-unused swimming pool in the basement. At the shallow end of the pool, the violets were light blue, and they grew darker and darker as the pool became deeper. The installation, called "Bloom," was open to the public for four days, and then the flowers were delivered to shelters, halfway houses, and psychiatric hospitals throughout New England.

"Bloom" was an immense success, not just as an art piece but also as a comfort to the staff. One of the senior faculty members said, "You turned a funeral into a celebration." As the department closed, my wife Susan and I gave a dinner for the senior staff and several of the residents who had trained with me. It was a sad time for us all. As MMHC was closing and I was leaving my job, the associate dean of the medical school to whom I reported said to me, "You were exactly the right person at the right time for this job." I felt good that my work had been recognized, but I was sorry to leave. It was the best job I ever had.

* * *

I have tried in this chapter to use my experience to give the reader a picture of life in a teaching hospital. I close with a story that illustrates the depth that relationships in this setting can reach: my supervision with Dr. Octavio Gutierrez. This was an experience that would change both our lives. Dr. Gutierrez had traveled a great social distance to arrive at our training program in Cambridge. He grew up in a project in Newark, New Jersey, in a single-parent home. Octavio's father, who was an alcoholic, was intermittently present and physically abusive to Octavio when he was around, to the point that Octavio needed several hospitalizations. His mother suffered with recurrent severe depression, and when she was ill, Octavio was in and out of foster care.

In Newark, where drug dealing and violence were endemic, Octavio stayed out of trouble. He was bright enough to receive a private school scholarship and went on to succeed at Yale. Five years after college, he opted to pursue a career in medicine and attended the University of Pennsylvania Medical School. After graduating, he did his psychiatric residency at Cambridge, where, in 2007 and 2008, I supervised him.

Octavio is a superb psychiatrist with a strong commitment to the public sector, and, unlike many psychiatrists, he has retained his knowledge of general medicine. In 2016, as we reviewed our experience together, Octavio described our work: "My supervision with Jim started during my third year of residency. During the two years prior, I found most supervision valuable, but I was beginning to take issue with focusing only on the patient's symptoms with a lack of attention paid to the bigger picture of who the patient was, his social context, why he got sick when he did. I rarely had the opportunity to discuss these issues with my colleagues and advisors, and when I did, it was often after a tragedy, or during the rare odd hour when we had a moment to reflect.

"I was increasingly concerned about my career being an endless repetition of treatment algorithms and diagnostic criteria; I craved the opportunity to know the patient, to form a strong bond, and to better understand the human condition, especially working in an underserved setting. As I grew professionally, I was having a crisis of vocation.

"This was my situation when I prepared to meet with Jim for the first time, and I began to discuss my case. I presented as I had many times before, noting age, sex, sexual identification, psychiatric and medical history, history of presenting illness, social and family history and so on. Jim listened carefully, but I noted his brow become increasingly furrowed as he listened to my presentation. After a few minutes, Jim interrupted abruptly to say, 'Stop, stop, stop. You've told me all about the diagnosis, but you haven't told me who the patient is. I can't imagine him at all.'

"He had me start over, this time encouraging me to discuss more about my patient's past. As I presented, Jim would interrupt with questions like, 'Where did he grow up?' 'What does he like to do?' 'How are his relationships?' Under his supervision, my patient came alive again, as I contemplated his body language, his childhood, his profession, and how all of these things informed my patient's presentation."

Our supervision grew into friendship, and we began to share stories about our lives. After Octavio finished residency, he moved to New York City, where he worked in a clinic dedicated to serving the underserved. Our personal relationship grew and deepened, and Octavio continued to seek my advice informally as a supervisor.

Octavio came to experience me as the father he never had. He had not been looking for a father, and I had certainly not been looking for a son—yet that is the relationship we developed. I walked his mother down the aisle when Octavio got married. He and his wife, Anna, named their firstborn child Ruben James Gutierrez, after Anna's father and me.

The enduring satisfactions of academic medicine come from our work with patients, and from the relationships we develop with our trainees. My relationship with Octavio is perhaps the most dramatic example, but it is not the only one. As academic physicians, we are paid less than our colleagues in private practice, but for those of us who have chosen this path, the rewards more than outweigh the loss of income. If I had the choice to do it all over again, I would choose academic psychiatry in a heartbeat.

#####

Psychiatry has done a great deal of good in the world, relieving much human suffering, but like any human activity that has the power to do good, psychiatry has the power to do harm. In the next two chapters, I present evidence of that harm.

CHAPTER 15

PSYCHIATRY'S VIEW OF WOMEN: BLAME AND ABUSE

In the 1990s, Sara Hall, a married mother of three in her mid-thirties who was struggling to extricate herself from an emotionally abusive marriage, sought therapy from a psychoanalyst. Her husband had insisted that she limit her activities outside the home to those appropriate for a cloistered Episcopalian banker's wife.

Sara rebelled. Stealthily leaving the house in the very early morning while her husband was asleep, she learned to row a single scull, which is a twenty-eight-foot long, fourteen-inch wide boat weighing, perhaps, thirty pounds. It is designed to do only one thing—go *fast!*

When Sara described this activity to her psychoanalyst therapist, he interpreted this as a form of penis envy, an unconscious wish to be like a man that Sara should understand and give up. She, instead, recognized that her rowing was an important source of her developing self-esteem, and she fired this therapist.

This is not an isolated episode of a psychoanalyst attempting to undermine a female patient's quest for independence, nor by far the worst. Penis envy was a stick that psychiatrists used to beat women, sending a message meant to discourage them from achieving economic and social independence. That was not the only way psychiatrists harmed their female patients.

This chapter tells the disturbing story of how psychiatry understood and treated women for much of the second half of the twentieth century, reflecting a viewpoint that was fundamentally misogynistic. From the 1940s through the 1970s, psychiatry believed that mothers were the cause of much mental illness. Worse, organized psychiatry knew that some psychiatrists were sexually abusing their patients and did nothing.

In the course of my forensic practice, I interviewed a dozen women who gave me credible accounts of sexual encounters with their psychiatrists, but I heard the most egregious story during my residency. One of our part-time supervisors was a psychiatrist whom the residents mistrusted. He often came to the hospital in the evenings when he had no obvious reason for being there, wearing—in 1964—World War II sheepskin flight boots, and so presenting a very strange appearance. He would ask the resident on duty to recommend a patient whom he might interview. One of my fellow residents was making night rounds to ensure that everything was as it should be, and no patient required immediate attention. When he walked into the ECT suite, he found this psychiatrist having sex with a patient who was unconscious after having had ECT. The resident quietly closed the door and left. In the morning, he reported this to the psychiatrist-administrator in charge of the hospital, who told him not to do or say anything. Nothing resulted from this report, as far as I know.

Professional distinction does not guarantee patient safety—again, particularly for women. Another scandal that tarnished psychiatry concerned Jules Masserman, a president of the American Psychiatric Association (APA), professor of psychiatry at Northwestern, and author of fourteen books and hundreds of papers. Masserman treated some patients in the 1950s and 1960s with sodium amytal, a drug that rendered the patient unconscious. One woman, Barbara Noel, began psychoanalysis with Masserman in March 1960; in January of 1967, he persuaded her to begin sodium amytal treatment. Masserman repeatedly treated her with amytal until 1984, when she awoke while he was raping her. She sued, and Masserman settled out of court.[50] After five other women made similar claims, Masserman lost his license, but the APA allowed him to continue on its Board of Trustees, stating that the allegations were unsubstantiated. Unsubstantiated or not, insurance paid $350,000 to settle these claims.[51] Interviewed by Noel's writing partner, Masserman said, "I never did anything unethical to any patient."[52] The resulting lawsuits naming Masserman were not settled until the 1980s.

By the 1970s, the attitudes of male psychiatrists toward women, both as colleagues and as patients, began to change as more women came into psychiatry and the second wave of feminist writers began to speak out compellingly about the inequality of men and women in American society. When I entered training in 1964, women in psychiatry were a small and powerless minority; just one of the twenty-four residents in my cohort was a woman, and this was typical for that time. By the 1970s, twenty percent of all psychiatrists were women; now, in the twenty-first century, more than half of all new psychiatrists are women. Meaningful numbers of women psychiatrists argued for, and got, change.

The #MeToo movement beginning in the late 2010s has dramatically illustrated how powerful men in politics, entertainment, industry, and other professions have abused women, and psychiatry is no exception. Psychotherapy creates a unique imbalance of power between the patient who seeks help and the therapist whom she learns to trust. The intimacy that develops as the patient reveals painful secrets provides an opportunity for exploitation. A predatory or lovesick therapist can use his (occasionally her) power to initiate a sexual relationship with the patient. All physicians are required as a matter of ethical practice to inform patients of the risks and benefits of any treatment. For psychotherapy, disclosure of this risk is honored more in the breach than in the observance. Examples of therapist-patient sexual abuse appear later in this chapter, but first, some history.

* * *

Men blaming women for regrettable events goes back to the creation myth in the book of Genesis when Adam tells God, "The woman tempted me, and I ate." Fast forward to the twentieth century, when psychiatry found ways to blame women for mental illness, from schizophrenia to borderline personality disorder to combat-related psychological collapse, as the result of "bad mothering." A generation of mothers was told that their children were psychologically damaged by their negligence—mothers who lived for decades, often for the rest of their lives, with guilt and self-recrimination imposed unreasonably by psychiatrists.

Psychiatry's beliefs about women have reflected Western, and specifically American, culture's social attitudes as these changed over time. Before World War II, men took it for granted that they were in charge; they earned the money, or most of it, so they called the shots, which meant they controlled women's lives, and most particularly their bodies. The German phrase, "Kinder, Küche, Kirche" ("children, kitchen, church"), along with sex on demand, describes what many men wanted from women.

Important shifts in the position of American women began in the early 1940s. After America went to war late in 1941, more than ten million men were inducted into the armed forces, and to compensate for this and otherwise aid the war efforts, nineteen million American women entered the workforce. Well over a quarter of a million women joined the armed forces. By 1944, women comprised sixty percent of the American aircraft industry, as opposed to just one percent before the war.[53] This was a new experience for almost all these women, who either had been homemakers or restricted to jobs as secretaries, teachers, or nurses. Many were in their forties or fifties and would have been denied the right to vote earlier in their lives, as women only obtained suffrage in the United States in 1920.

After the war, many women were reluctant to give up the rewards associated with work, and they continued to work outside the home. Some observers saw this as pernicious—and described women, especially working women, as badly damaged by their new roles and identity. In their 1947 book, *Modern Woman,*

265

The Lost Sex, male sociologist Ferdinand Lundberg and female psychiatrist Dr. Marynia F. Farnham wrote, "We come now to the fact that the mother, under conditions of modern social change, is very often deeply disturbed. Although not a feminist or a courtesan, necessarily, she is herself afflicted very often at a deep level with penis-envy, which plays itself out in various ways with respect to children. She is disturbed, discontented, complaining, unreasonably demanding, aggressive and shows it directly or indirectly. The damage she does to boys as well as girls is great.

"[The married mother who works] must of necessity be deeply in conflict and only partially satisfied in either direction. Her work develops aggressiveness, which is essentially a denial of her femininity. . . . We are observing the masculinization of women and with it enormously dangerous consequences to the home, the children (if any) dependent on it, and to the ability of the woman, as well as her husband, to obtain sexual gratification. . . . The distortion of character under pressure of modern attitudes and upbringing is driving women steadily deeper into personal conflict soluble only by psychotherapy."[54]

The idea that it was harmful for mothers to work outside the home persisted for decades, despite evidence to the contrary. In the February 24, 1969, issue of *The Nation*, feminist historian Jo Freeman wrote, "Study after study has shown that children are not harmed by the fact that their mothers work (that, on the contrary, they frequently benefit), but employed mothers are still made to feel that they are shirking their maternal responsibilities." In the twenty-first century, the content has changed, but the issue persists: increased presence for women in the boardroom, in the executive suite, and in at least one male-dominated academic discipline, economics, comes with a price.

* * *

A theme runs through this history: many psychiatrists believed that women were the cause of mental illness. From the 1940s through the 1970s, we can sum up psychiatry's ideas on the cause of mental illness as, "It's your mother's fault." As a trainee in the 1960s, this is what I was taught and what I accepted—that is, mothers were to blame for schizophrenia and other severe mental illness. By the 1970s, I had enough clinical experience to know better.

Many of these perceptions came from Dr. Edward A. Strecker (1896-1959), a distinguished American psychiatrist, who served as a medical officer for a combat division in World War I. His ideas formed the basis for American military psychiatry during World War II. Between the wars, Strecker was professor of psychiatry at Thomas Jefferson University, the University of Pennsylvania, and Yale. In 1943, Dr. Strecker, then president of the American Psychiatric Association (APA), was named psychiatric consultant to the Secretary of War for the Army Air Force and to the Surgeon General for the Navy.

Strecker reflected on his war experience in his 1946 book, *Their Mothers' Sons: The Psychiatrist Examines an American Problem*.[55] He wrote, "500,000 men tried to evade military service, 1,825,000 were rejected for induction for neuropsychiatric reasons, 600,000 were invalided out as neuropsychiatric cases. In ninety percent of cases the cause was IMMATURITY."

As for the cause of this immaturity, Strecker said, "In the vast majority of cases a 'mom' is at fault." Strecker uses "mom" as a derogatory term for overprotective or otherwise bad mothers. Notably, "moms" were not just the cause of this alleged immaturity that left men too inadequate for military service, but also largely the cause, or so Strecker suggested, of homosexuality and, schizophrenia. From our twenty-first-century vantage point, Strecker's ideas are absurd. But for the next several decades, they were regarded as the opinions of a respected psychiatrist, good clinician, leader of the profession, and national resource in the war effort.

* * *

From about 1920 until the 1970s, American psychiatry's understanding of the cause of mental disorders was largely derived from psychoanalysis. In 1920, we had no treatment for schizophrenia; but in this wasteland, psychoanalysis offered new hope. If, as psychoanalysts suggested, schizophrenia could be understood as a reaction to life events, specifically as a reaction to pathogenic early life experience, then it was treatable.

Beginning in the 1940s, the specific concept of the mother who caused schizophrenia—the schizophrenogenic mother—entered the mainstream of psychoanalytically oriented psychiatry. Women themselves accepted this perspective: Freda Fromm-Reichmann, a Viennese psychiatrist and psychoanalyst who left Austria in 1936, was a gifted psychotherapist who worked with severely ill patients. In 1948, she wrote, "The schizophrenic is painfully distrustful and resentful of other people, due to the early warp and rejection he

268

encountered in important people of his infancy and childhood, as a rule, mainly a schizophrenogenic mother."[56]

Psychologist Sybil Escalona had a different view. In 1948, she discussed seventeen psychotic children treated at the Menninger Clinic, a psychoanalytically oriented psychiatric hospital. Escalona wrote, "Most of the mothers spontaneously commented that there was something puzzling and 'different' about these children from a very early age on. . . . The more one studies the early life history of psychotic children, the more one is impressed with the atypical and pathological reaction of the children to perfectly ordinary maternal attitude. . . . These early developmental disturbances [should be] regarded as arising in large measure from the pathology within the child rather than from parental attitudes per se."[57]

Psychoanalytically oriented psychiatrists and psychologists paid no attention to this report, nor to this perspective. They insisted that bad mothering caused schizophrenia and urged these mothers to look into themselves to see what had caused their child's devastating illness. A group of Yale psychiatrists published their first paper on this topic in 1948, summarizing their work in *Schizophrenia and the Family*.[58] They described mothers of patients as "strange, near-psychotic or even overtly schizophrenic." The mother "distorts her perceptions [and] is impervious to the needs of other family members. . . . [She has] psychotic or very strange concepts. . . . Her communications are vague, stereotyped, fragmented." All the mothers of male patients were seen as "dangerous figures to males. They were engulfing, castrating, or chronically dissatisfied with their husbands," while the mother of daughters with schizophrenia was characterized as "disillusioned about her marriage, filled with hostility toward her husband... and deficient in feminine warmth and affectionate qualities." These psychiatrists emphatically rejected the alternative explanation that what they observed in the mothers might be a result of her difficulty in responding to a child with a severe illness.

Most psychiatrists abandoned the schizophrenogenic mother theory over the next few decades, as cognitive neuroscience documented with increasing specificity what was wrong in the brains and minds of people with schizophrenia. Despite this evidence, some psychoanalysts clung to the theory that early experience in the family caused schizophrenia. The Yale group even insisted that the genetic data were wrong and that their understanding was correct!

Schizophrenia was not the only disease attributed to bad mothering. Mothers were also blamed for causing autism and borderline personality disorder. Dr. Leo Kanner, the first self-described child psychiatrist in this country, headed the nascent child psychiatry service at Johns Hopkins, and in 1943, he wrote the first paper describing autism in children as a recognizable disorder.[59] He coined the phrase "refrigerator mothers" to describe the mothers of his patients. Many years later, when it became clear that autism was a genetic disorder, Kanner apologized for his earlier use of this term.

In the 1930s, psychoanalysts erroneously blamed borderline personality disorder (BPD) on bad mothering. When first described, BPD was thought to be a variant of schizophrenia; later, it was understood as lying on the border between neurosis and psychosis, hence its name. Patients with BPD often have intense but unstable personal relationships, marked emotional dysregulation and episodes of self-destructive behavior. They are impulsive; make frantic efforts to avoid real or imagined abandonment; become inappropriately angry; experience feelings of emptiness; and may become transiently dissociated or psychotic. They often abuse substances, and when someone disappoints them, they may make frantic efforts to manipulate that person into meeting their demands. These patients are extremely difficult both to live with and to treat, and many psychiatrists avoid them when they can.

In 1938, psychoanalyst Adolph Stern wrote an early paper explaining the backgrounds of many patients with BPD: "In at least seventy-five percent [of borderline patients], the histories show that one or more of the following factors were present from earliest childhood. The mother was a decidedly neurotic type. . . . These mothers inflicted injuries on their children by virtue of a deficiency of spontaneous maternal affection. Actual cruelty, neglect and brutality by the parents of many years' duration are factors in these patients.... [BPD patients experience] very early periods of psychic starvation and insecurity due to lack of parental, chiefly maternal, affection."[60] This assessment would set the stage for continued attributions of BPD to maternal failings.

In treating BPD, analysts focused on the intrapsychic life of the mother—i.e., on what was wrong with her. They ignored her life experience, which often included an abusive man. Later, they went beyond a narrow focus on the internal life of the mother and developed the concept of attachment as key to the development of the psychologically healthy adult. For adult health, they posited, the child needed an attachment to a "good enough" mother or to another "good enough" adult. Parental abuse or neglect can

271

lead to damaged infant attachment, and we now understand damaged early attachment as present in BPD and other adult psychopathology. We also understand that BPD arises in people with genetic vulnerability and potentially damaging early life experience.[60]

In 1989, psychiatrists Judith Herman, Christopher Perry, and Bessel van der Kolk, my colleagues at Cambridge Hospital, wrote the first paper reporting substantial incidence of childhood abuse and neglect in patients with BPD.[61] They reported that all types of self-harmful behavior—including cutting, burning, overdoses, and suicide attempts—were more common in patients with BPD than in other severely ill patients, and the extent and severity of adult self-harm was strongly correlated with history of childhood abuse or neglect. Later studies repeatedly confirmed these results. But the reasons for parental neglect varied well beyond maternal psychopathology. These could include an abusive partner or the stresses of poverty or racism.

BPD occurs equally often in men and women,[62] but psychiatrists in clinical practice diagnose BPD in three women for every one man.[63] We do not know whether this is because women with the disorder more often seek treatment than men, or because men are commonly misdiagnosed with PTSD or depression, or because psychiatrists more readily recognize the disorder in women.[62] Uniquely among all diagnoses, psychiatrists may use "borderline" as a pejorative adjective applied to a woman they don't like, as in 'she's a borderline,' said in a disparaging tone. 'Borderline' can also be used as an explanation for why a patient is difficult, as heard in the 21st-century on the ward of a Harvard teaching hospital: "Her mother is a borderline."

Patients with BPD are notoriously difficult to treat because of their rage when anyone disappoints them, and the resulting fragility of their relationships. I was asked to consult on the case of a woman with BPD who had been in the hospital for more than two months. She also had been hospitalized for more than three additional months in the past year. Her psychiatrist and his team were at their wits end. They knew that long hospitalizations would only create a chronic patient, but this woman repeatedly threatened suicide with sufficient credibility that the team felt they had no choice but to hospitalize her for her own safety.

At the time I saw her she was in her mid-30s, and she had been struggling for years. She was quite bright and had graduated from a good small college. Shortly after graduation she became suicidally depressed. She recovered from the depression, but since then she had worked in a series of marginal jobs that were well below her capabilities. She had functioned primarily as a psychiatric patient either in the hospital or, when living at home, as an outpatient.

What made her particularly difficult to treat besides her threats of suicide was her almost constant rage. Like many patients with BPD, she was not able to connect her emotions with the events that had triggered them. When she was angry she had no idea why she was so angry; she was just angry. Her anger often took the form of abusing her caregivers. She would call them terrible names and she would threaten violent action. For example, as an outpatient she would call her psychiatrist in the middle of the night and say, 'If you don't see me right now I am going to cut myself.' She would count down, and when the psychiatrist refused to get out of bed and drive half an hour in order to see her, she would cut herself, then present to the hospital emergency service and be re-admitted. This is an example of the kind of behavior that leads many psychiatrists to avoid these patients if they can.

When I saw her I had the clear impression that she was refusing to take responsibility for her own life. When I reviewed the history, she never had a plan to commit suicide. She just repeatedly told the staff that if they discharged her she would kill herself. I understood this suffering woman to be chronically suicidal but not an acute suicide risk. These patients are among the most difficult for us to treat; many psychiatrists are afraid to trust their own judgment that the patient is not an acute risk, so these patients are repeatedly admitted, typically briefly.

I told the patient honestly what I thought, that if she were really going to kill herself there was nothing any of us could do to stop her. I said that this decision was her responsibility. I saw that she suffered a great deal. I noted also that, although she was often miserable, she had considerable strengths, and, in my opinion, she had a very good psychiatrist. I saw a basis for hope, and I hoped personally that she would decide to stay alive and do what she could for herself.

I told the staff in her presence that I thought they should discharge her because she was not an acute suicidal risk, recognizing that if this plan were successful this would be at best a difficult treatment experience for her and her treating psychiatrist.

This story illustrates that I am willing to trust my own judgment and that I am not afraid to have difficult conversations with patients, but that is not why I tell it. I tell it because it illustrates a successful psychotherapy with a BPD patient. This woman's insurance policy paid for all her hospitalizations but provided only limited coverage for outpatient treatment. Her psychiatrist made the argument to her insurance company that it would be cheaper for them to make an exception and pay him to provide outpatient treatment, rather than to continue with her current policy limits. To their credit, the insurance company agreed.

Two years after my consultation the patient continues in psychotherapy with her psychiatrist, and she has been hospitalized exactly 5 days! Over the course of this psychodynamically based therapy, the patient was able to tell her psychiatrist about her abuse history, including a long sexual relationship with a high school teacher. With the help of her psychiatrist, she could begin to make the connection between her rage and what had been done to her. She began to feel much better. At follow-up, she was working full-time in a position that involves caring for abused children, and she was planning to go on to graduate school.

This case primarily illustrates that psychotherapy by a committed psychiatrist can be helpful for a patient with BPD, but this case also illustrates the role of the insurance industry in dictating what care psychiatrists can and cannot provide. Regrettably, in the American healthcare system as a whole, it is very rare that patients like this have access to outpatient psychotherapy that is clearly indicated for them.

Since the days of the schizophrenogenic mother, the mental health professions have refocused their view of motherhood from its pathology to its strengths. We now understand that healthy mental development depends on "good enough" mothering. We recognize that failures of motherhood are often the result of external pressures—including partner abuse, poverty, racism, and beyond—rather than the results of psychopathology. Maternal character problems can be pathogenic for BPD, but therapy of the patient with BPD must also consider social determinants of bad mothering.

By the latter half of the twentieth century, women had had enough, and they fought back. Feminist writers of the 1970s and '80s protested vigorously that psychoanalytic ideas about women and women's health represented cultural stereotypes that served to maintain the status quo that kept women in an inferior social position. In her 1980 book, *Therapy with Women,* psychologist Susan Sturdivant wrote, "Freud's impact, ultimately, was to legitimize sex-role stereotypes by embodying them in a 'scientific' theory. His theories sanctified the oppression of women.... Psychoanalytic mythology passing as human traits.... Unfortunately for women, the majority of American psychotherapists continue to adhere to a psychoanalytic orientation to therapy."[64]

* * *

Regrettably, the portrayal of the mother as the root of mental illness was not the only problem. Sexual abuse of patients occurred but organized psychiatry chose to ignore it. Male physician–initiated sexual behavior with patients has been recognized as a problem in medicine for millennia. Hippocrates, who practiced 2500 years ago, cautioned against sex with patients. In the eighteenth century, King Louis XVI of France appointed Benjamin Franklin to head a commission to address sexual misconduct by physicians. The commission's report warned that the physician "is responsible, not merely for his own wrong-doing, but for that he may have excited in another."[61] By the twentieth century, the vast majority of American psychiatrists believed that sex with patients was wrong, but the profession knew what was going on and did nothing. When change came, it was the result of three social forces: the activism of female8 psychiatrists, the voices of women in American society, and the power of lawsuits.

The first agents of change were feminist writers and abused patients. In the 1970s, the writers called attention to the sexual bias in therapists' ideas of mental health. Many patients spoke out about the sexual abuse they experienced and organized to confront the issue. Gaining strength and confidence, they brought lawsuits alleging that sex with patients was malpractice, and they filed complaints with state boards of medicine. As women became psychiatrists in increasing numbers, they forced the profession to address the issue.

Jan Wohlberg was one of the first women to publicly address her sexual abuse; I interviewed her about these experiences in 2014.[62]

In 1973, Jan, [now a good friend], was a married, well-educated mother of two when a psychotic patient fatally shot her psychiatrist husband. Wohlberg called her former psychotherapist, Dr. Lionel A. Schwartz, seeking crisis counseling. Dr. Schwartz, a psychoanalyst and not so incidentally the director of mental health services at Wellesley College, told her his schedule was very full

---

8 Despite its biological connotations, strict grammarians prefer 'female' over woman or women because it is a full-fledged adjective, rather than shoehorning a noun into the role of an adjective. Referring to men, one would be far more likely to refer to "*male* psychiatrists" than to "*men* psychiatrists." To maintain a parallel structure, I have chosen to use 'female;' but the shame is that the qualification needs to be made at all.

and he was not sure if he would have time to see her. "I will call you back," he told her, "if I can find a slot."

Schwartz did call back, and within a couple of sessions, he offered himself as a source of the intimacy that Wohlberg was so afraid of losing with her husband's death. After a few sessions, he suggested she provide him with oral sex, and she obliged. For most of the psychotherapy sessions during the following year, she serviced him, and Schwartz provided sex toys for her. He would clean up, they would talk for ten minutes, and she would leave. Wohlberg said later, "I essentially became his sexual slave. I knew I was in a bad situation, but I didn't have the strength to leave, and I didn't know where else to go." Schwartz continued to send bills for psychotherapy, and Wohlberg and her insurers continued to pay them.

Eventually, she found the strength to move on, and a little over a year later, she phoned Schwartz seeking acknowledgement that what happened between them was not therapy. She asked him to return the money she had paid him. "Nonsense," he told her. "It was therapy, and you got a great deal out of it." When she was seeing Schwartz, Wohlberg had asked "Have you ever done this with anyone else?" He acknowledged that he had. "Aren't you concerned that someone will report you?" she asked. "No," he responded, "I pick my people carefully."

With Wohlberg, he had not been careful enough. Finally, with the help of one of her late husband's colleagues, she brought an ethics complaint to the Boston Psychoanalytic Institute. Before a committee of analysts, including one woman, she told her story. The members of the committee listened stone-faced. "It was clear that not one of them believed me—that they were looking for my pathology," she said. She finally challenged, "If you have any questions about my story, ask Dr. Schwartz to drop his pants. He has a large inguinal hernia, and there is only one way I could know that." *That* was damning enough evidence to change the analysts' attitudes.

In the end, the committee asked Schwartz to reimburse Wohlberg for the $1,760 she had paid for therapy, to go into therapy himself, and to have his work supervised by another analyst for three years. They did not report him to the medical board or to Wellesley College.

A decade later, the Massachusetts Board of Registration in Medicine wrote to Wohlberg asking whether she would be willing to speak with them about her relationship with Schwartz. "Just seeing the return address on the envelope, I knew," she told me. "My hands began to shake, and I said, 'He's done it again.' " Indeed, he had: two former Wellesley students had filed claims against him. Wohlberg appeared as a corroborative witness at the board's hearing. Despite the three known cases, the board dragged its feet.

Frustrated by its inaction, Wohlberg wrote a letter to the *Boston Globe* detailing what had happened to her. She agreed to let her name be used to give the story "a face and a soul," and in 1989, the *Globe* ran several well-documented stories about Schwartz's repeated abuse of female patients. Faced with this dramatic, credible account, Schwartz surrendered his license.

A physician who loses his license can no longer practice medicine, but he (usually he) may still hang out a shingle with the designation "MD" after his name because the Board of Medicine has no legal authority to order him to remove the degree granted by a medical school. In Massachusetts, no license is required to practice psychotherapy, so these men can continue to practice as psychotherapists after they no longer have a license as physicians.

Schwartz was a predator. As soon as the *Globe* published the articles, other abused women began contacting Wohlberg, and they agreed to meet. Five women came to the first meeting of what would become TELL, the Therapist Exploitation Link Line.[63] By the third meeting, there were more than thirty. At times, the group exceeded fifty. The pent-up need for a place where women could break the isolation of this experience was clear.

The TELL founders group met in the Boston area for four years and then expanded internationally through a website9 where volunteers from the United States, Canada, Australia, and Europe, who had themselves been exploited in psychotherapy or other health care settings, could provide support. Clearly, the problem has not gone away; the group's website gets more than forty thousand visits a year.

Concerned about possible lawsuits for libel or slander, the original five founders invited Boston attorney Linda M. Jorgenson to attend the meetings as a resource. Her work with TELL led to a long, distinguished career as a plaintiffs' attorney and as an advocate for abused psychotherapy patients. I first learned about the problem when she hired me as an expert to evaluate the psychological damage to an abused client. I worked with her on other cases of therapist abuse, some perpetrated

---

9 As of the publication of this book, the URL for TELL is http://www. therapyabuse.org.

by psychiatrists, but others by psychologists, social workers, self-identified Christian counselors, and priests. Hearing these women's stories changed my view of what men are capable of, and of the limited power of ethical standards to control behavior. I felt deeply for these women and would have liked to do more, but my role was limited to listening to them, and then telling their stories in their lawsuits.

* * *

Therapists commonly experience sexual attraction to patients; the issue lies in how the therapist deals with that attraction. I was strongly sexually attracted to two patients over the course of my career, but I maintained my boundaries. The first was a young woman with borderline traits whom I saw as a first-year resident, admitted after she made a suicidal gesture. As our therapeutic relationship continued, I felt too guilty to discuss my sexual attraction to her with my supervisors. She mostly talked and I mostly listened, but we never talked about my sexual feelings, or hers. After some months, she improved enough to leave the hospital.

I saw the second patient in midlife. She was a professional woman a few years younger than I, depressed with borderline personality traits. I found her attractive, and I had persistent sexual fantasies about her. Like many patients with borderline traits, she had a strong need for affection, and she repeatedly expressed her wishes to be close to me both emotionally and physically. The day came when she asked to sit on my lap, telling me that this would help her deal with her needs.

281

I refused her request, not because I was concerned that it might be bad for her—although it probably would have been—but because I did not trust myself in that situation. I continued to maintain appropriate boundaries in this therapy in spite of my sexual fantasies and the anxiety they caused me. I was able to resist the temptation to gratify these impulses through a combination of Jewish guilt and an adult sense of right and wrong. The therapy appeared to have been useful to the patient. On follow-up several years later, she told me that she was happily married and working successfully.

I did have one experience with sexual undertones that ended badly. I met Donna (not her real name) when I lectured first-year residents on forensic psychiatry at Cambridge. We talked afterwards about some of her work issues, and we connected. She expressed the hope that we might continue meeting as supervisor and supervisee. That was our only contact until some months later, when she requested to see me and told me weeping that she had recently had a severely distressing experience at work. She could not tell me what happened, because, she said, the memory was too upsetting

Some months after that, she was assigned to me for weekly supervision for the next academic year, I believe at her own request. We were doing well together until I made an ill-advised observation that caused her great distress, and that I continue to regret. We were discussing the relationship between the patient and the therapist, when I told her that many men would find her attractive and that, when she felt able to do so, it would be important for the progress of therapy to give her male patients permission to discuss their relationship. I went on to tell her that if I were a generation younger and a patient of hers, I would have found her to be attractive. That was the extent of this conversation, and we went on to discuss other issues.

Several weeks later, the training director called me into his office to tell me that Donna had made a complaint about me. She reported that she had been distressed by this discussion and found it to be inappropriate. She did not want to initiate any formal action against me, but she wanted the training director to know about this discussion and how it had made her feel.

In hindsight, I saw that I had brought this up when it was my issue, rather than waiting for her to raise it when she experienced it. The timing reflected my attraction to this young woman and my difficulty in focusing on professional issues as her supervisor. I wanted to meet with Donna once more to apologize and to try to repair the damage I had done. Through an intermediary whom we both trusted, I sent this message, but she refused to meet, and we never spoke again. Supervision, like psychotherapy, can be a close relationship, and even well-intentioned supervisors can fail to recognize the extent of their own involvement.

I think it is easy to imagine that a therapist who was single or who was in an unsatisfactory relationship could have behaved differently with a patient or with a supervisee, with a very different result. One distinguished psychoanalyst called such men "lovesick therapists." In the course of my forensic work, I evaluated two such therapists who were in deeply unhappy marriages. Each lacked the capacity to tell his wife how he felt, becoming increasingly enraged and, at the same time, increasingly needy. In each case, a patient, with her own needs for love and closeness, told the psychiatrist repeatedly that he was wonderful. Eventually, she asked for a hug;

the therapist provided the hug, biology asserted itself, unethical conduct was conveniently justified, and it was downhill from there.

In time, the men developed some capacity to be comfortable with their anger, and both were able to raise marital issues with their wives. One decided to remain with his wife, and when he told the patient he would not leave his wife for her, the therapy came to an abrupt, angry end. She made a formal complaint, which led to my involvement with him.

The second case was unique in my experience. It was not a case of mine, but the report came from a reliable source whom I knew well. This psychiatrist did leave his wife, and he and his now former patient established a household. His children chose to live with them, and on two-year follow-up my informant told me the new family was doing well.

* * *

One of the questions observers often ask is: "How do intelligent, well-educated women fall into the trap of a sexual relationship that is often profoundly damaging?" Some part of the answer is that a therapist provides a vulnerable woman with unconditional acceptance, or something close to it, possibly for the first time in her life. She often responds by forming an intense emotional attachment to the therapist, so that maintaining this relationship becomes a very strong motive, and she may do whatever he wants in order to preserve the relationship.

Some patients believe they are special for the therapist, telling themselves that the psychiatrist cares more about them than about his other patients, or that he is more interested in her than in his wife. When the therapist tells this patient that he is in love with her, she is ready to believe him.

Abusers, in turn, carefully groom their patients. The prospective abuser will encourage the patient to believe that he cares deeply for her—that she is special in a way that his other patients are not, that sex is part of therapy, and that it is what the patient needs in order to heal. After the predatory therapist has initiated the sexual relationship, he will encourage the patient to believe that she is responsible for the relationship and for nurturing and caring for him. The predatory therapist will typically attempt to isolate his victim from other support systems, foster dependence, and then threaten the patient with abandonment, public exposure, or other dire consequences, should the victim try to end the "therapy."

The therapist may promise an enduring relationship, and the patient sues after she discovers that the therapist is unwilling to make good on his promise. At this point, she becomes enraged, realizes that she has been exploited, and breaks off the relationship, then makes a formal complaint either to the board of medicine or as the plaintiff in a lawsuit.

The emotional repercussions that women suffer as a result of the sexual manipulation can be catastrophic. The abused women in my forensic practice were all badly damaged. They described recurring nightmares, frightening flashbacks, guilt, disrupted sleep, severe depression, and loss of trust in themselves. One woman killed herself.

More damaging than the anxiety and depression is the change in how these women view themselves. Many suffer a profound loss of self-esteem, and they have lost trust in their ability to evaluate other people. Many entered a sexual relationship believing that they were special to the therapist, or that he loved them—or even, perhaps, that they loved him. When they discovered that the therapist had lied, they were enraged and lost their belief in their judgment about people.

All of us as social animals rely on our belief that we can accurately assess the motives of others. When we lose that, we are helpless to protect ourselves from possible exploitation, and we are terrified. A person can put a bad sexual experience behind them; a loss of basic trust can last forever.

When it is even possible, subsequent therapy can be a challenge both for an abused patient and for the new therapist. As with any patient, the new treating therapist wants to help the new patient, but if the new patient arouses feelings of anger or guilt about past misdeeds of the profession, the new therapist can be ambivalent about the patient. This can occur without the therapist having any conscious awareness of these feelings, and how they limit the therapist's engagement with the patient, badly damaging their capacity to be helpful.

Some therapists remain under-involved, doubting that the sex ever happened or blaming the patient if it did, urging the patient to "get beyond" the experience, rather than helping the patient to process it. Others may become over-involved, believing the patient's story, and feeling deeply for her. These therapists can focus sympathetically on the patient as victim to the exclusion of helping the patient process the past experience or to deal with early experience that may have led to her vulnerability.

What abused women want and need from a subsequent treating therapist is first validation—acceptance that the relationship occurred, with a clear statement that it is the responsibility of the therapist, not the patient, no matter how much she feels that she initiated it. The therapist must make clear to the patient that this new therapeutic relationship will not be sexual and that boundaries will be clearly stated and maintained. Further, the therapist needs to acknowledge how much difficulty this patient will have in trusting them or any other subsequent treating therapist.

* * *

Throughout the latter half of the twentieth century, even as evidence mounted that women were being severely damaged, the APA continued to ignore psychiatrist sexual exploitation of patients. One senior psychiatrist in the APA leadership stated openly that sex with patients or with students was "just something that happened" and "nothing to be concerned about." A president of the APA told attorney Jorgenson that he was advising psychiatrists who wanted to have sex with their patients to terminate the therapeutic relationship so that they could then have sex with their now former patient. Jorgenson responded by organizing symposia on patient-therapist sexual abuse at the APA. I served on several of these symposia, and I also served with her on a Massachusetts legislative committee that drafted legislation to make patient-therapist sexual contact illegal in Massachusetts. The proposed bill failed in committee, in part because feminist activists opposed it, arguing that women should be able to have sex with whomever they wanted.

As the proportion of women in psychiatry increased in the 1970s and '80s, they were appointed to important committees, and for the first time, male psychiatrists heard their voices. Two female psychiatrists, Nanette Gartrell and Judith Herman, were largely responsible for forcing the APA to acknowledge that sex with patients is wrong.[51] They had both embraced a radical feminist view of the role of women in contemporary American society as an oppressed underclass. They understood male supremacy as a fundamental problem, and they were sensitive to the numerous ways in which men kept women in their place.

Dr. Herman was a member of our department at Cambridge Hospital when she heard from several credible informants that one of the senior psychiatrists in our department had initiated sexual relations with several of his female trainees, and then a another resident came to her in great distress and revealed how this professor had tried to seduce her. When Dr. Herman reported this to the residency training director, his first reaction was to ask whether this could possibly be a misunderstanding. Herman denied this, stating that the professor had asked the resident in so many words to go to bed with him. The training director imposed no discipline on the professor, who outranked him academically, but after this conversation, the training director assigned no other female residents to this supervisor.

A footnote to this story: some years later, when I was working at the Cambridge District Court, I saw this professor in the company of a defense attorney, looking very frightened. Several months later, this supervisor died of a heart attack. It may have been a coincidence, but I knew of other psychiatrists who had died of heart attacks when they were defendants in lawsuits involving allegations of sexual misconduct with patients.

Male administrators accepted these sexual advances as part of life, but from a feminist perspective, Dr. Herman understood the power dynamics of sexual misconduct with a young trainee as similar to the dynamics of incest. Like the adolescent female powerless to resist the older father figure, a trainee can feel forced to submit to the wishes of an older more powerful supervisor. Dr. Herman had done original work establishing that incest between young female children and older male relatives was far more common than the "one in a million" that psychiatrists believed. [65]

Like sex with patients, incest was not something that troubled even recognized leaders of the profession. Otto Kernberg was a distinguished psychoanalyst with an international reputation. When Dr. Herman asked him at a national meeting about incest in the histories of patients with borderline personality disorder, he responded matter-of-factly that incest histories were very common in these patients, but he appeared to attach no significance to this fact.

When I was a resident, Dr. Elvin Semrad inspired me, as well as many other generations of psychiatric residents. I was present when another resident presented the case of a psychotic young woman who was particularly agitated and so disorganized that she could not engage in psychotherapy. Dr. Semrad was able to connect with her, and she told him about having had sexual intercourse with her father from the age of sixteen. In his discussion of the case after the patient left the room, Dr. Semrad suggested that perhaps she was so disorganized because she felt guilty that she had enjoyed the experience. I clearly remember Dr. Semrad's smile as he told us this, as if he were telling us something that we residents would not have understood without his help. I also remember how we nodded our agreement and looked at each other thinking how wise he was. In retrospect, this case showed that Dr. Semrad had the limitations of his time of which we, sharing the same limits, were completely unaware. Now, a generation after this discussion, we know better. We know that women who had sexual relations with their fathers are victims. We know that the physical sensations during intercourse, whatever these may be, are the least important part of what this experience means. I know from my own clinical experience at Metropolitan State Hospital that incest can lead to the most intractable psychoses that we see in a state hospital population.

When Dr. Herman joined Dr. Gartrell on the APA Committee on Women in 1982, the APA insurance carrier was receiving increasing numbers of malpractice claims alleging damage to patients as a result of sexual contact with their psychiatrist. Working with a third member of the committee, Silvia Olarte, the three women proposed that APA study the issue. The legal advisors to the APA were in favor of doing the study, not because they had a more finely developed moral sense, but because the APA malpractice insurance was paying out too many claims in these cases. Men at all levels of the APA hierarchy opposed doing the study, and the board of trustees rejected the proposed study, saying it would create bad publicity, and "destroy the credibility of the profession."

Undeterred, these three women decided to perform the study anyway. Since the APA was unwilling to provide a membership list, Dr. Gartrell purchased the mailing labels for every 5th U.S. psychiatrist (alphabetically, under the age of 65) from the AMA. The survey was mailed out to this random sample of 5,574 psychiatrists, and 1,423 of those contacted returned questionnaires.[66]

Psychiatrists were asked whether they had had any sexual relationships with patients, and those who answered in the affirmative were asked how many patients, and whether they considered the sexual relationship(s) to have been appropriate or inappropriate.

After completing their study, the authors had to fight to have their findings published. The *American Journal of Psychiatry*, the official journal of the APA, initially rejected the paper, but later accepted it for publication after the authors informed the editor that the American Psychological Association was prepared to publish it if the APA did not.

The findings were published in 1986 and 1987.[65, 66] Eighty-four psychiatrists—more than seven percent of the men, and more than three percent of the women who responded—reported having had some sexual contact with a patient. These eighty-four reported they thought that sex after termination was all right, and that romantic love could justify sex with a current patient. Sixteen of these eighty-four respondents acknowledged sex with more than one patient, and they claimed that sex with patients could be therapeutic.

The publication of these two papers essentially forced organized psychiatry to acknowledge this problem and to respond. It took years, but organized psychiatry ultimately did what was right. In 1993, the APA took the official position that sex with a patient is never acceptable.

* * *

Yet patient-therapist sexual relations still occur. It is difficult to know how large the problem is, or even whether the number of cases increases or decreases from year to year. A 2007 book reports estimates that between seven to twelve percent of psychologists had engaged in sexual behavior with one or more patients.[67]

Professional distinction remains no bar to immorality. In September of 2017, the Massachusetts Board of Medicine denied a senior Boston psychoanalyst the right to renew his license. Breaking new ground for outrage, three women sued psychiatrist Keith Ablow, alleging that, at his urging, they engaged in "degrading sexual activity, bondage, and in one case getting a tattoo of her doctor's initials to show that he 'owned' her."[68]

Clearly, predatory therapists still exist, and there will always be some men for whom emotional and sexual desires are stronger than conscience, but when there are consequences, some men will be deterred from doing wrong. In psychiatry, countervailing power was required to end the abuse of power. Strong feminist psychiatrists, feminist writers, and organizations of the patients themselves, such as those in TELL, generated the countervailing power that forced psychiatry to change. And just as women have slowly changed psychiatry, women in the #MeToo movement are forcing changes in the larger society. If we are successful as a society in limiting sexual predators, it will be because women organize to insist on their freedom from unwanted sexual demands. I know the damage that women have suffered from the predators in my own profession; I hope women will be successful in their larger battle.

#####

CHAPTER 16

HOMOSEXUALITY: HOW WRONG WE WERE

Homosexuality is not now—and never has been—a disease, but until 1973, organized psychiatry insisted that it was and treated it as such. The psychiatrists, largely white, heterosexual men—who held these views had grown up in the 1930s and 1940s, when homosexuality was widely vilified. Virtually all gay men and women kept their sexual orientation secret for fear of consequences that could, in some states, lead to a prison sentence. It is a fair inference that psychiatrists in the 1950s had no *openly* homosexual friends or acquaintances; knowing no identified gay people, they knew nothing or close to nothing about homosexuality.[10]

Some psychoanalysts claimed that they could cure homosexuality through "conversion therapy." These analysts subjected innocent people to years of abusive treatment in which

---

10 See Lillian Faderman's history for an account of how psychiatric attitudes changed.

success meant that the patient acknowledged a pathological or defective sexual orientation and then rejected it. The conversion therapist's goal was for the patient to give up his core sexual identity and replace it with one that the patient did not recognize as a part of himself.

For straight society, psychiatry's approach to homosexuality reinforced the view that gay men were sick and that what they did was disgusting. Gay people also received this authoritative medical opinion, and for them, the message was especially destructive. It told them that their natural impulses were a sign of psychopathology. Believing this, some gay people actively sought conversion therapy. The heterosexual reader can perhaps begin to imagine how damaging it would be to seek the solace of therapy, only to have the therapist identify your sexuality as pathological, and then inform you that the goal of your therapy would be to convert you to homosexuality.

The most optimistic case studies of conversion therapy report a 30 percent conversion rate. Most patients failed to convert, and they were left worse off than before treatment. They had come to therapy hoping to be cured of what they were told was psychopathology, only to learn that they were incurable—now with a permanently damaged identity as a person whom society viewed with opprobrium. Rather than help the patient deal with this burden, the conversion therapist added to it by treating this as a failed therapy.

I have never treated a patient who had been subjected to conversion therapy, but there are published accounts by therapists who have. These later therapists described patients conflicted about their sexuality, often suffering from severe depression and anxiety. The later therapists viewed these symptoms as the direct result of the conversion therapy experience.

Psychiatry's understanding and treatment of homosexuality was an intellectual failure by an entire profession. This failure damaged American society by perpetuating angry prejudices against gay people and it inflicted substantial psychological harm on gay people by defining them as sick at the core. This did slowly change, and finally end.

* * *

The change in twenty-first century society's acceptance of homosexuality is remarkable. Less than two generations ago, homosexuals were denigrated, rounded up and arrested for their private consensual sexual behavior. Today, the discrimination they face has lessened, and most Americans support same-sex marriage. Gay marriage is legal throughout the United States as a result of the landmark 2015 U.S. Supreme Court decision (*Obergefell v. Hodges*), which ruled that the due process and equal protection clauses of the Fourteenth Amendment guaranteed same-sex couples the fundamental right to marry. This change did not come about by accident; it was fueled every step of the way by gay and lesbian activists who pushed successfully for incremental changes in how society viewed and treated them.

Regrettably, organized psychiatry was an influential institution against which these activists had to fight. In 1952, the American Psychiatric Association (APA) published its first *Diagnostic and Statistical Manual of Mental Disorders* (*DSM-I*), which designated homosexuality as a "sociopathic personality

295

disturbance." For decades, the APA actively opposed attempts by individual psychiatrists to de-pathologize homosexuality. The second version of *Diagnostic and Statistical Manual of Mental Disorders* (*DSM-II*), published in 1968, continued to list homosexuality as a sexual deviation—a pathological condition. This was a milder description than the 1952 labeling, but the stigma of mental illness remained.

As early as 1956, scientific data argued strongly that homosexuality was not pathological. Evelyn Hooker, an experimental psychologist at Johns Hopkins, planned to study a male homosexual and his partner, as well as several lesbian women. [69] When she mentioned this to a psychologist friend, he said, "You must do it! We don't know anything. What we know about are the sick ones."

Dr. Hooker recruited a group of homosexual men and a comparison group of heterosexual men of comparable age, education, and social status. She administered the Rorschach test, the Thematic Apperception Test, and other standard psychological tests. She gave their test results to expert psychologists, who were blind to whose they were reading—that is, these blind raters did not know whether the protocols they had received were from the gay or the straight study participants. These blind raters were unable to distinguish between the two experimental groups. Dr. Hooker concluded that there was no basis in her data to conclude that homosexual and heterosexual men were psychologically distinguishable, and thus there was no evidence that homosexuality represented a distinguishable, pathologic condition. Dr. Hooker's work became critically important in the 1970s, when individual psychiatrists were struggling to de-pathologize homosexuality while others in the APA fought to keep its designation as a mental disorder.[70, 71]

The psychoanalytic view of homosexuality was more complex than psychiatry's yes-or-no struggle on whether homosexuality was or was not a pathological condition. Freud understood homosexuality as a developmental arrest in childhood that affected sexual instincts and prevented the development of a more mature heterosexuality, a view that implied that an adult homosexual might, if sufficiently mature and sufficiently motivated, become heterosexual. Around 1940, psychoanalysts turned away from this view. Instead, they understood homosexuality as a phobic avoidance of the other sex caused by parental prohibitions against childhood sexuality. This shift led some analysts to conclude that psychoanalysis could treat and potentially cure homosexuality.

In 1962, American psychoanalyst Irving Bieber and colleagues published *Homosexuality: A Psychoanalytic Study*, which described a pathogenic family type as the cause of homosexuality.[72] Homosexuality, they wrote, resulted from early experiences with a detached and rejecting father and a close-binding and domineering mother, and, therefore, it was something that analysis might cure.

Psychiatric and psychoanalytic writing about homosexuality focused almost exclusively on male homosexuality. Little discussion of the etiology of female homosexuality existed in the early psychoanalytic literature. Often, homosexuality in women was simply treated as a mirror image of homosexuality in men. This is one example of the misogyny common in medical literature. Until quite recently, medical research and medical writing focused almost exclusively on men.

While psychiatry was moving glacially, dramatic changes were taking place in the gay community. The civil rights movement of the 1960s showed women that political activism could be a constructive route to social and political change. Later, the women's movement taught the same lesson to the gay community. Beginning in the 1960s, gay people increasingly organized and campaigned for recognition as healthy adults entitled to equal social and political status and treatment.

In the 1970s gay activists directly attacked the APA position that homosexuality was pathological. They argued that homosexuality was a normal human variant and that there was no evidence to support the position that it was pathological. Their top priority was to overturn the APA's classification of homosexuals as pathological. In discussions among themselves, gay activists noted satirically that APA position on their community was to call them "crazies." Unless homosexuals were acknowledged to be as mentally sound as the average heterosexual, they argued, they would never be first-class citizens. The campaigns finally led APA to drop the classification of homosexuality as a pathological condition.

In her book, *The Gay Revolution*, author Lillian Faderman, an internationally known scholar of LGBTQ+ history, described the 1971 APA annual meeting in which gay activists heckled psychiatrists who talked about conversion therapy.[73] Psychiatrists yelled back, "Paranoid fool." Gay activists chanted, "Psychiatry is the enemy." A few psychiatrists were sympathetic and promised that at the 1972 APA annual meeting, there would be a booth for gay representation, which the activists would later name, "Gay, Proud, and Healthy: The Homosexual Community

Speaks." Later in the 1970s, gay psychiatrists began to come out of the closet, startling many of their colleagues.

In 1973, APA took the official position that homosexuality was not an illness. The third version of *The Diagnostic and Statistical Manual* (*DSM-III*), published in 1980, removed homosexuality from its list of mental disorders, but this provoked strong opposition. The decision to remove homosexuality was upheld by a 58 percent majority of voting APA members—a dramatic change from the 90 percent of members who, when polled a few years earlier, said they thought that homosexuality was an illness.

Some psychoanalysts continued to pathologize homosexuality. The following quote from Otto Kernberg, one of the most distinguished psychoanalysts of his generation, is an example of what the gay community had to deal with. Kernberg understood male homosexuality as caused by "the projection of pre-genital aggression reinforce(ing) oedipal fears of the father and castration anxiety in particular, further reinforcing, in turn, pre-genital aggression and fear."[74]

By 1980, the majority of psychiatrists believed that homosexuality did not belong in the *Diagnostic and Statistical Manual*, but rather than force this opinion down the throats of the opposing position, they offered a new category—"ego-dystonic homosexuality" (EDH), a diagnosis created to satisfy the minority opposition. EDH referred to hypothetical homosexuals whose sexual orientation caused them distress; this was a sufficient basis for a diagnosis.

Gay psychiatrists opposed this diagnosis with a brilliant counterproposal. They offered to accept this diagnosis if an additional diagnosis was added: "ego-dystonic heterosexuality." The straight majority could not stand this idea, and so they abandoned "ego-dystonic homosexuality." Ironically, the proposed diagnosis of heterosexual dysphoria could have applied to transgender or bisexual individuals, but neither society nor psychiatry were ready to consider this possibility in the 1980s.

The 1988 revision of the *DSM-III* dropped EDH, completely removing the designation of homosexuality as any kind of pathology, and from that point on organized psychiatry's views on homosexuality changed. Instead of labeling homosexuals as sick, psychiatry became supportive of constructive social action. In 1988 also, the APA publicly opposed employment discrimination based on sexual orientation; in 1989, it opposed discrimination against homosexual people in the military. Over the next decades, the APA would go on to support the right to privacy in relations between consenting adults; urge its membership to actively take a position against statements or actions against gay people; end its support of conversion therapy; recognize the legitimacy of same-sex partners as parents; and finally, in 2005, endorse same-sex civil marriage.

The American Psychoanalytic Association, which had taken a harder line against homosexuality, also dramatically reversed its earlier positions. It opposed discrimination against gay people and directed that sexual orientation not be considered in evaluating candidates for training as psychoanalysts. It also took a strong position against conversion therapy and stated that same-sex couples should be considered equally with other couples as possible adoptive parents.

This history reflects a generational shift. Older psychiatrists born in the 1930s saw homosexuals, none of whom they knew personally (or, at least, realized they knew), as damaged others. The push for change within APA came from younger members who had more personal experience with gay people. As gay people, including gay psychiatrists, came out of the closet, the older psychiatrists could see that gay men whom they knew and whose work they admired were surprisingly "normal." In contrast, lesbianism was not even on psychiatry's radar screen; what had become accepted in men had not yet been recognized as an issue for women.

Like my colleagues who were born in the 1930s, I was unaware that some people I knew were homosexual. Despite clear evidence that several of my teachers in college were coupled, it never crossed my mind that these might be sexual relationships. My first-year English teacher, well known in my generation but no longer widely read, was the poet and novelist May Sarton. I knew her well enough that she often invited me to afternoon tea in her home. She lived with another woman, but that never registered.

I worked closely with my tutor Roger Brown for three years. I wrote my undergraduate honors thesis with him, and I visited him at home a few times. On several occasions, I met his roommate Al, who taught English at Boston University. To me Al was just Roger's roommate.

I was not alone in my naïveté. The wife of my undergraduate house's faculty dean, Florence Hammond, gave a weekly tea for members of the house, and one week, she teased Roger—who was a tall, handsome man, saying, "Oh Roger, when are you going to get married?" Roger laughed and passed off her question.

I graduated from medical school with my ignorance intact. At Harvard Medical School, there had been no discussion of sexuality, gay or straight, as part of the curriculum. At Massachusetts Mental Health Center (MMHC), where I began my psychiatry training in 1964, the faculty taught me what I accepted as true: that homosexuals were immature and damaged as a result of early experience with a distant, detached father and a domineering, overinvolved mother. Years later I learned better.

I applied this "knowledge" only once, when I served on a citizens committee in Lexington, Massachusetts, in the 1970s that was tasked with evaluating candidates for superintendent of schools. One of the candidates was known to be gay, and I remember pontificating that we could not afford to have a superintendent of schools who was psychosexually immature. My committee members nodded their acceptance of my sage opinion, and we discarded this candidate. This anecdote clearly illustrates the damage psychiatry did based on psychoanalytically derived false beliefs that confirmed the homophobia of the larger society. My beliefs damaged both the individual who did not get a fair hearing and the town of Lexington that was unreasonably deprived of a potentially strong school superintendent.

Somehow, I walled these beliefs off from other aspects of my professional life. I was aware that some of the trainees in our department were gay, but I never paid any attention to that fact, and I ignored the teaching that homosexuality was pathological. Gay or straight, I accepted our trainees as the professionals they were. It is an inconsistency of thought and action that I cannot explain.

It was not until 1987, when a friend's son came out to him as gay, that I realized that psychoanalytic ideas on homosexuality were wrong. I knew the parents very well. The father was not distant; he was the opposite—warm, engaged with his children, a loving husband committed to his family. His wife was a dedicated mother with a life centered on her family, as available as anyone could wish and in no way overbearing. On this basis, I concluded that the psychoanalytic view of what caused homosexuality must be wrong. Still later, in the dark days before homosexuality began to be accepted in American society, a clinic patient said to me bitterly, "Being homosexual isn't something you choose," and I began to have a different understanding of what homosexuality might represent—something closer to our current understanding: one biological variant among the many that distinguish one human being from another.

* * *

While the APA was debating its views on homosexuality, our psychiatry department at Cambridge Hospital never had a problem. Thanks to the attitude of our first chief, John Mack, we accepted and welcomed gay residents, faculty, and staff members.

We trained our first openly gay resident, Bob Cabaj, beginning in 1974. Bob had known he was gay since his early adolescence. He attended Notre Dame for college, where he came out to a few close friends. When he applied to medical school, one homophobic priest wrote that he should not be admitted to any medical school because he was gay. (That priest was later arrested for sexual activity with young boys.) The secretary who processed

303

medical school applications destroyed this letter, and Bob was admitted to Harvard Medical School.

At medical school, Bob was not "out," but he had a circle of friends who knew he was gay, and he received the support of several gay faculty members. He applied for residency at MMHC, but a senior faculty member rejected him for being gay. Two other faculty members intervened to reverse the rejection, and Bob was placed on the waiting list. Bob had also applied to our department at Cambridge, and we were happy to accept him.

Bob was immediately comfortable with us; he arrived already knowing two of our gay faculty members. He did well with us, and he went on to organize gay and lesbian psychiatrists in New England, and later he served as president of the National Association of Gay and Lesbian Psychiatrists (AGLP), [now the Association of LGBTQ Psychiatrists]. At sixty-seven, Bob was professionally active. He had been with his partner for thirteen years, married for three. Sadly, Bob died in February 2020.

Our department was so gay-friendly, in fact, that we lost at least one residency applicant. He came to lunch wearing a kippa, identifying him as an observant Jew. As the banter including gay and lesbian members of the department went on around him, he abruptly pushed back his chair and said, "I don't think this department is for me," and rushed out of the dining room.

We never let sexual orientation dictate hiring practices, and our department was the stronger for it. In the mid-1980s, young openly gay psychiatrist applied for a job with us. He was concerned about being 'out' and told the department chairman about his apprehension. The chairman assured him, "We not only want you; we need you." This psychiatrist became our training director and then our acting chair. At one time, across a span of several years, our training director, assistant training director, and training program administrator were all openly gay.

In the larger world of organized psychiatry, changes in gay representation were occurring as well. In 1991, the APA elected its first openly gay president, Lawrence Hartmann, a long-time, respected member of the Boston psychiatric community. By electing him, psychiatry demonstrated that not only had its intellectual and social ideas about homosexuality changed, but also that organized psychiatry now practiced what it preached. In the 21st century, psychiatry's views on homosexuality reflected those of the American social consensus.

#####

CHAPTER 17

PSYCHIATRY NEAR THE END OF LIFE

I spent the last seven years of my professional life working as a palliative care psychiatrist, caring for people who were near the end of life or suffering from chronic illness. What drove this career shift was the almost five years I spent caring for my wife, Susan, who suffered from progressive dementia. After Susan died, I thought that I might put that terrible experience to some constructive use, and I offered my services to the Cambridge Hospital as a palliative care clinician.

If there is any experience more awful than watching your wife of forty-three years lose her mind, I don't know what it might be. Susan had a lot of mind to lose; she knew that she was losing her capacity to think and to remember, and she hated it.

The disease struck in 2004 shortly after Susan and I sold the home in Lexington where we'd raised our now adult daughters and moved into a townhouse in Cambridge. We were pleased with our move, but in December of that year, Susan appeared depressed. We looked for a psychiatrist, and we chose one on the advice of several knowledgeable friends. This psychiatrist would be a great source of strength for Susan through the following five pain-filled years.

By March of 2005, it was clear that something else was wrong, and our longtime internist thought that Parkinson's disease was the likely diagnosis. Over the next several months, Susan experienced few of the motor symptoms that characterize Parkinson's disease, but intellectually she was beginning to show signs that all was not well.

Wanting to do all I could, I researched the symptoms Susan was increasingly showing, and I learned that Parkinson's and Lewy Body Disease (LBD) appeared to have similar pathology, but they attacked different parts of the brain. Parkinson's primarily attacks the motor systems in the brain, while LBD causes a relatively rapid dementia—like Alzheimer's, only faster. Based on the clinical picture, I thought it more likely that Susan was suffering from Lewy Body Disease rather than Parkinson's. A neurologist at Massachusetts General Hospital (MGH) confirmed my impression later that year.

For the first year, Susan's motor function was good enough that she was physically able to drive, but as her intellectual function deteriorated, my daughters questioned whether she had sufficient judgment to continue. To be honest, my daughters had a better sense of the risk her driving represented than I did, but when I saw that they were right, I told Susan she could no longer drive. She was furious when I took away the car keys.

There was one positive aspect to this terrible situation. Before her illness, when Susan did something that I didn't like, I criticized it directly, and that did not contribute to a happy marriage. After she became ill, I decided that anything she did that was at all troubling to me was a result of her illness. I resolved never to be critical of anything she did, and I think I was largely successful in that effort. The result was that our relationship was better in that way than it had ever been. The irony that it took this catastrophic illness to teach me to be a more sympathetic person was not lost on me.

Susan continued to deteriorate over the four-plus-year course of her illness to the point that, by the end, she had lost almost all mental capacity. She could not speak; she recognized no one; and she could walk only with assistance from me or from one of the women we hired to look after her. Over the last months of her illness, Susan developed terrible lower abdominal pain, but by that time, her dementia left her unable to cooperate in the necessary diagnostic assessment, so we never found out what was wrong. As Susan moaned with every breath, our family—our two children, Susan's two sisters, and I—all agreed that pain management was our primary concern. The physicians managing her illness prescribed antianxiety medication that was effective: when she took it the moaning stopped.

* * *

During the last several years of her illness, I tried to travel infrequently because when I was away, Susan got anxious which in turn made her caregiver anxious, and they would end up in the emergency room at Massachusetts General Hospital. Typically, they would spend the day; but by the end of it, the staff would tell them there was nothing to be done and send them home.

I could not avoid one overnight trip, and when I returned in the early evening, I learned that Susan had again gone to the MGH emergency ward with the usual result. That evening, Susan was moaning in pain and I gave her the prescribed Ativan. She was comfortable for forty-five minutes; then she awoke and began to moan again. She needed the Ativan four more times over the course of that night, and she fell out of bed twice, which had never happened before. After the fifth dose of Ativan, she slept through the night and through the following day. I thought that I had over-sedated her, but when she did not wake up the second day, I became concerned.

One of our care team, a geriatric social worker, came to the house, took one look at Susan, and said, "This is a dying woman." I had had no experience of death or dying since internship many years before; this assessment took me totally by surprise. The social worker recommended that we call our hospice nurse, who came the next day. She too said: "This is a dying woman." We watched as Susan remained unconscious through the last week of her life.

At that time, our older daughter, Deborah, was between jobs. She was seeking teaching positions in the classics at the college or university level, and there were exactly two jobs in the whole country for which she was a good fit. Deborah called during the last week of Susan's life to say that she had been offered one of the two jobs and that she had accepted. Susan had been unconscious continuously and apparently comfortably for five days. Her breathing was even and regular. I whispered in her ear, "Deborah got her job," and Susan's breathing noticeably changed. Two days later, she died. We were in bed together, which was the way I wanted it.

Watching my wife of many years, the woman I loved, slowly become an angry non-person was awful. I could avoid the misery by not thinking about her when I went to work, but when I was with her and could see what she had become, the misery seemed endless.

The end, when it did come, was a blessing for everyone, most importantly for Susan. For the last several months of her life she had endured severe pain while losing her mind, a process that no one could stop. For the family, her death meant that Susan's ordeal was over.

The literature is clear that 75% of families who care for a demented member at home become depressed, and a similar number acknowledge that they are relieved when the ordeal is over. None of us became depressed, but we understood how this could happen to more vulnerable people, and we could acknowledge the sense of relief we felt when death finally came.

* * *

As I reflected on the entire gut-wrenching experience of caring for a loved one at the end of their life and trying to bring what comfort I could, I thought I could put it to some use. A few months after Susan died, I went to the chief medical officer at Cambridge Hospital and told him that I wanted to do palliative care at the hospital. His response was so characteristic of Cambridge Hospital

311

that it almost made me laugh. He said, "You can't do palliative care here because we have no palliative care service. So, if you want to do palliative care here you will have to start the service, and by the way there is no money and there never will be any money."

I had enough experience at the hospital not to be surprised and enough confidence in my ability to navigate the system that I thought I could probably manage, and I did. Palliative care consists of pain management, emotional support for the patient and the family, a religious experience for those who want it, and extended social services that foster connections with helping agencies in the community. I knew that, with some help, I could successfully provide all these things, since with some help I had provided them for Susan.

To prepare, I took a course in pain management. I had been offering emotional support for my whole professional life and had just been through this harrowing experience myself. For religion, I reached out to an old colleague who was both a psychologist and a nun, and she was happy to volunteer her time. I relied on the social workers at the hospital to provide the social service these patients and their families would need.

Palliative care psychiatrists and nurses have written extensively about the importance of introducing palliative care early in the course of a chronic illness that places huge stress on patients and their families, especially a potentially life-threatening illness. Palliative care can help with the emotional burden and the pain—not just near the end of the course of illness, but from the beginning.

But in the culture at Cambridge, palliative care was seen as appropriate only for patients near death. I did palliative care in this setting for three years, and it was a mixed experience. The feedback I got was good, but I received few referrals. Cambridge Hospital had a relatively small medical service—just thirty beds—so there were relatively few patients sick enough that the staff would consider palliative care. At this time, the majority of interns and residents were women, and my impression was that these young women were more attuned to the emotional issues of patients and families than were the men, with the result that they handled many of these cases themselves.

The critical event came when I asked the staff physician in charge of medical education whether I could have one hour a year to teach palliative care, and he said no. That showed me what value the hospital placed on my service. Fortunately, another opportunity presented itself.

The Spaulding Rehabilitation Hospital (SRH), a 130-bed, long-term acute care hospital for patients admitted from acute care hospitals was (and still is) just down the street. One of the hospitalists at Cambridge was also on staff at Spaulding, and he invited me to come with him to their monthly staff meetings. After some months, the chief physician at Spaulding offered to hire me ten hours a week to do palliative care. Given my experience at Cambridge, I was happy to accept.

Spaulding has a long history. It opened in 1894 as "The Holy Ghost Hospital for Incurables," staffed by the Sisters of Charity of Montreal (Grey Nuns), and it is now the continuing-care arm of Partners Health Care[11], a large organization of Harvard-affiliated hospitals including Massachusetts General and Brigham

---

11 Partners changed its name to **Mass** General Brigham in 2019

and Women's hospitals. Its mission statement reads, "We are committed to delivering compassionate care along every step of your rehabilitation journey, from inpatient care to outpatient services and wellness programs, all designed to help you recover from, or learn to live fully with, illness, injury or loss of ability." In my experience, the hospital more than lived up to this mission statement. The patients who came to Spaulding had been lying in bed, typically for months, during a long, often chronic, illness. These patients urgently needed rehabilitation. They had muscle atrophy, weight loss, and physical weakness.

The medical and nursing care is excellent, but it is Spaulding's rehabilitation services that distinguish this hospital from others. Physical, occupational, and speech therapists provide therapy tailored to the individual needs of each patient, as often as three times a day. There is a huge "gymnasium" on each of the three floors where the physical and occupational therapists work with the patients. Typical scenes include a therapist carefully helping a sitting patient move each forearm backward and forward from the elbow. Another therapist supervises a patient while he slowly, laboriously pedals a stationary bicycle. In the hallway, a procession of three slowly makes its way: the patient is walking and wheeling his IV pole; the physical therapist walks beside him, encouraging him; behind the patient, an aide pushes his wheelchair so that if the patient tires, he can immediately sit down. A group of patients may be seen painting pots.

I worked happily as a palliative care psychiatrist at Spaulding for three and a half years, seeing patients and families on referral from their physicians. The referrals were for psychiatric assessment, diagnosis, and treatment, the last of which, in these cases, meant emotional support for patients and families making difficult decisions. My forensic psychiatry background was useful in assessing a patient's capacity to make medical or end of life decisions. I left that job to write this book.

In my years at Spaulding, I learned a lot about the resilience and determination of patients with chronic disease. People's will to live is strong enough that they almost always want to continue living with what function they have left. No matter how much people have lost, most do not become discouraged enough to want to die. They make their peace with what they have.

People with chronic illnesses often did become discouraged about their situation, but I rarely recommended antidepressants or other psychoactive medication, because this was not depression. The patients typically had not lost their interests, which is a hallmark of severe depression. Many were grandparents, and when I asked them about their grandchildren, typically their eyes would light up and they would become enthusiastic. Usually, they slept as well as their pain and the noise of the hospital would allow, and they made up for nighttime loss with daytime naps. When patients complained of poor appetite, it was usually related to the underlying illness or to complaints about hospital food. Based on these markers, emotional support was my usual recommended treatment.

As a palliative care psychiatrist, the most important thing I do for patients is provide emotional support, not by offering empty words of encouragement, but by showing the patient that there was a hospital physician interested enough in them to spend time together. When I first saw a new patient, I always began by sitting and asking the patient, "What would you like me to call you?" Most patients wanted to be called by their first name. I remember only two who did not. The first was a drug dealer who asked me to call him Mr. Smith. The second was a man in his seventies who had been a congressman many years earlier. He said, "Call me Congressman."

I sat down for three reasons. The first was to show the patient that I was not in a hurry, that I was there to spend some time with them. The second was to show that I was not in a superior position. We both knew that psychosocially I was in a superior position, but I wanted to send the message that at least physically we were on a level. The third reason is that I don't like to talk with people while I am standing up.

As we sat, I learned as much as I could about them, so that we could talk about their interests, rather than about their present situation. One patient who illustrates my approach was William Murphy. At our first interview, I met a bluff, hearty man who was clearly weak and tired, but he quickly and firmly told me he had little interest in talking to a psychiatrist—his biggest problem was constipation. He was a retired manufacturing executive in his seventies when he received a new kidney after a long history with kidney disease. He had been transferred to our hospital after a months-long acute-care hospitalization.

Nursing staff reported that he could be quite irritable, even angry—and as we met regularly and I got to know him, I could confirm that. He complained to me about the long course of his illness and was at times dismissive of the young nurses and therapists taking care of him: "They don't know anything," he said. Bill had no interest in discussing his mental life, but he was interested in the function of his bowels, so I addressed that. I spoke to the nurses about his constipation; Bill got some treatment, the constipation improved, and he was marginally less irritable.

If I waited for Bill to talk, he would ask me how I was, listen to my response, and then lapse into silence. I broke that pattern after he told me he was an avid sports fan who closely followed Boston professional sports teams, especially the Red Sox. We spent almost all our time together talking about these teams, about which I knew next to nothing until I began to read the *Boston Globe* sports section, so that I was able to keep up my end of our conversation. I lost contact with him when he was re-hospitalized at MGH. Loss of contact was common because the hospital had no system for following most discharged patients.

Another important lesson I learned was that patients varied enormously in how much they wanted to know about their medical condition. Some patients knew little or nothing and made clear that they did not want to know more—sometimes out of fear of what they might learn, and sometimes out of the urge to deal with their situation through denial.

Peter Moran was a cheerful denier. He had terminal pancreatic cancer, and we expected him to die in the hospital, but that was not his expectation. When I first visited him, he explained that he was in the hospital until he was strong enough to go home. He was a single, retired pipefitter in his early sixties who lived close to the Boston waterfront. He had the occasional visit from one of his buddies, but he was largely alone except for hospital staff. I visited Peter twice a week.

Fishing was his passion, and that is what we talked about. I was not (and still am not) a fisherman, but I learned a great deal from him about different kinds of fishing rods and the many different ways to catch fish: surf casting, trout fishing in streams, ocean fishing from small boats close to shore and from big boats farther out. We talked often about the fishing Peter would do when he got home. Peter got weaker over the weeks we talked, but he never complained, and his interest in going home to fish never faltered. I grew quite fond of Peter and looked forward to our conversations. When I came into his room, Peter was always in bed waiting for me, until the day when I arrived, and his bed was empty. The nurses told me he had died the day before. In the days that followed, I missed our conversations, and I never learned anything more about fishing.

Some of the most complicated situations involved families whose members had different ideas about how to handle the medical situation. Roberto Gonzalez was a ninety-year-old man who spoke limited English and suffered from terminal metastatic lung disease. I worked mostly with Roberto's son who was visiting from the west coast. He told me that, based on the advice of the patient's longtime primary care physician, he and his siblings had decided it was not in their father's interest to know his diagnosis, since he had a long history of anxiety attacks; knowing his diagnosis would only make him more anxious.

The children knew the prognosis, and their mother understood that her husband had a terminal illness, although she did not know the diagnosis. The children thought—and I agreed—that there was no need for the patient or his wife to know the exact diagnosis since the wife understood that he was terminally ill. I never learned what the patient knew about his condition: the family had a meeting over a weekend when I was not present and decided to take Roberto home with hospice until the end of his life. He had improved enough that he was alert and oriented when he was discharged from Spaulding.

Patients have the right under American law to decide how much to know about their situation, such as whether or not to be told their diagnosis. In this case, the family ignored this right, and I agreed to ignore it with them. His family was clear about what they wanted, and when the family are decent people who love each other and want the best for the patient, I go with what they want if what they want appears reasonable.

Families from other cultures could also present a challenge to me in helping them make a decision that conforms strictly to American law. I evaluated one patient named Mohammed Shazad who had terminal metastatic cancer. He was a man in his seventies from a country in the Middle East. His son, who had decision-making authority as the health care proxy, told me that, in his culture, the family made health care decisions without necessarily explaining the diagnosis or prognosis to the patient. This created a conflict under American law, first articulated in 1914: "Every adult of adult years and sound mind has the right to decide what shall be done with his own body."[75] If a patient is of sound mind and wants to know, we are legally obligated to tell him. Therefore, I wanted to interview Mohammed with an interpreter so I could assess his capacity to understand his situation and learn whether he wanted to know more than he did.

Mohammed's daughter-in-law had come from her home in the Middle East in order to be with him, and I was impressed with her intellectual capacities and commitment. I used her as a translator, although I knew from my work at the court clinic that it is not best practice to use a family member. Rather than wait for a professional translator, I decided to go ahead with her.

She told me that her father-in-law was a little tired and that he had a little pain, but that his mind seemed perfectly clear. He knew what was in his bank account and made good sense about whatever they talked about. I accepted that he had the capacity to make decisions for himself. When I asked, through the interpreter, about his condition, he told me that the doctors had told his son what was the matter with him, and he was fine with his son making treatment decisions.

I recognize that this was a sketchy evaluation, but in this situation, I think it was appropriate. I telephoned the son and explained that we could accept him as the decision maker, and I then went on to explain the difference between full code and DNR (do not resuscitate) and DNI (do not intubate).

The decision for full code versus DNR/DNI is one of the hardest choices a patient or their family must face, and the implications of each choice are not necessarily apparent. Full code means that if a patient begins to die, we will do everything we can to prolong life. This often means cardiac resuscitation, but to resuscitate a failing heart, we climb on the patient's chest, and we must push so hard that we can break ribs. If we are successful, the patient lives—usually not for much longer—with moderate to severe rib pain. While the instinct can often be to do anything to save the patient, from the perspective of a medical professional, it is not always the best choice.

The other choice is "do not resuscitate/do not intubate," which we abbreviate as DNR/DNI. This is a legal order authorized by the patient or his health care proxy stating that no life-saving measures will be taken if a patient's heart stops beating or he stops breathing. The patient (or health care proxy) who agrees to a DNR/DNI order acknowledges that the end of life is near and chooses to let it come when it does. Unless there is a DNR/DNI order in place, hospital staff are legally obligated to try to resuscitate the patient. Authorizing a DNR order is a difficult decision, and not surprisingly, many patients and families are not ready to make it.

I discussed the options with Mr. Shazad's son and told him that, in our opinion, full code was not a good choice for someone as sick as his father; but the son decided to continue his father on full code anyway.

This case required balancing an assessment of what the law required with what appeared to be emotionally reasonable. Given that this patient, who apparently had the capacity to make this decision, did not want to know any more than he already did, and that he wanted his son to make his health care decisions, I was content to leave this family system of decision-making intact. This was my effort to respect cultural differences in how loving families approach the health of their member's without becoming too involved in American legal questions. After this conversation, the patient's hospital course was uneventful, and my further services were not required.

* * *

I also assessed capacity to make treatment decisions distinct from DNR/DNI. In another case, which involved a patient named Georgine Williams, I evaluated her capacity to decide whether she should go home or stay in the hospital. I interviewed Georgine and her husband together, and I found that Georgine clearly had the capacity to make treatment decisions for herself.

Her basis for making decisions, however, was unusual. She and her husband were devout Christians who had organized their lives around what they understood God wanted for them. This came into play in a critical way during Georgine's battle with terminal cancer, which oncologists believed would respond to chemotherapy and palliative radiation. They recommended after she got stronger, that Georgine have three weeks of radiation, and a course of chemotherapy, and she initially agreed, but she was put off by the thought of so much radiation. She prayed to God for guidance, and God told her to accept two weeks of radiation; after those two weeks, it was God's will that she goes home.

As far as her understanding of her situation, Georgine stated clearly that she had a terminal illness. She knew that palliative radiation and chemotherapy were the only treatments, and she had made her peace with the idea that death might be near. She accepted God's will for two weeks of radiation, and if it was God's will that she die after that, then so be it. At my recommendation, the hospital honored Georgine's request, and she received two weeks of radiation and then went home. Often, hospital staff—myself included—would lose all contact with the patient and family after discharge; that was true with Georgine, so I never found out how she did.

Perhaps the most dramatic case I was involved with, and the one that imposed the most responsibility on the staff, was that of John Simmonds, a fifty-two-year-old married man with a severe chronic disease that prevented him from breathing on his own. He was connected to a mechanical ventilator and had an indwelling tracheal tube. This was not the way John wanted to live: he repeatedly told his family and me that he wished to remove the ventilator, stating clearly that he wanted to die. This made his wife sad, but she accepted his decision because she could see this was his choice.

I did not question his capacity to make this decision. He was unable to speak because of the indwelling tracheal tube, but he communicated by writing clearly and forcefully on a whiteboard and by appropriately shaking his head 'yes' or 'no' in response to questions. He denied any depression, smiled appropriately, and made good eye contact with me. He wrote that he understood that his decision required an affirmative act to remove the tracheal tube and to disconnect him from the ventilator.

The couple had discussed what this would entail, and they agreed that his wife would be present at the end. John repeated his wishes in three different conversations with me over a period of two weeks. John's wife confirmed that this had been John's consistent wish for several months.

It was clear that John had the capacity to make a competent decision to end his life, but unlike the usual decision to offer comfort measures only, this decision required direct staff action in removing the supports that were keeping him alive. After consultations with all involved, from the clinical director on down, all involved staff accepted the responsibility to honor the patient's wishes.

After the social workers and I worked with hospital staff to provide the necessary support, staff implemented the patient's wish, and he died peacefully with his wife present. Years later, I can still picture that courageous man and his wife in my mind's eye. They were one of the two families with whom I was most deeply involved.

* * *

Nurses have written extensively about the importance of touch, especially in terminal cases, and from my own experience at Spaulding, I know they are right: human touch was sometimes the most comforting support I could offer. Nothing could take away the pain of death and dying, but I could share the experience and create a bond with the suffering person and their family that went beyond speech.

Sam Robbins was a vigorous man in his late sixties who sat day after day with his dying wife, Jennifer. She had an incurable cancer, and all involved—the doctor, the patient and her husband—had agreed that the time had come for comfort measures only. We had stopped tube feeding and started her on a morphine drip to help her breathe comfortably and reduce her pain. To the surprise of her doctor she was still alive after a week on this regimen. This was very hard on her husband, and the doctor asked me if I would see him.

When I first met Sam and his sister-in-law, I began, as I always did, by encouraging them to sit, and then I sat with them. I told Sam that I thought this must be very hard for him. He nodded and teared up as he told me how hard it was. With an occasional question, I learned about the history of their marriage, how happy they had been together and how hard it was now for him to see her go.

324

The sister-in-law, with whom Sam was clearly very close, had brought family photo albums going back to childhood, and the two took turns telling me family stories. When I left, we all three hugged.

The three of us repeated this experience for more days than any of us had anticipated. Despite being on a dose of morphine that should have helped quietly end her life, Jennifer remained in a coma, and Sam suffered greatly through this extended deathwatch. Finally, after two weeks, staff told me she had died the evening before. I was sorry not to be there at the end. When I had left the two of them with our usual goodbye hugs, both told me how much it had meant to them that I had shared this experience. For all of us, physical contact anchored in memory our participation in Jennifer's death.

I found palliative care psychiatry to be different from any other psychiatry I had practiced. Much of what I provided was what a friend would offer, not what I typically did as a traditional therapist. I was much more open about my own personal experiences, and I was ready to offer sympathetic or comforting contact to my patients. Early on, I told a few family members of patients about my experience with Susan, and it was immediately clear that this established a bond between us beyond what empathic listening alone could have accomplished. I knew chronic illness, and I could understand what they were going through. Despite strong emotional connections with these patients and their families, I never lost the sense of a professional relationship. When I chose to share my story or to hold someone's hand or give them a hug, it was after I had reflected and decided that it was appropriate for this patient in this situation.

My furthest departure from usual practice came in the case of Cecil, a Haitian American Haitian in late adolesence with sickle cell anemia. He had been in and out of hospitals since childhood, and, as it turned out, he would spend the rest of his life in a bed at Spaulding.

Sickle cell is a genetically determined disease that preferentially attacks African American and Hispanic people, producing damaged red cells that clump up in the blood vessels and cause extremely painful episodes. The pain can be chronic, and the oxygen deprivation can cause tissue damage. Cecil had had one hip replaced after a failed surgery to ameliorate severe hip pain, and for the last year of his life, he had required an indwelling tracheal tube through which he received the oxygen he needed to survive. He could speak with the aid of a plug that he inserted into the tracheal tube, but this interfered with the flow of oxygen, so he could only use it briefly. Once every three weeks, he went to the acute care hospital, where he received a total body blood transfusion. He also went there when he got sick enough to need the ICU.

When I heard his story, I thought Cecil had the hardest row to hoe of any patient in this hospital, and I started spending time with him every week for the four years until he died. We met twice a week, typically for twenty-five minutes. Cecil was a poet, and initially we spent most of our time together reading Maya Angelou or an anthology of the best poems in the English language. Sometimes we'd sit quietly together; sometimes we'd talk.

Cecil eventually came to refer to me as his "grandpa." He would put out his arms for a hug and a kiss on the forehead at the end of every visit, and this goodbye was an important part of his experience with "grandpa." Cecil wanted to know personal facts about me, and in a way that I had not done with any other patient, I told him almost anything he wanted to know. I told him about my wife, Elisabeth (I remarried in 2015), how we celebrated the holidays, where we went on vacation, and the vicissitudes of our daily life. Knowing these facts about me and my life helped Cecil keep me as a presence in his life.

Four years after I met him, Cecil became sicker and sicker, with more pain and more weakness. Ultimately, he died in the ICU. For the four years that we knew each other, he was an important part of my life. I looked forward to our visits, and I miss him deeply now that he is gone. Outside of my relationships with my family and my closest friends, it is this relationship and a few others that provided the deepest meaning to my life.

* * *

What did I learn from these experiences? Susan's illness taught me more about suffering, both hers and mine, than I had ever known. For Susan, realizing that she was losing her capacity to think meant losing her identity. She had come fully into her own as a judge. Her colleagues admired her, and they were vocal in praising her work. Losing this made her intensely angry. The professional loss is what she struggled with as long as she could. Susan had been a person who valued control, and knowing there was nothing she could do about this process made it worse. Her family had shared her life for many years but losing us was not what hurt her most.

I learned from this experience that I could deal adequately with whatever life threw at me. There are challenges that you choose, and challenges that choose you; Susan's dementia chose me. I did what I could, but I hope I never have to face anything like that again. Watching my wife of many years, whom I loved, slowly disintegrate cut me to the bone. Now, many years after her death, the painful picture of Susan with her stuttering gait being led by her night attendant remains vivid.

At Spaulding, I learned that there are as many ways to deal with chronic illness and approaching death as there are people. Some of those ways seem to me to be better than others, but I was impressed at how often these methods worked for the people who chose them. Cases of severe illnesses were far more difficult for the family members than for the patients who appeared to have made their peace with their situation. Perhaps because it was late in the course of these illnesses, I did not see the angry patients that Kubler-Ross described as typical in her book, *On Death and Dying*.

Friends have asked me if I found the work at Spaulding to be emotionally draining. I did not; it was the opposite. Almost sixty years earlier, when I was an intern, I had participated in the experience of patients who were dying, and at the time I felt that it was a privilege. I feel the same way now. When I was able to enter the lives of these patients and their families, it was a deeply moving experience, and one of which I never tired. The experience at Spaulding built me up, it never tore me down. I saw firsthand what palliative care can mean to patients and their families near the end of life.

My work in palliative care psychiatry led me to reflect on my life in psychiatry. I am grateful for what I experienced, when managed care forced so many younger colleagues into unsatisfying professional lives. To a large extent, I was an observer, not a participant in these troubles. My core professional experience was teaching residents and other trainees in a public sector psychiatry department that reflected my values. Our psychiatry department at CHA took responsibility for treating those who needed us, no matter how sick or how poor.

If I had to summarize what I contributed, it would be the clinical teaching that understanding the experience of even the sickest patients is the core of our work. With that understanding, or as much understanding as we have at whatever our level of clinical experience, we can begin to form the patient-physician relationship on which treatment is based. I did other professional work over the course of my working life that I think was valuable, but I experienced my teaching as a calling in the full religious sense. It is my teaching for which I hope to be remembered.

The last few years have been personally fulfilling beyond what I could have imagined. Two years after Susan died, I met my current wife, Elisabeth, at a stand-up cocktail event before the annual meeting at the Cambridge Boat Club. Elisabeth was sitting down because she had a broken ankle; I was sitting down because I hate stand-up cocktail parties. Seeing Elisabeth improved my state of mind, and it improved more when I sat next to her. I thought she was the most attractive woman there.

Psychoanalytic psychotherapy during and after Susan died helped me deal with the challenges of her death, and my aging, and helped to clear out the psychological underbrush that was impairing my capacity for intimacy. These changes have helped to make my life with Elisabeth what it has been, and my life with Elisabeth has made me the happiest I have ever been. Elisabeth and I were together for eight years until an illness compelled us to separate. I never imagined that my ninth decade would be the happiest of my life, but so it has been, and for that I am profoundly grateful.

#####

PART THREE

PSYCHIATRY IN TROUBLE

CHAPTER 18

PSYCHIATRY TRANSFORMED

In its quest for scientific respectability, psychiatry made major changes in diagnostic practice—changes that would be in some ways constructive but would also have unexpected consequences. Since the second world war, diagnostic practice had been based on the psychoanalytic idea that the way to understand a patient was to listen quietly, saying little or nothing while waiting for patients to reveal themselves. But a small group of psychiatrists, mostly in the Midwest, maintained that accurate diagnosis could only be achieved based on replicable observations. Reliable psychiatric diagnosis could not be based on hypothetical underlying psychological conflict. Their position received dramatic support in the 1970s, when two articles using quite different methods arrived at the same conclusion: in comparison with diagnostic practice worldwide, and particularly in the United Kingdom, the American diagnosis of schizophrenia was unreliable.[33, 76]

In parallel with these new intellectual developments, mainstream psychiatry was becoming disillusioned with psychoanalysis.[77] Non-analysts were concerned that theoretical constructs within psychoanalysis were untestable and that psychoanalysts rejected any scientific investigation of their therapy. The analysts in turn believed that any kind of measurement would alter the therapeutic situation and so invalidate the tests. With this approach, psychoanalysis relegated itself to the scientific dustbin.

Thoughtful psychiatrists came to believe that the midwestern group was right—that diagnosis based on the assessment of signs and symptoms was the necessary first step in transforming psychiatry into a scientific medical specialty. Signs are the clinician's observations: poor hygiene; rapid, pressured speech, and so on. Symptoms are the patient's complaints, such as pervasive tiredness, convictions that others are stealing their thoughts, and others. Assessment of signs and symptoms as the basis for diagnosis led to a focus on medication as treatment, and to a corresponding increase in the influence of the drug industry on psychiatric practice.

In the 1970s, as a first step toward accurate diagnosis, the American Psychiatric Association (APA) appointed a committee to revise the *Diagnostic and Statistical Manual of Mental Disorders II* (*DSM-II*). The *DSM* contains the official description of mental disorders. APA sought an "objective" description of signs and symptoms of mental disorders that would enable psychiatrists to reliably agree on a patient's diagnosis. The *DSM-III,* published in 1980, represented a major step toward more consistent diagnoses of mental illness.

This approach has been successful, enabling psychiatrists to agree on what they see. Two independent psychiatrists who interview the same patient can more consistently agree on diagnoses of schizophrenia, bipolar disorder, and major depression, and these diagnoses appear to be stable over time when the same patients are re-interviewed. This reconstruction of the *DSM* represented a major step toward the goal of scientific legitimacy.

While the *DSM* addressed this, it said nothing about the meaning of the observations. The committee's approach to defining mental illness had the strength of consensus, but the weakness of ignorance. The committee did not have a scientific basis for their description, and neither did anyone else. For example, a committee created the list of symptoms that they said defined schizophrenia, but, as changes from one edition of the *DSM* to the next illustrated, that list was arbitrary.

The *DSM-5* the criteria for the diagnosis of schizophrenia unaccountably omit cognitive impairment! Cognitive impairment has been recognized as a core symptom of schizophrenia since Kraepelin first described dementia praecox and has been included with other core symptoms in every edition of the DSM since *DSM-III* in 1980. This omission is a dramatic illustration of the poverty of the science underlying the DSM approach.

Essentially, the DSM committees didn't know—and we still don't know—what specific brain structures or mechanisms cause the symptoms. We know, for example, that schizophrenia is a brain disease, but almost nothing more. Fundamentally, we know very little about how the brains of people with schizophrenia differ from the brains of everyone else. For that matter, we know very little about the brains of "everyone else". We are a great deal more ignorant about the brain than we like to acknowledge.

When internists name an illness, physicians know the biological science that underlies that named illness. When psychiatrists name an illness, it represents only the constellation of signs and symptoms that a committee decided to name; there is no underlying biology—psychiatric illnesses represent phenomenological descriptions, nothing more. This was true in 1980, and it is still true forty years later, a fact that has important implications for treatment. We treat the phenomena, i.e., the signs and symptoms of mental disorder, almost independent of diagnosis. Delusions all get treated with an antipsychotic medication whether the diagnosis is schizophrenia, psychotic depression, bipolar disorder, or borderline personality disorder.

In their 2015 book, *Psychiatry Under the Influence*, medical journalist Robert Whitaker and psychologist Lisa Cosgrove [78] make a different point; they argue that the *DSM-III* was a self-serving enterprise because it defined what psychiatrists treat as mental illness—meaning that psychiatrists could bill insurance companies. In my opinion, Whitaker and Cosgrove were wrong about the motivation for the *DSM-III*: it was not developed in order to make more money for psychiatrists. It was what its developers said it was—an attempt to make psychiatry scientific. The insurance industry's use of it for billing was secondary, but this usage of the *DSM-III* and its later revisions would play a major role in the further transformation of psychiatry.

Other critics noted that half the men who developed the *DSM-III* were paid as consultants to the drug industry. These men had to have been aware that symptom-based diagnoses would lead to increased prescriptions of psychoactive medications and therefore to increased sales and profits for drug companies. When signs and symptoms define the illness, medicine is the treatment of choice.

Insurance companies saw the *DSM-III* as a vast improvement over the *DSM-II*, because the newer version made diagnosis more precise, allowing insurance companies to see what they were paying for. As insurance companies required a *DSM-III* diagnosis, the new edition became the *de facto* basis on which physicians and other mental health professionals would be reimbursed. As a result, every practice that treated mental disorders would require an up-to-date edition of the *DSM*. It did not take APA long to realize that if they could repeatedly revise the *DSM*, it would be a huge moneymaker. The APA revised the *DSM* five times between 1968 and 2013, and its sales earned the APA $5 million a year, accumulating to approximately $100 million by 2012.[79] These revisions would have been justified if they presented new information, but psychiatry had learned almost nothing to justify the changes between one edition and the next—the differences between revisions are almost meaningless. The *DSM* and the 269 spin-off publications related to it serve primarily to make money for the APA.[80]

Distinguished psychiatrists have observed the unintended consequences of *DSM*. Nancy Andreasen, a past president of APA and one of the Midwestern group, wrote in 2007, "Since the publication of *DSM-III* in 1980, there has been a steady decline in the teaching of careful clinical evaluation that is targeted to the individual person's problems and social context and that is enriched by a good general knowledge of psychopathology. Students are taught to memorize *DSM* rather than to learn complexities from the great psychopathologists of the past." [81] The descriptions of people, their social context, and the time course of their symptoms were lost. Psychiatric assessment had become nothing more than inquiry about a list of signs and symptoms. Andreasen was surprised by this turn of events and uncertain as to why it had happened.

My own experience supports her concerns. A resident told me that she presented a case to a supervising psychiatrist at a major Boston area teaching hospital, and as the resident described the social history, the supervisor stopped her by saying, "I have no interest in social history." In another teaching hospital, a supervisor taught a resident that a psychiatric evaluation consists of assessing symptoms of anxiety, depression, obsessive-compulsive disorder, substance abuse, and psychosis, but nothing more—literally, diagnosis by 'laundry list.'

I observed a resident interview Patricia, a woman in her twenties, who had been hospitalized for problems with alcohol addiction and depression. The resident was thorough in asking about symptoms of depression: mood, sleep, appetite, feelings of guilt, thoughts of suicide, and so on. When describing her symptoms, Patricia said that she had trouble with the law, but the resident ignored this. Patricia said that what had led her to the hospital was partly a wish to stop drinking and partly because, "I had a fight." The resident ignored the fight. Patricia referred to her boyfriend, but the resident let that pass. When I questioned the resident further about the patient and her life, he acknowledged that this was not something his teachers had stressed. Asked for his ideas about treating her, he ventured that he would "give her antidepressants and 'therapy,'" but he appeared to have no understanding of "therapy". To me, these anecdotes illustrate the most troubling aspect of our focus on signs and symptoms: we have lost sight of the person who seeks our help.

* * *

In her 2007 paper, Andreasen wrote about psychiatry as if it were self-contained, existing in a silo uninfluenced by any outside pressures.[81] But psychiatry does not exist in a silo, and the twenty-five years that Andreasen wrote about are the twenty-five years in which the pharmaceutical industry increasingly influenced the practice of psychiatry.

Initially, the pharmaceutical industry had very little interest in psychiatry. The first psychoactive medications, developed in the 1950s and early 1960s,[82] treated symptoms of psychosis, hence "antipsychotic" medications. These medications were appropriate for, at most, 5 percent of the population.[83] These patients often could not manage a medication schedule, and many stopped taking them altogether.[84]

The economics changed dramatically beginning in 1954 with the introduction of Meprobamate (marketed as Miltown), the first drug that effectively treated anxiety.[85] Miltown was followed by Librium in 1960 and Valium in 1963.[86] Miltown was found to cause dependence, and it was reclassified as a sedative in 1970, but Librium and Valium continue to be prescribed for anxiety well into the twenty-first century. Between 1969 and 1982, Valium was the most prescribed drug in America, and it was "the first drug to reach $1 billion in sales."[87]

In response to pharmaceutical industry advertising to physicians and to the public, antidepressants, anti-anxiety and anti-psychotic medication have all been over-prescribed. This over-prescription by physicians and resulting overuse by patients should not lead us to avoid their appropriate use. All three classes of psychoactive drugs are effective when prescribed as indicated for symptoms of illness.

Antidepressants, anti-anxiety and anti-psychotic medications have greatly ameliorated human suffering. Pharmaceutical industry marketing that obfuscates physician decision making should not lead us to undervalue these medications or to fail to provide them when the indications are present. These are medications for which there is no substitute when used appropriately.

.Pharmaceutical company advertising to the public has made it more difficult for the person who is suffering to make a good judgment about when these medications are indicated, and when they are not., so that it is hard for the patient to know when to ask the doctor for one of these medications. Patients who are aware of this over prescribing, and who can ask their doctor appropriate questions, are more likely to receive medications they need, rather than medications the pharmaceutical industry persuades them they need. It is worth repeating that these are powerful and effective medicines for the symptoms of anxiety, depression and psychosis when prescribed appropriately and taken as prescribed. But they all have side effects, and when taken for no good reason the risks can outweigh the benefits.

In the 1950s, the pharmaceutical industry developed new drugs that effectively treated depression as well as anxiety. Tofranil, released in 1957, and Elavil in 1961 were the first, and they opened up a huge market.[88] Almost everyone gets anxious from time to time, and many people feel depressed at some point, so the potential market for these medications was—everyone!

These early antidepressants were effective, but they had unpleasant side effects, including blurred vision, dry mouth, and drops in blood pressure so sudden that they sometimes caused people to pass out. For this reason, they were not an easy sell. Prozac was the first of a new chemical class of antidepressants (selective serotonin reuptake blockers or SSRIs) that were effective without these troubling side effects, although these medications were later found to have troubling side effects of their own. When Prozac was introduced in 1987, the pharmaceutical industry saw a potential blockbuster drug.[89] By the 1990s, antidepressants were marketed as treatment for chronic anxiety as well as depression. As of 2011, antidepressants and anti-anxiety agents were the third most commonly prescribed class of medications in the United States;[90] just a year later, they were in second place.[91] More recently, other classes of drugs have taken over the top spots, but at least through 2014 antidepressant use continued to increase, and they were still the third most commonly prescribed drugs.[92]

Data in a U.S. government survey report that from 2011–2014, 12.7 percent of all Americans were taking an antidepressant. [92] Three decades earlier, it had been less than one in fifty. The use of antidepressants increased with age and reached nearly 19 percent in adults sixty-five years and older, but primary care physicians would write these prescriptions for patients in all age groups.[93]

In her book *The Truth About Drug Companies*, Marcia Angell, a distinguished physician and first woman to be editor-in-chief of

341

the *New England Journal of Medicine*, the most prestigious medical journal in America wrote that in 2001, the pharmaceutical industry profit was 18.5 percent as a percentage of sales, versus 3.3 percent for other companies in the Fortune 500.[94] In 2007, 73 percent of all antidepressant prescriptions were written without any basis in a mental disorder.[90] Physicians were prescribing antidepressants off-label for conditions not approved by the FDA—not approved because there was not sufficient evidence the medication would be effective. The introduction of medications effective (in some cases) against anxiety and depression, coupled with the trend toward diagnosis based on signs and symptoms of those disorders, was proving to be a bonanza for the pharmaceutical industry.

* * *

Since their advent, drug companies have sold billions of dollars of antidepressants. These drugs have helped some people with depression, but not as many as the drug companies would have consumers believe, and they have important, sometimes damaging, side effects. In this section, I have tried to present a more realistic picture of what these medications do.

SSRI medications are the treatment of choice for depression in America, although some distinguished psychopharmacologists consider that the new SNRI[12] antidepressants (duloxetine,

---

12 This may be TMI for the general reader for whom this book is intended, but I include the information for those who may be interested. Depression is characterized by a relative paucity of two neurotransmitters in the central nervous system: serotonin and norepinephrine. The selective serotonin reuptake inhibitors [SSRI] work by increasing the available amount of serotonin. They do not affect the available amount of norepinephrine. SNRI medications, Serotonin and norepinephrine

venlafaxine) are superior, and this opinion is supported by evidence.[95]

In considering treatment for depression, psychiatrists commonly assess major depression[13] using the Hamilton Depression Scale (HAM-D).[96] The HAM-D is a twenty-one-item, clinician-administered questionnaire scored as 0-7, no depression; 8-13, mild; 14-18, moderate; 19-22, severe; and 23 or over, very severe. (The HAM-D is in an appendix at the end of this chapter). The level or degree of depression is important to know, because different degrees react to treatment quite differently.

Importantly, several large studies have found that only people with *severe* depression improve on antidepressants.[97, 98] These studies do not find evidence that antidepressants help people with moderate or minor depression—these patients improve on placebo almost as often as they improve on antidepressants.[97] Complicating this picture, many mild or moderate depressions spontaneously remit without any treatment: 23 percent remit after three months, 32 percent after six months, and 52 percent after one year.[99] These remission rates mean that many less severe depressions, if left untreated, will get better. Most depressions are not severe; only between 4 and 11 percent are.[100] Taken altogether, these data tell us clearly that physicians—psychiatrists and primary care physicians—are prescribing antidepressants for vast numbers of people for whom they are not helpful.

---

reuptake inhibitors, increase the amount of both these neurotransmitters, and are consequently more effective against depression.

13 The DSM uses the term "major depression" to identify clinically meaningful depression, which includes mild, moderate, and severe depression. Since the term "mild major depression" is confusing, I have omitted the word 'major' unless it clarifies.

The line between severe and moderate or between moderate and mild depressions can be difficult to draw; and, reasonably enough, patients want something done when they feel depressed. If doctors suggest that they should wait a month without medication to see if they improve, patients may object. Uncertainty about which patients would benefit from medication can provide a rationale for physicians to prescribe medication for any depressed patient, but there is a risk: all medications have side effects. Antidepressants can have unpleasant—and, in some cases, harmful—side effects. Impairment of sexual function is common; even more serious is the metabolic syndrome: unhealthy abdominal weight gain, high blood pressure, high blood sugar, and abnormal cholesterol levels. Taken together, these increase the risk for diabetes, heart attack, and stroke.

A skeptic might argue that this is beside the point. If a person takes an antidepressant and gets better at the risk of side effects, this is a reasonable choice. Who cares whether this is a drug response, a placebo response, or spontaneous remission? This rationale, whether implicit or explicit, supports the overprescribing of antidepressants.

It is a truism of medical practice that every drug has two effects: the one we know about, and the one we don't. In 2019— almost sixty years after Valium was introduced—compelling new evidence was published showing that benzodiazepines (the name of the drug class for Valium, Librium, Xanax, Ativan, and others), when taken along with antidepressants in the first trimester of pregnancy, significantly increased the risk of major fetal malformations.[101] The clinical significance of this is unclear, but it complicates decision-making for pregnant women.

Ultimately, the research is clear: *on average,* antidepressants do not help the mild depressions from which most people suffer. An average includes some people who get better and some who get worse, and we cannot predict how any individual will respond. The fact that a few will improve on these drugs complicates the choice of whether to try an antidepressant for a mild or moderate depression. The evidence for improvement of moderate depression is at best mixed.

Patients often take antidepressants for many years in part because there are limited, and conflicting, data on when or whether to stop.[102] Continuation is most clearly useful for patients for whom the drug was useful in the first place, i.e., people with severe depression who responded well to drug treatment. In one large study, almost two-thirds of patients were continuing to take antidepressants after six years. Importantly, in this study, some people who discontinued antidepressants on long term follow-up showed an improvement in the metabolic syndrome two and six years later.[103] But, when an antidepressant is stopped abruptly, a discontinuation syndrome can occur characterized by flu-like symptoms, insomnia, nausea, imbalance, sensory disturbances, and hyperarousal.[104] Any psychoactive medication should be discontinued slowly; the longer it has been taken the slower the discontinuation.

Despite incontrovertible research, psychiatrists continue to overprescribe antidepressants, partially because they have received institutional support to do so: 2010 APA guidelines for the treatment of mild depression explicitly supported overprescribing. They state: "An antidepressant medication is recommended as an initial treatment choice for patients with mild to moderate major depressive disorder."[105] Later APA publications obscured the issue further. The 2017 edition of the APA's *Textbook of Psychopharmacology* discusses antidepressant treatment of major depressive disorder without distinguishing severe from moderate or minor depression, leaving the clinician with the impression that antidepressant medication is an effective treatment for any major depression, a conclusion unsupported by good evidence.[106] More recently, one of the two authors of the textbook has corrected that recommendation, explicitly stating that antidepressants are not recommended for mild depression.

Another reason for the increased use of SSRI medication has been their increasing use as treatment for anxiety disorders. The evidence for effectiveness against anxiety is not substantial, but the shift has been fueled by the reluctance of physicians to prescribe benzodiazepines for anxiety disorders,[107] because of the risk of habituation or possible addiction and, the fear that benzodiazepines may exacerbate or even cause Alzheimer's disease, especially in the elderly.[108] Again, the evidence for this is not substantial,[109] and distinguished psychopharmacologists continue to prescribe benzodiazepines, with the result that their anxious patients avoid the significant sexual side effects and metabolic syndrome that develop in many patients taking SSRIs.

* * *

The reported level of antipsychotic drug sales appears to reach far beyond evidence-based treatment, and far beyond the number of people with psychotic disorders, i.e. people with schizophrenia, bipolar disorder, psychotic depression, and some others who have the delusions and hallucinations that these antipsychotics are designed to treat.[14] In short, they too are overprescribed. Recognizing that relatively few people become psychotic, the pharmaceutical industry encouraged doctors to prescribe antipsychotic medication for a wide range of emotional and behavioral problems in children and adolescents.[110] By 2011, the antipsychotic Abilify was the fourth largest selling pharmaceutical in this country at $5.2 billion, and Seroquel was sixth at $4.6 billion.[111]

Children and adolescents who take antipsychotic medications can have severe side effects requiring emergency room visits, followed in some cases by hospitalization or even death.[112, 113] Yet year after year, more antipsychotic drugs are prescribed for children and adolescents despite the serious risks.[114] There was a 660 percent increase in these prescriptions between the 1990s and the 2000s.[110] These drugs can be essential treatment for certain children with severe behavioral problems, but a 660 percent increase appears to relate more to marketing than to clinical value.

Behavioral problems are difficult to control in the demented elderly—assault, intruding on the space of others, yelling, wandering occur, and antipsychotics are the only effective medication we have for these problems. Their use in the demented elderly is associated with significant harm—cognitive decline, uncontrolled movements, sedation and increased risk of

---

14 Antipsychotics may also be useful as adjunct treatment of severe major depression when the depression fails to respond to antidepressants alone.

death[115-119], but when behavioral management tactics fail, the physician's hand is forced.

Physicians are also prescribing antipsychotics off-label for anxiety and insomnia in this population[113, 120, 121], a practice not supported by evidence, or forced by management problems. The large volume of pharmaceutical industry marketing has been associated with, and likely led to reliance on medication rather than on more labor-intensive social efforts to deal with these problems. Again, these drugs are enormously useful when appropriately prescribed but pharmaceutical industry marketing has led to overprescribing these potentially damaging drugs for the young and old; overprescribing that continues to this day.

Overprescribing one unnecessary medication to a patient is bad enough; but polypharmacy, or the practice of giving a patient more than one antipsychotic at the same time, has also increased. As far as I know, no pharmaceutical company has recommended this. Rather, psychiatrists and other physicians do this when prescription of one antipsychotic drug does not lead to improvement. There is no evidence to support this practice, and I can only surmise that doctors do this because they have no idea of what else to do.

* * *

Overprescribing appears to be a direct result of pharmaceutical industry marketing to physicians and to the general public. To reach individual physicians, the industry employs tens of thousands of sales representatives who call on physicians armed with money and perks—food, junkets, and more. Pharmaceutical companies reported making payments to more than 607,000 of the estimated 700,000 physicians in the U.S. in 2014.[122] Payments ranged from small gifts and lunches to thousands of dollars for sponsored lectures and promotional appearances. (For a discussion of how these sales representatives work and how they influence the practice of even the most responsible psychiatrists, see Carlat (2010).[123])

In March 2013, ProPublica released a report showing that the industry paid more money to psychiatric consultants than to consultants in any other medical specialty.[124] Included were the names of twenty-two physicians who had each received $500,000 or more in speaking and consulting fees. Twelve of the twenty-two, including the first, third, and fourth biggest recipients, were psychiatrists, and four of the twelve held academic appointments. [124] These are the men modeling professional behavior for psychiatric residents.[125] When he was apprised of this report, Dr. James Scully, the chief executive officer of APA, said, "My immediate, honest response was that this boggles the mind. It surprises me because we've made so many changes in what we have done here at the APA."[126] Some consultants may be providing useful information in return for these large sums of money, but when the chief executive officer of APA says that these practices "boggle the mind," other reasonable minds may be boggled as well.

It's not just big money—it's medium money and small money. According to a 2016 article in ProPublica, doctors who took $5,000 or more from drug companies wrote 30 percent of their prescriptions for the company's brand-name drugs, compared to 20 percent by doctors who refused drug company money.[127] That may not seem like a big difference, but viewed another way, this is a fifty percent change, which is *huge*. According to a 2016 article in the *Journal of the American Medical Association*, when doctors accept even just a lunch costing $20, it affects their prescribing practices.[128]

The industry also tries to influence trainees by sponsoring teaching conferences in academic departments. One small study examined the practice of residents prescribing brand-name drugs in relation to teaching conference sponsorship by drug companies. The study reported a significant correlation between company sponsorship and brand-name prescribing.[129] In response, some academic departments have canceled drug company sponsorship of teaching conferences.[130]

These are at least legitimate business activities, but the pharmaceutical industry has repeatedly crossed legal and ethical lines in marketing psychoactive drugs, paying billions of dollars in fines or to settle lawsuits. Examples include:

- GlaxoSmithKline paid $3 billion for illegally promoting the antidepressant Paxil.
- Johnson & Johnson paid $2.2 billion for promoting unapproved drugs, including the antipsychotic Risperdal.
- Abbott paid $1.5 billion for illegally promoting the anti-seizure and antimanic drug Depakote.
- Lilly paid $1.42 billion for illegally promoting the antipsychotic Zyprexa.
- Warner-Lambert (Pfizer) paid $430 million for illegally promoting Neurontin, an anticonvulsant.[131, 132]

In addition to courting individual doctors, drug companies have wooed institutional psychiatry. Beginning in the 1970s, the drug industry paid millions of dollars to support APA annual meetings. In return, the APA offered drug companies all the space they wanted at the meetings. By 1974, the board of APA was concerned that the "APA's relationships with pharmaceutical companies were going beyond the bounds of professionalism and were compromising our principles."[133] Those worries did not stop APA from giving the pharmaceutical industry almost unlimited access to psychiatrists at the annual meeting. Beginning in 1980, APA allowed drug companies to sponsor symposia. In 2004, the industry sponsored fifty-four symposia, paying $50,000 for each. [78] With this drug company support, the APA made millions of dollars each year.

After 2004, the APA no longer permitted industry booths in the same area as the professional displays. Instead, it rented space in other areas to the pharmaceutical industry and other advertisers. Personally, I found the drug company presence so objectionable, and the whole spectacle so troubling, that I stopped going to the APA annual meeting in the mid-1990s. I went back in 2018 to find that the drug companies are still heavily represented, but in a separate commercial area where psychiatrists can see exhibits and talk with company representatives.

Drug companies also pay for advertising in APA journals. At its peak in 2008, the APA received $65 million in advertisement sales from drug companies.[134] After a Senate investigation of the industry opened in 2008, advertising revenues declined, and the drug companies phased out their support of APA symposia. Moderate advertising by drug companies continues in the *American Journal of Psychiatry* and in the pages of other psychiatry journals, as it does in the professional journals of all medical specialties.

The pharmaceutical industry also advertises directly to consumers, mounting massive media campaigns on television and in the print media.[135] These are designed to convince the public that these medications could fix not just their symptoms, but also their lives. American television stations air eighty ads for prescription drugs every hour of every day.[136] The U.S. and New Zealand are the only two countries that permit direct pharmaceutical advertising to consumers.

The drug company Eli Lilly spent heavily to promote Prozac to consumers, as did the industry for other antidepressants—and it appears to have worked: a 2005 study reported in the *Journal of the American Medical Association* (JAMA) found that patients who referenced television ads when asking for an antidepressant were more than twice as likely to receive one (76 percent) when compared with those who did not (31 percent).[137] It is a reasonable inference that this consumer-directed advertising is one of the drivers of the 73 percent of prescriptions doctors write for which there is no evidence base. Shortly after Lilly's advertising push, Prozac had about forty million users and accounted for a quarter of Lilly's $10.8 billion in sales and more than a third of its $3 billion profit in 2000.[138]. As sales of psychoactive medications increased, the pharmaceutical industry became by far the most profitable industry in the United States.[139]

* * *

The pharmaceutical industry has transformed psychiatry for good and for ill. In bringing drugs to market that are effective against the symptoms of psychosis, depression, and anxiety, the pharmaceutical industry has made a huge contribution to human health and quality of life. We have emptied out state hospitals largely because antipsychotic medications are effective. We have ameliorated pain and suffering for millions of people with severe major depression and diagnosable anxiety disorders.

These benefits do not change the fact that these medicines are vastly overprescribed. The drug companies have encouraged the inappropriate use of these drugs through targeted marketing. They have urged patients to ask for, and doctors to prescribe, these medicines. Doctors have responded by writing prescriptions for these drugs, all of which helped the company's bottom line but help for patients was not always so clear. So long as the pharmaceutical industry continues its aggressive marketing and there is no countervailing pressure from organized psychiatry or from the FDA, inappropriate prescribing will continue. The failure to confront this problem is an institutional and societal failure of the highest level. For psychiatry, it's worse than passive avoidance—it looks more like closet collaboration.

I have worked hard in my teaching and in my practice to avoid overprescribing. Like the midwestern psychiatrists, I have stressed the importance of careful evaluation of signs and symptoms, and the importance of targeting prescriptions to these observations. I have especially urged residents to avoid polypharmacy and instead to engage with the patient in a discussion that might help lead to more effective treatment. In my practice as a palliative care consultant, I resisted the requests of internists to prescribe antidepressants, once again choosing to rely instead on a careful evaluation of signs and symptoms.

There is nothing magic about what I taught and how I practiced. We can avoid overprescribing by doing careful evaluations and prescribing only for what we observe. This would go a long way to limit the unnecessary use of psychoactive medications; but sadly, I am not optimistic that one book will have much impact when opposed by the many communications from the pharmaceutical industry. A more limited goal for this chapter is that its readers will be more informed patients; more able to appreciate when medicine may help, and when help from a pill is unlikely.

#####

Chapter 18 Appendix (HAM-D)

HAMILTON DEPRESSION RATING SCALE (HAM-D)
(To be administered by a health care professional)

Patient Name _____   Today's Date _____

The HAM-D is designed to rate the severity of depression in patients. Although it contains 21 areas, calculate the patient's score on the first 17 answers.

1. **DEPRESSED MOOD**
   (Gloomy attitude, pessimism about the future, feeling of sadness, tendency to weep)
   0 – Absent
   1 – Sadness, etc.
   2 – Occasional weeping
   3 – Frequent weeping
   4 – Extreme symptoms

2. **FEELINGS OF GUILT**
   0 – Absent
   1 – Self-reproach, feels he/she has let people down
   2 – Ideas of guilt
   3 – Present illness is a punishment; delusions of guilt
   4 – Hallucinations of guilt

3. **SUICIDE**
   0 – Absent
   1 – Feels life is not worth living
   2 – Wishes he/she were dead
   3 – Suicidal ideas or gestures
   4 – Attempts at suicide

4. **INSOMNIA - Initial**
   (Difficulty in falling asleep)
   0 – Absent
   1 – Occasional
   2 – Frequent

5. **INSOMNIA - Middle**
   (Complains of being restless and disturbed during the night. Waking during the night.)
   0 – Absent
   1 – Occasional
   2 – Frequent

6. **INSOMNIA - Delayed**
   (Waking in early hours of the morning and unable to fall asleep again)
   0 – Absent
   1 – Occasional
   2 – Frequent

7. **WORK AND INTERESTS**
   0 – No difficulty
   1 – Feelings of incapacity, listlessness, indecision and vacillation
   2 – Loss of interest in hobbies, decreased social activities
   3 – Productivity decreased
   4 – Unable to work. Stopped working because of present illness only. (Absence from work after treatment or recovery may rate a lower score).

8. **RETARDATION**
   (Slowness of thought, speech, and activity; apathy; stupor.)
   0 – Absent
   1 – Slight retardation at interview
   2 – Obvious retardation at interview
   3 – Interview difficult
   4 – Complete stupor

9. **AGITATION**
   (Restlessness associated with anxiety.)
   0 – Absent
   1 – Occasional
   2 – Frequent

10. **ANXIETY - PSYCHIC**
    0 – No difficulty
    1 – Tension and irritability
    2 – Worrying about minor matters
    3 – Apprehensive attitude
    4 – Fears

HAMILTON DEPRESSION RATING SCALE (HAM-D)
(To be administered by a health care professional)

11. ANXIETY - SOMATIC
Gastrointestinal, indigestion
Cardiovascular, palpitation, Headaches
Respiratory, Genito-urinary, etc.
0 – Absent
1 – Mild
2 – Moderate
3 – Severe
4 – Incapacitating

12. SOMATIC SYMPTOMS -
GASTROINTESTINAL
(Loss of appetite , heavy feeling in abdomen;
constipation)
0 – Absent
1 – Mild
2 – Severe

13. SOMATIC SYMPTOMS - GENERAL
(Heaviness in limbs, back or head; diffuse
backache; loss of energy and fatiguability)
0 – Absent
1 – Mild
2 – Severe

14. GENITAL SYMPTOMS
(Loss of libido, menstrual disturbances)
0 – Absent
1 – Mild
2 – Severe

15. HYPOCHONDRIASIS
0 – Not present
1 – Self-absorption (bodily)
2 – Preoccupation with health
3 – Querulous attitude
4 – Hypochondriacal delusions

16. WEIGHT LOSS
0 – No weight loss
1 – Slight
2 – Obvious or severe

17. INSIGHT
(Insight must be interpreted in terms of patient's understanding and background.)
0 – No loss
1 – Partial or doubtfull loss
2 – Loss of insight

TOTAL ITEMS 1 TO 17: _____
0 - 7 – Normal
8 - 13 – Mild Depression
14-18 – Moderate Depression
19 - 22 – Severe Depression
≥ 23 – Very Severe Depression

18. DIURNAL VARIATION
(Symptoms worse in morning or evening.
Note which it is.)
0 – No variation
1 – Mild variation; AM ( ) PM ( )
2 – Severe variation; AM ( ) PM ( )

19. DEPERSONALIZATION AND
DEREALIZATION
(feelings of unreality, nihilistic ideas)
0 – Absent
1 – Mild
2 – Moderate
3 – Severe
4 – Incapacitating

20. PARANOID SYMPTOMS
(Not with a depressive quality)
0 – None
1 – Suspicious
2 – Ideas of reference
3 – Delusions of reference and persecution
4 – Hallucinations, persecutory

21. OBSESSIONAL SYMPTOMS
(Obsessive thoughts and compulsions against
which the patient struggles)
0 – Absent
1 – Mild
2 – Severe

CHAPTER 19

BURNOUT

A few years after completing his psychiatric training, Dr. Richard Saunders (a pseudonym) is burning out. Dr. Saunders works in a large East Coast city in a university-affiliated hospital clinic. He is a public sector psychiatrist in his thirties, committed to delivering high-quality health care to an underserved population. His burnout is a result of external pressures brought by managed-care insurance and recent electronic medical record (EMR) requirements. Unfortunately, Dr. Saunders is far from alone.

Medicine has become industrialized, and burnout is a direct consequence.[140]Like assembly-line work, medicine has become a high-demand, low-control occupation: too many patients to see (high demand) and no physician influence on patient scheduling or conditions of practice (low control).

Burnout among physicians, including psychiatrists, has reached crisis proportions. According to a 2018 Physicians Foundation report,[141]more than three-quarters of the surveyed doctors reported feelings of burnout; of those, 40 percent indicated that they felt it frequently or all the time. Two-thirds felt that insurance company demands and electronic medical records (EMR) requirements affect patient care adversely, and 60 percent felt that they had little or no ability to influence the health care system.[141] More than three-quarters expressed pessimism about the future of medicine, and more than half indicated that they would not recommend a medical profession to their children. Half are planning to work less— by retiring, leaving clinical practice, or working fewer hours.

Burnout produces poor morale, increased medical errors and patient dissatisfaction.[142-146] These working conditions and the resulting physician response to them are bad for both the quality and quantity of available care. Doctors are leaving clinical practice, and those who remain are working fewer hours. There are approximately one million working physicians in the United States, but estimates suggest a shortage of 130,000 physicians in 2030.

We already have a physician shortage in many areas. In five mid-size U.S. cities, the average waiting time to see a new primary care appointment varies from 72 to 153 days.[141] Access to physician services is worse for poor people; 30 percent of physicians refuse to see Medicaid patients because reimbursement rates are so low.[141] The attitudinal repercussions of burnout in so many of the physicians who are available only make this shortage worse.

Dr. Saunders's working conditions are a good illustration of what many physicians face. His contract offers him a yearly salary, but payment is based on meeting productivity standards. The clinic requires him to see at least seventeen patients a day. Initial patient visits can be forty minutes each; outpatient follow-up visits are set at twenty minutes, severely limiting the care he can give. In twenty minutes, he can check signs and symptoms and note the progress of an illness, but he has only a few minutes to do what he hoped to do as a psychiatrist: attend to the patient as a person. Some insurance plans pay only for a fifteen-minute follow-up visit.

On some days, though, Dr. Saunders sees more than seventeen patients. The clinic has a no-show rate of 35 to 40 percent—typical for clinics serving the urban poor.[147] To meet his seventeen-patient quota, Dr. Saunders must schedule twenty-four patients. When more than seventeen show up, he stays as late as necessary to see all of them. That can make him late for dinner with his wife and young family, causing disruption at home with expectable emotional consequences. His work schedule allows no time for the emergency visits that occur frequently in the low-income patient population he works with, nor time to discuss difficult patients with colleagues, attend staff meetings, take a break for coffee or lunch, or even attend to his own hygiene.

Too many and too brief patient visits are only part of the story; Dr. Saunders must also meet rigorous reporting requirements. Like all doctors working under managed care, he must use the EMR to describe each patient visit.[148] For every patient encounter, the EMR requires a rigid system of Current Procedural Terminology (CPT) codes to rate the complexity of evaluation and management. Separate ratings are required for the patient history, for the physical exam and counseling, and for the amount of time spent with the patient. This information is used to determine reimbursement rates.

Complicated problems take more time and pay more, but when a doctor records one of these, he bills for more time, and records additional codes to justify the time spent and the greater expense. This may trigger an audit by the insurance company, or even a refusal to pay. An audit can be so time-consuming that Dr. Saunders might bill at a lower rate, rather than risk an audit, and make up the difference by working a longer day in order to see his required seventeen patients. Psychiatrists in private practice have told me they handle complicated visits similarly for the same reason.

* * *

Electronic medical records (EMRs) were introduced with great fanfare in the 1990s as an innovation that would improve medical practice by permitting physicians to have instant access to their patients' entire health records. The EMR does that, but the cost in the physician's time needed to fill out the EMR is far out of proportion to the benefits the patient receives. The EMR documents both clinical and billing data, and many physicians believe that billing data, rather than clinical information, drive the use of the EMR. Doctors list the EMR as one of the biggest causes of dissatisfaction with their working conditions.[141, 149, 150] The second biggest is insurance regulations and requirements. More than half of surveyed physicians say these decrease their efficiency.[149]

The average physician work week now includes an estimated twenty-three to thirty hours [141] of required EMR data entry, an average of almost six hours a day,[151] essentially imposing an administrative function on the physician. The EMR requires that the physician answer more than 100 questions for an established patient visit and more than 400 for an initial evaluation.

Almost two-thirds of physicians report that the EMR has meant less time spent with patients and that it is one of their two greatest sources of professional dissatisfaction;[150] the other is the conditions of practice under managed care. Physicians who practice in a private office, a clinic, or on a hospital ward all report this problem with EMR. Some settings even require their physicians to take notes on their computers while they are talking with patients, leading physicians with whom I have spoken to complain bitterly that splitting their attention between the keyboard and the patient damages the doctor-patient relationship. These working conditions have led Dr. Saunders to plan to leave his job for a private practice limited to patients who can pay out of pocket.

The EMR burden begins in the training years. Psychiatric residents spend an average of twenty-two hours a week on the EMR,[152] and the emotional cost is high. Residents report that hours required by the EMR are the most significant source of emotional exhaustion, more important than sleep deprivation, lack of exercise or clinical load.[150]

Physicians recognize the potential value of the EMR, but Epic, the leading EMR firm with 28 percent market share as of April 2019,[153] is extremely difficult to use. I have trained on Epic and have firsthand knowledge that it provides no guidance on how to navigate from entry to entry; it is all rote memorization, and if you get it wrong, Epic offers no help to point you right. Beyond its technical inadequacies, Epic also requires billing information of no clinical relevance. In short, physicians want an EMR—but we want one that works for us, not one that burns us out.

* * *

Managed care is an insurance system designed to control the costs of medical care, and it is ubiquitous. If you, reader, have health insurance, nine times out of ten, some aspect of your health care is managed.[154] There are varieties of managed care, and many plans carve out mental health care. This practice directly affects the experience of psychiatrists (and other physicians), and so indirectly affects the experience of patients.

Many managed-care insurance plans carve out benefits for mental health services. That is, they separate mental health reimbursement from general medical reimbursement, and they assign the responsibility for payment for mental health services to an external insurer. These insurers accept some portion of the risk of paying for mental health services so that if they save money on patient care, they keep some of it. Carve-out plans typically offer fewer benefits for mental health services than they offer for medical or surgical services, and they pay less for the ones they do offer, discriminating against, and potentially harming, patients with a mental illness.[155, 156]

There is concrete evidence to show that carve-out reimbursement policies specifically discriminate against psychiatry. They pay psychiatrists 20 percent less than primary care physicians and 17 percent less than other specialists for the same services, that is, for identical CPT codes.[157] This is true for both adult and pediatric patients, contributing to less care for people of all ages with mental disorders.[158] Medicaid programs in thirty-eight states carve out mental health services,[159] typically to an independent for-profit insurance organization.

These conditions of practice fall more heavily on the poor. A March 2019 *New York Times* article about a major effort to improve mental health care in New York City reported, "Even as the city has poured money into mental health programs and training, nonprofit directors said they still struggle with providing treatment, citing inadequate Medicaid reimbursement rates and even less generous reimbursements from commercial insurers. Some have closed their doors; others have chosen to stop providing mental health services."[160]

Managed care not only tells the psychiatrist how much time to spend on each patient visit, but it also largely determines how we will spend that time. The system has done that in the most direct and brutal way: insurance companies pay relatively well for drug treatment and relatively badly for psychotherapy. If the psychiatrist sees a patient who is in trouble and who needs more than the 15 or 20 minutes managed care will pay for, the psychiatrist faces a hard choice: donate their time to respond to the patient with what her training has prepared her to do, what she would like to do, and why she became a doctor, or she can ignore her patient's need. Imagine the psychiatrist who confronts this choice almost daily over months or years.

Most insurance plans deter physicians from providing psychotherapy by limiting the number of sessions they will approve per year and/or limiting the dollar amount they will reimburse for psychotherapy in one year. Even when a physician accepts this reduced reimbursement, the managed-care company may refuse to approve payment; or if they do pay, they demand that the psychiatrist fulfill onerous requirements explaining why psychotherapy is necessary. These policies effectively limit patient access to physician-delivered psychotherapy. Psychologists and social workers face the same onerous documentation requirements, but managed care pays them at rates closer to what they earn in private practice, which mitigates the pain.

Psychiatry training programs reflect the bias in managed care against psychotherapy. As early as 1991, psychoanalytically trained psychiatrists were noting the decline of psychotherapy training. [161] More recently, accredited residency training programs have been required to certify that residents attain competency in a range of subjects, including psychotherapy—but the required "competency" training for psychotherapy is a bad joke, requiring the resident to treat fewer than five patients with psychotherapy, unless the psychotherapy is combined with drug treatment. Then the requirement is ten patients, clearly reflecting how psychotherapy in itself has been devalued and how training aligns with what the market will pay for.

Older psychiatrists who were trained in psychotherapy and want to offer it have adapted to these conditions as best they can. A colleague in private practice who accepts insurance told me, "Many of us have adapted the therapy component of our work to twenty or forty minutes once a month, much as one would work with issues with a medical patient with a chronic illness. This therapy has a heavy cognitive component, but it's far from just handing out meds or advice about diet and exercise, and it gives us much more time than our medical colleagues to talk to patients about what's bothering them and how they're dealing with symptoms and handicaps."

It's not just poor payment for psychotherapy—reimbursement programs can damage patients and systems in other ways. Insurance refuses to pay for community health workers (CHWs), a policy that has hurt us badly at Cambridge. Our ACS program for serving the severely and persistently mentally ill in the community once relied on CHWs, and they did a superb job until insurance refused to pay for them. As a result, we had to pay more for social workers who were over-trained for the job. We also lost a pipeline of future health care professionals, as many of our CHWs had gone on to train as health or mental professionals.[162] A recent *New England Journal of Medicine* article documents the value of CHWs and urges insurance to write procedure codes to cover them.[162]

Drug company marketing and managed care together propelled psychiatry in a new direction, but there is a psychological difference for individual practicing psychiatrists in how these influences are perceived. They may have doubts about how much medicine they are prescribing, but it was a choice they made, albeit strongly influenced by the pharmaceutical industry. Managed care was forced on the physician and is experienced as an external force hostile to the practice of good medicine. The fact that this condition has been externally imposed, as much as the substance of what it imposes, demonstrates a loss of control and perpetuates burnout.

Burnout is getting worse. Psychiatry is in trouble, and burnout is a big part of the problem. Fighting burnout requires radical action, but some of our problems are self-inflicted and these are

within our power to change. The next, and last, chapter offers
strategies for change.

#####

CHAPTER 20

CONCLUSION: A WAY FORWARD

Psychiatry is failing. We are not giving our patients the time and attention they deserve. Within living memory, we were the physicians who were defined by our listening skills. Now, most psychiatric practice is limited to pushing pills little else.

This is the psychiatry pushed by the pharmaceutical industry. It is easy to learn and simple to practice. But this is what far too many psychiatrists practice, and this is who they are. They can get by knowing only the effects, side effects, and interactions of the medicines they prescribe. They can manage perfectly well without current knowledge of brain structure and function and without the empathetic understanding needed to spend serious time listening to patients, let alone provide psychotherapy. When I ask applicants for our residency program at Cambridge why they chose psychiatry, more than one has told me, "Because it's easy."

Given that much psychiatric practice today is limited to prescribing for signs and symptoms, with little time available for patients, what does that say about current psychiatric training? To me, it says that three years of training for such limited activity is a waste of two good years of a young physician's time and of the social resources spent in training. Opinions of other physicians about psychiatry reflect this view.[163]

In studies going back many years, physicians consistently appraise psychiatry as a low prestige medical specialty.[163] In 1974, when psychiatrists primarily practiced psychotherapy, other physicians held the opinion that non-physicians could provide this psychotherapy equally well. In a 1982 survey, physicians opined that psychiatry was unscientific and imprecise, that many psychiatric patients did not need a doctor, and that practicing psychiatrists did not make full use of their medical training.[164] Medical students in 1982, and again in 2010, did not think that a medical education was necessary in order to care for the patients that psychiatrists see [164, 165]. This opinion is consistent with much current psychiatric practice—prescribing for patients with minor disorders, or even without any psychiatric diagnosis at all. Most current psychiatric patients do not need a psychiatrist.[93]

As for the public, according to a recent paper, most people do not understand what psychiatry is or how it differs from other mental health professions. This paper summarized the results of 462 opinion surveys of the general public worldwide.[166] The surveys asked what type of *professional* would be a good choice to treat someone with schizophrenia. More respondents (85 percent) chose psychologist/psychotherapist than chose psychiatrist (83 percent)! Substantially fewer people—68 percent—selected a general practitioner. These results illustrate that the public appreciates that a mental health professional is a better choice than a general practitioner to treat schizophrenia, but the more important finding is that the public does not distinguish between psychiatry and psychology—almost equal numbers of people think that both these professions are appropriate and qualified to treat schizophrenia. This finding strongly suggests that psychiatry has failed to make its case that we are the professionals uniquely trained to treat schizophrenia and other psychotic disorders.

When asked about treatment for people with schizophrenia, given choices of psychotherapy or medication, 85 percent of respondents selected psychotherapy and 67 percent selected medication. We in the profession know that essential treatment for schizophrenia is medication, with the addition of psychotherapy. Clearly. we have not communicated that to the public. Taken together, these results suggest that psychiatry has failed to make its case with the general public.

These opinion surveys also asked who should treat people with depression. More people chose a general practitioner to treat depression (81 percent) than chose psychologists (76 percent) or psychiatrists (70 percent).[166] Currently, primary care physicians write the great majority of prescriptions for antidepressants,[167] and these results indicate that the public Is comfortable with this.

When asked about treatment for depression, 76 percent picked psychotherapy and 49 percent picked medication, showing that respondents preferred psychotherapy to medication as a treatment for both schizophrenia and depression [166]; a modality of treatment that psychiatrists rarely provide, but there is some evidence to suggest that by psychotherapy, the subjects meant something closer to 'any therapeutic relationship,' rather than referring to a more formally defined psychotherapy.

The consistent finding over fifty years is that other physicians think psychiatry is unscientific, that a medical school education is not necessary to treat many patients whom psychiatrists treat, and that the public has no clear idea of who psychiatrists are professionally or what we are best equipped to do. These data send a message for how psychiatry should change. **Psychiatry should be the specialty that treats patients with severe mental disorders: schizophrenia, bipolar disorder, major depression, severe PTSD, and others.**

Resident training for this specialty should focus on clinical work with these seriously ill patients. Academic training for this new approach to psychiatry should include neurobiology, a field that represents what we know about brain structure and function. Increasingly, as neurobiologists elucidate the functions of individual nerve cells and understand how cells are organized within the working brain, neurobiology will be clinically relevant to the understanding and treatment of severe mental illness. To date, our knowledge of neurobiology has played only a minimal role in our development of new treatments, but that will change, especially for severe illness.

In this vision, psychiatry would focus on assessment and treatment of severely ill patients, with clinical practice anchored on a base of knowledge of brain structures and functions. When we base our assessment and treatment in neurobiology, psychiatry will be recognizable as a scientifically based specialty, treating a seriously ill patient population. This new psychiatry will be more closely integrated with medicine, rather than occupying, as it does now, an often-dismissed left field of its own. A more radical proposal along the same lines would be, as others have suggested, developing integrated training in psychiatry and neurology for a new specialty in neuropsychiatry.

The National Association on Mental Illness (NAMI) has fought for years to overcome the stigma that people with severe, persistent mental disorders face. The new psychiatry as a medical specialty focused on severely ill patients will help society understand that our patients are not people with some personal or moral weakness, but rather people afflicted with one or another serious illness with causes in biology and unfavorable life experience. When psychiatry is the branch of medicine that cares for the severely mentally ill on a scientific base, mental illness might be less stigmatized; and then perhaps—just perhaps—society will be willing to allocate more resources to the treatment of people with severe mental illness.

Such a model of psychiatry may induce greater acceptance in other areas as well, including, importantly, payment for services. Current insurance carve-out plans pay less for the evaluation and treatment of mental disorders than for other illnesses.[168] This is unfair and unreasonable, as severe disorders like schizophrenia or severe depression are illnesses in the same way that pneumonia and cancer are illnesses. Limiting psychiatry to the treatment of severe mental illness would argue for parity. When psychiatry is the specialty that treats serious mental illness, and *only* serious mental illness, this is a strong argument that insurance should reimburse psychiatrists on the same basis as other medical specialties.

To that end, my proposal specifically rejects a role for psychiatry in treating minor mental disorders or the anxiety and distress of everyday life. These are meaningful problems for the people who experience them, but primary-care physicians already write more than half of all antidepressant prescriptions for ambulatory patients,[90] and I hear no outcry that they are not competent to do so or that the practice has led to a flood of malpractice suits. A primary-care residency can teach the necessary skills for the treatment of these conditions; psychologists and social workers can provide the psychotherapy these patients need.

However we psychiatrists define our areas of practice and our expertise, we should be empathetic listeners, and we should have a dynamic understanding of human psychology. I believe that every mental health practitioner should have some familiarity with the psychodynamic understanding of human psychology regardless of their specialty, the population they treat, or what therapy they employ. Those of us who want to offer psychotherapy should have the necessary training to do so, but in the new psychiatry this would be psychotherapy for the severely ill, tailored to their needs.

In my clinical experience treatment with severe mental disorders need support and medication management from their physician until their acute episode of illness is brought under control. Until that happens, they are not candidates for any kind of psychotherapy. When the acute episode of illness is under control, psychotherapy may be useful in the context of an existing supportive patient physician relationship.

There is little research support for the use of psychodynamic psychotherapy with this patient population, so that clinicians like me who are dynamically trained must rely on their own clinical experience and the experience of their teachers for guidance.

Research supports the use of cognitive behavioral therapy for psychosis (CBTp) as a treatment for some of these patients,[169] and so we should teach both standard CBT and CBTp alongside a dynamically informed supportive psychotherapy, recognizing that "supportive psychotherapy" is essentially what empathetic physicians have always provided for their patients. This support, whether we call it psychotherapy, is essential to helping patients and their significant others manage the burden of severe mental illness.

Despite its fall from clinical and intellectual grace, my belief is unchanged that psychoanalytic theory has value and that a psychodynamic understanding of human psychological functions is an important part of the therapeutic armamentarium for physicians who wish to provide support for their patients. Going beyond this psychodynamically informed support, there are patients with severe disorders who may, when their illness is stable, benefit from psychodynamic psychotherapy.

Severely ill patients have a character structure the same as everyone else, and just as adults generally may have character problems or character disorders, so may our patients. When their illness is stable, selected patients with these problems may benefit from psychodynamic psychotherapy or even psychoanalysis. Academic coursework in the new psychiatry curriculum can provide an introduction to this therapy. Faculty drawn from the ranks of the relatively few psychodynamic psychotherapists who have experience with sicker patients can teach the basics to all residents and offer an advanced elective for trainees who want to learn more.

To be clear, this proposal explicitly rejects training psychiatrists as psychodynamic psychotherapists for the broad range of what were called 'neurotic problems' before the *DSM-III* abolished the term and renamed these problems as anxiety disorders and depressive disorders. Psychiatrists who want to treat neurotic patients could elect to pursue a post-residency fellowship in psychotherapy. Those few psychiatrists who want to become psychoanalysts could take that additional training.

Young adults who think they want to provide psychotherapy for less severe disorders might consider training in one of the non-medical mental health professions rather than in medicine. I do not believe it is a great loss for society if most psychiatrists are not offering psychotherapy for these patients.[15] Other professionals do this well.

This proposal has public health implications given America's shortage of physicians and psychiatrists.[170] A 2018 study found that major depressive disorder (MDD), according to *DSM-V* criteria, is "highly prevalent, disabling" and badly undertreated, i.e., many patients receive little or no treatment.[171] Focusing psychiatry on the care of very sick, underserved people who need us most is an efficient use of scarce psychiatric resources. Mental health care is a system, and this proposal allocates professional resources efficiently within that system.

I am not alone in making this proposal. Anne Harrington, the Franklin L. Ford Professor of the History of Science at Harvard University, has made essentially the same proposal in her book *Mind Fixers: Psychiatry's Troubled Search for the Biology of Mental*

---

15 It was a struggle for me to come to this position. I wanted to be able to argue that medical training was essential, or at least an advantage, for professionals treating neurotic and other less severe disorders, but I could not convince myself. The four years of medical school and four more of residency training are an inefficient use of scarce human resources.

Good doctors are committed to their patients in a way that may not always characterize other healthcare professionals. We don't turn off at 5 o'clock Friday afternoon (or at least we didn't when we were self employed). We should be able to teach this commitment to other professionals.

Illness.[172] She suggests a strategy for enabling psychiatry to emerge from its current status as a poorly respected field with little or no scientific base: "[Psychiatry] could decide to return to... a profession concerned principally with the most severe forms of mental illness." She goes on to suggest that psychiatry could leave psychotherapy to the non-medical psychotherapists.[172] When two people from different disciplines reviewing the same history come to the same conclusion, it suggests that the recommendation has value.

My proposal for the new psychiatry tracks closely with much of my own work as a psychiatrist. I taught our trainees what a general psychiatrist should know about how to evaluate and treat severely ill patients, especially patients with schizophrenia. Many patients with schizophrenia do not understand that they are ill, despite being afflicted with a dreadful chronic disease. This makes it very difficult to treat them, and the skills necessary to treat these patients require a specially trained physician. We are the professionals best able to help these patients, and we should not divert our unique skills to tasks that others can do at least equally well. I know from my own experience the value of what I am recommending for others.

* * *

To this point, I have written about what psychiatry can do for itself, but we do not control our conditions of practice. Changing those conditions requires direct confrontation with the insurance industry and managed care. American medicine has a long history of independent private practice, but that has changed. Ninety percent of American physicians practice at least in part under some form of managed care.[173, 174] The practice of psychiatry and all medicine under managed care is a miserable experience for many physicians and not what it should be for our patients. Good medical care requires a strong physician-patient relationship, but managed care works against providing one. We must have more time with our patients.

And we need more than just additional time; we need flexibility and agency. It is not just a metaphor to say that current medical practice is an industrial occupation. Doctors in settings like Dr. Saunders', where salary depends on 'productivity,' have neither enough time with patients nor the agency to determine how to spend what time they have.

What is to be done? The history of labor relations provides an answer. Profit-driven management gives up nothing to labor until labor forces it to do so. Employees improve working conditions when they organize. Organized labor has the power to challenge employers to negotiate better working conditions. The American Medical Association (AMA), a guild organization that represents physicians in private practice, is unlikely to morph into the organization that employed physicians will need. We need a union.

An article in the psychiatric literature stresses the importance of social connection for psychological health and the ability to fight stress.[175] Beyond its potential for improving working conditions, our union would provide social connection that in itself would benefit physicians who join.

The idea that we should unionize will be new to many physicians, and one that initially will generate little enthusiasm. Medicine is a profession, and we physicians have always thought of ourselves as professionals. We are professionals, but professionals whose payment is dictated by managed care and insurance companies are members of the working class—a professional working class, but a working class, just the same. It will not be easy for most of us to accept this re-definition of our social role, but it is accurate.

A subset of doctors in California has already formed a successful union. The Union of American Physicians and Dentists (UAPD) is an affiliate of the one million, three hundred thousand–member American Federation of State and County Municipal Employees (AFSCME). As an AFSCME affiliate, the UAPD has access to their lobbying, research and organizing resources. The National Labor Relations Board recently recognized a new UAPD union in Washington State.

Beyond the AFSCME-UAPD, there exist other unions organizing on behalf of physicians. The Doctors Counsel in New York is affiliated with the Service Employees International Union (SEIU). The Committee of Interns and Residents is a national union for house staff, with 17,000 current members. Physicians are not the only health care professionals who are organizing. The California Nurses Association (CNA) union has successfully negotiated improved working conditions for nurses in California, and CNA has expanded nationally. The success of these unions can serve as a template and an inspiration for psychiatrists.

* * *

I have tried to suggest a way forward for psychiatry through making substantive changes in how we define our profession, and in how we might change our working conditions. I believe change is possible, and I am hopeful that it will occur. If we take a longer historical view, we see that at different times over the past several centuries, there have been improvements in the treatment of the mentally ill, often followed by a decline—repeated cyclical changes that offer a basis for hope that current conditions can improve.

Nineteenth-century asylums at their best were humane institutions for the treatment of the severely mentally ill, until they morphed into the desperately overcrowded state hospitals of the early twentieth century. We dealt with that overcrowding with Thorazine and with the promise of community mental health centers. This combination let us empty out the state hospitals.

In the 1960s, community mental health centers offered meaningful treatment for severely ill patients in the community. But that promise failed as the centers used their resources to treat the 'worried well', which they did until they exhausted their federal money and went out of business. The result was little or no treatment for seriously ill patients in the community, many of whom ended up on the street or in jail, either untreated or with medication their only treatment.

These are illustrations of cycles in treatment *facilities*, but similar observations can be made about treatment *methods*, both organic and psychosocial. Psychosurgery and psychoanalysis serve as the most dramatic examples. Each was seen initially as a breakthrough treatment, and each was ultimately recognized as not just ineffective, but in the case of psychosurgery, as actively harmful, with devastating consequences for many patients. Psychoanalytically oriented treatment of schizophrenia was ineffective for the disease and, beyond that, it badly damaged the mothers of the patients.

* * *

I want to end by reflecting on what psychiatry represents at its best. Using tools, we have now, we can and we do ameliorate a great deal of human suffering. For the first time in history, we have medicines that do more than dull the brain—psychoactive medication targets and effectively treats the delusions and hallucinations of psychotic mental disorders. Minimizing these symptoms helps patients to become more comfortable psychologically, and this comfort reduces the disruptive behavior that often leads to their rejection in society. By accomplishing improvement in these symptoms, we can, in collaboration with other mental health professionals, help these patients to maintain meaningful lives in the community.

We also prescribe medication that is effective against the most severe forms of depression, and perhaps also against some of the less severe. Depression is one of the leading causes of disability worldwide, a disability for which psychiatry has effective treatment. Similarly, we have effective medication against anxiety.

As important as our somatic treatments, psychiatry developed psychotherapy. Based on Freud's theories and techniques of psychoanalysis, psychiatrists developed psychodynamic psychotherapy. Later a psychiatrist who was a psychoanalyst developed cognitive behavioral therapy [CBT], a contribution that has made psychotherapy accessible to many millions of people for whom psychodynamic psychotherapy was out of reach. As we reflect on what psychiatry represents, count psychotherapy among our contributions. If we psychiatrists no longer deliver psychotherapy, it is not through choice; it is because society has chosen others to do this work.

Psychiatry is a field of medicine with its own uniquely valuable skills and tools. If we are to apply these optimally, then both psychiatry and society must change. I hope that with time, and with concerted efforts, American society can be induced to provide the resources, and that American psychiatry will focus its efforts on treatment of the severely ill people who need us most. These are ambitious goals, but worth the effort needed to attain them.

#####

Afterword

My life did not stop after Susan died. I worked in palliative care psychiatry for three years while I began the research for this book, and that experience led me to reflect on my life in psychiatry. I am grateful for what I experienced , when so many of my younger colleagues were forced into the unsatisfying professional lives I have written about. To a large extent, I was an observer, not a participant in these troubles. My core professional experience was teaching residents and other trainees in a public sector psychiatry department that reflected my values. Our psychiatry department at Cambridge took responsibility for treating those who needed us, no matter how sick or how poor.

If I had to summarize what I contributed, it would be my clinical teaching. That understanding the experience of even the sickest patients is the core of our work. With that understanding, or as much understanding as we can manage at whatever our level of clinical experience, we can begin to form the patient-physician relationship on which treatment is based. I did other professional work over the course of my working life that I think was valuable, but I experienced my teaching as a calling in the full religious sense. It is my teaching for which I hope to be remembered.

These last few years have been personally fulfilling beyond what I could have imagined. Two years after Susan died, I met my current wife, Elisabeth, at a stand-up cocktail event before the annual meeting at the Cambridge Boat Club. Elisabeth was sitting down because she had a broken ankle; I was sitting down because I hate stand-up cocktail parties. Seeing Elisabeth improved my mood, and it improved more when I sat next to her. I thought she was the most attractive woman there.

Psychoanalytic psychotherapy has helped me deal with the challenges of aging and helped me to clear out the psychological underbrush that was impairing my capacity for intimacy. These changes have helped to make my life with Elisabeth what it has been, and my life with Elisabeth is principally responsible for my present happiness. Elisabeth and I were together for eight years until an illness compelled us to separate. I never imagined that my ninth decade would include the happiest years of my life, but so it has been, for that I am profoundly grateful.

Appendix: Seeking Professional Help

Seeking Help

If you are wondering whether you or someone in your life might benefit from treatment, or if you are just curious, this chapter is for you.

Technical Point

I write this during the COVID-19 pandemic, which has led to a dramatic change in the provision of all health services including mental health services. Mental health services short of those requiring hospitalization, are now delivered online. Whatever service you decide on will be delivered online rather than in person. If/when conditions ever return to "normal" online options will almost certainly continue.

When should you seek help from a mental health provider?

- You should definitely seek help: when you feel an overwhelming and prolonged sense of helplessness and sadness or depression, and your problems do not seem to get better despite your efforts and the efforts of family and friends.
- If you are having any thoughts of ending your life, please do not wait. Seek help immediately.
- National suicide hotline: 800 273 8255, 911 or your primary care physician (PCP) or mental health provider, if you have one.
- If you are experiencing anxiety or distress that is seriously interfering with your relationships or with your ability to fulfill your daily responsibilities, whatever these are.
- If you are feeling miserable all the time or almost all the time, for no good reason.
- If you or someone close to you thinks that you have changed in a way that makes you difficult to get along with—you are irritable, having speeding thoughts or unclear thinking, or are much more anxious than usual.
- If you are unable to concentrate or think clearly or your memory is bad to the point that it is difficult to carry out everyday activities: for example, you are unable to concentrate on assignments at work, or you are having trouble with everyday activities.
- If you worry excessively, expect the worst or are constantly on edge.

- If your actions are harmful to yourself or others: for instance, you are drinking too much, abusing drugs, or becoming overly argumentative and aggressive.
- If something bad is happening. You're not sure what, but you're frightened.

If you feel that any of the above are making you, or someone you love, miserable, or are interfering with your personal relationships or with your work, then the problem is serious enough that you should get a consultation from your PCP, if you have one, or a psychiatrist or other mental health professional.

If this informal survey leaves you uncertain, you can try one of the widely available self-report checklists available on the internet. These are free and available to the public.

The first is the PHQ-9. PHQ stands for Patient Health Questionnaire. This is a nine-item questionnaire that asks you to rate your symptoms of depression. You rate yourself on each symptom from not at all (zero) to nearly every day (three). To find your depression score, you add the numbers for each of the nine items: score of 0-4, no depression; 5-9, mild; 10-14, moderate; 15-19, moderately severe; and 20-27, severe. *A score of 10 or higher is an indication to seek professional help.*

The GAD-7 is a scale for rating anxiety; GAD stands for Generalized Anxiety Disorder. The score is calculated by assigning scores of 0, 1, 2, and 3 to the categories of "not at all", "several days", "more than half the days", o "nearly every day", and then adding the scores of the seven answers together. Scores of 5, 10 and 15 are taken as the cut-off points for mild, moderate and severe anxiety. *Further evaluation is recommended when the score is 10 or higher.*

Treatment guidelines exist for depression. For mild to moderate depression (scoring 5-14 on the PHQ-9), The American Psychiatric Association (APA)-recommends psychotherapy with or without added medication. For more severe depression, a PHQ-9 score of 15 or higher, the recommended treatment is a combination of both medication and psychotherapy.

If you use one of these scales, they will give you an estimate of severity. Severity can also be judged along two other dimensions: psychological distress, and impaired social function. I imagine that almost every reader has been asked by a physician to rate pain on a scale from 1 to 10, where one is no pain at all and 10 is the worst pain you have ever had or the worst pain you can imagine. You can rate your distress in the same way. A seven on either of these is an indication that a consultation may be helpful.

If you have decided that help is appropriate, the next question is where to look. Your choices will depend on the resources available in your area and your own finances. If you can afford to pay for treatment out of pocket, you will have independent choices, but if you are depending on private insurance or Medicaid or Medicare, your choice will be limited to what your insurance will pay for, and your choice of providers will be limited to those who accept this insurance or who are in the network of providers approved by the insurer.

- If you have health insurance, your insurance policy may have a list of specific mental health providers who are covered, or it may only cover certain types of mental health providers.

- Check ahead of time with your insurance company to find out what types of mental health services are covered, identify the covered providers in your area, and also be sure to check your benefit limits, including what co-pay your program requires from you.
- If paying out of pocket, any initial consultation should include a discussion of fees. Many mental health professionals, especially those who limit their practices to self-paying patients, charge fees on a sliding scale, where the rate depends on your income. Some provide an initial free consultation. Clinics at non-profit agencies also usually have sliding scales, but these clinics often have a long waiting list.

After you have determined the practical aspects of your situation, the next step is to think about what treatment makes sense, and then to find a treatment resource.

What kind of provider should you seek? People with mental health problems often have strong ideas about treatment. Some people put their faith in medicine. Others believe that putting any foreign substance, including medicines, into their bodies is a bad idea. Some people want to talk; others are not interested in talking about their problems or discussing what bothers them. These different beliefs will influence where you will look for help.

If you are a person who would rather take medicine then talk about a problem, then you need a professional who is licensed to prescribe medication. This might be a primary care physician, a psychiatrist, an advanced practice nurse, or in a few states [Idaho,Illinois, Iowa, Louisiana, New Mexico] a specially trained psychologist.

If you would rather talk and would prefer to avoid medicine, then your options definitely include psychologists, social workers or mental health counselors, and possibly psychiatrists. Although psychiatrists are trained to provide psychotherapy as well as pharmacological treatment, and some do both, many others today provide medication management only. It's a good idea to ask.

As a good rule of thumb, the more severe your symptoms, the more likely it is that medicine can help. If you and your PCP decide that the best treatment for you includes medicine and psychotherapy you might see a physician[16] or certified, licensed nurse practitioner for medicine and a psychologist or social worker for psychotherapy. In this case, you want a pair of practitioners who have a strong working relationship and a history of successfully sharing patients.

In looking for a treatment resource, your PCP or nurse practitioner can refer to a mental health specialist, but PCPs often treat mental health problems themselves, so your search may end here. If you don't have a PCP, making the effort to find one is a good idea, because if you do get sick it is important to have a doctor who knows you. I realize that in some regions This could be your PCP or a psychiatrist of this country finding a PCP may not be easy.

Thinking you want or need psychotherapy strongly suggests that you would like to change something about yourself or your situation—how you feel, how an important relationship is going,

---

16 This could be your PCP or a psychiatrist.

or your functioning socially or at work. To put this another way, at this point in your life you are not happy, and you have at least some idea that you are a part of the problem. If you don't have some idea that you are a part of the problem, therapy may help, but it could be a long process.

[17]Remember that the pharmaceutical industry has persuaded many physicians, PCPs and psychiatrists, that medicine is the primary treatment for anxiety and depression. Remember also that evidence does not support medication as treatment for minor depression or for sadness or life distress. There is abundant evidence that CBT is effective for both anxiety and depression, and there is also evidence the psychodynamic psychotherapy is effective as well.

The Internet can be very helpful in learning about who is available in your area. I found Psychology Today.com to provide useful information about different types of mental health professionals and services, including telepsychiatry, listed by ZIP Code or by state. Each listed professional provides a picture and a statement.

Choosing a Therapist

If you have decided psychotherapy is your treatment of choice, how do you find a therapist? You can begin by consulting your (PCP) or licensed nurse practitioner for recommendations. If

---

17 Throughout this chapter, 'physician' or 'PCP' should be understood to include licensed nurse practitioners.

you have already been a patient and you were satisfied with that experience, then you may want to begin again with that therapist. If you were not satisfied with your prior experience or if you think it would be worthwhile to try with someone new, then you should do that. If a new person doesn't work for you, you can always return to your original provider.

Going online (see above) for, 'how to choose a psychotherapist' will produce many leads. Many therapists have websites that provide enough information about themselves to give some indication of whether you might like to talk with them. Again, asking trusted sources who might know or know about one of these therapists can be helpful.

After you have a name, [or names], the next step is calling the possible therapist(s). If the first therapist you talk with seems like the right person for you, then you are done. But you may find it useful to have initial interviews with more than one potential therapist simply because people differ and your 'chemistry' with one potential therapist may be quite different from that with another.

There are many schools of psychotherapy, with different names and different theoretical orientations. You should certainly ask any therapist to tell you what kind of therapy they practice, something about how their therapy works, and the theory on which it is based. What the therapist says should make sense and should not sound like mumbo-jumbo. If it does not make sense, look elsewhere.

Important facts about any therapist include:

- How long has the therapist been practicing?
- What is the therapist's professional education?

- What specific training has he/she had in psychotherapy, including postgraduate training?
- What is the therapist's opinion about what makes a good therapist?
- What is the usual structure of psychotherapy: length of each session, number of sessions per week, usual length of time over which therapy occurs?

Three major types of psychotherapy are currently in use: 1) CBT or cognitive behavioral therapy; 2) IPT or interpersonal psychotherapy and 3) psychodynamic psychotherapy. CBT and IPT are focused on present problems or symptoms and are designed to be completed in twelve to eighteen sessions. Psychodynamic psychotherapy is usually more open-ended and less structured and takes longer. Many types of therapy are available, and a longer list is beyond the scope of this discussion. Any in which you are interested will have its own website.

Both CBT and IPT have been studied intensively for depression. CBT has also been used extensively for anxiety disorders and obsessive-compulsive disorder. Both are used for adolescents as well as adults. CBT is a structured therapy that typically includes homework assignments—exercises for you to practice, observations to make in your life between sessions. CBT tries to help you change maladaptive thoughts with the expectation that a corresponding improvement in symptoms will follow. CBT helps identify symptoms with a goal of getting rid of them. IPT focuses on helping you improve current personal relationships through a focus on those. Like CBT, it is present- and problem-focused. Psychodynamic therapy is less structured than either CBT or IPT, often lasts longer, and may include some investigation of how your current difficulties relate to past experience.

Psychodynamic therapy does not mean 'Freudian.' Freud's observations and theoretical understanding are the historical basis for a psychodynamic understanding of human psychology, but psychodynamic understanding and psychodynamic based psychotherapy have developed well beyond Freud.

There are no clear guidelines or indications that would help any potential patient choose one therapy over another. The therapists with whom I spoke who are trained in both CBT and dynamic psychotherapy said that the choice of therapy depends largely on what the patient wants, rather than on some formal assessment of the value of one therapy over another. Therapists may incorporate elements of several therapies to tailor the treatment to the individual patient's needs. Increasingly, therapists are introducing mindfulness exercises into their therapy.

Even before Covid 19 psychotherapy provided over the internet was widely available because many mental health practitioners have incorporated this kind of distant treatment into their professional profile. Studies of online CBT, both therapist-guided and self-guided, have shown positive outcomes (see below). A 2013 publication [176] reports on successful online therapist guided dynamic psychotherapy.

If you have begun therapy, how do you decide if the therapy is working? If you and your therapist have decided on goals during your first few meetings, then if the therapy is working, you should experience some progress towards those goals. A paper I read early in my career suggested that you should have a clear sense after six sessions that either the therapy is helpful, or it isn't. Minimally, a helpful therapy is one in which you feel better after you leave a session. Feeling better is good, but it is not enough. A helpful therapy helps you move toward your goals and encourages some understanding of yourself in a way that offers you the possibility of constructive change.

Feeling better is not the same as feeling comfortable. You may leave a session feeling troubled, sad, or angry, but at the same time feeling that useful work is being done. Feeling troubled, sad, or angry repeatedly without a corresponding feeling that the session has been useful is an indication to get consultation from another psychotherapist.

If after six sessions you feel that little or nothing has happened—you don't feel (even a little bit) better and you have not begun to understand how something about yourself has led to the difficulties that brought you to therapy—you should discuss this issue as forthrightly as you are able with the therapist. If this discussion leads to a change so that you do begin to feel that therapy is helping, well and good. If you continue to feel that little is being accomplished, this is an indication to obtain a consultation from another therapist, and possibly a reason to end this relationship while looking further.

In a successful therapy, you should be able to identify change and to link the change to the therapeutic experience. If change has occurred, then important people in your social network should have noticed, although not everyone may like the change.

The above discussion relates to outcome, but you can also evaluate the process of therapy. You should always feel that the therapist accepts you as a person the way you are. This is true for all types of therapy. The basic attitude of the therapist toward you should be one of unconditional positive regard.[18] This does not mean the therapist is uncritical about what she observes, but you should always feel that critical judgment refers to particular behavior or issues, not to you as a person.

You should never feel that the therapist is being judgmental about you. If you do feel judged, it is critically important that you discuss this with the therapist. There are patients who have serious problems with trust, who can feel judged when no judgment is intended. Alternatively, there are therapists who, in the words of my daughter's second grade report card, 'need improvement'. Sorting this out in the individual case can be difficult but is important for the progress of therapy.

If your feeling of being judged is accurate, this is an indication that the therapist has departed from the basic therapeutic attitude. No patient who feels he is being judged will feel safe enough to share what is most troubling or anxiety provoking.

It is possible for the therapist to be critical of some behavior or attitude without being critical of the person, and if the therapist is a good one, this distinction should be clear to you. An example: You tell the therapist that you lent money to a cousin but you now regret it. The good CBT therapist might say, "what can you remember about the situation in which you agreed to lend the money?" The dynamic therapist might ask a similar question, and could go on to ask, "does this situation remind you of anything earlier in your life?" Or, "this reminds me of the story you told me about how x did y." The bad therapist might say, "Your judgment

---

18   This was first stated by psychologist Carl Rogers who developed his own school of psychotherapy that stressed the importance of the principle. Rogers was right; this attitude is fundamental to any successful therapy.

about that loan was not so good." Worse yet, "this is the kind of mistake you make too often."

If you are satisfied that the therapist genuinely accepts you, the next question is, do you feel understood? When you tell a story, does the therapist understand how that story made you feel.? If the therapist accepts you but does not appear to understand your feelings, this therapist will probably be of limited help.

The technical concept is the 'therapeutic alliance'. If the patient feels that the therapist cares about them, genuinely accepts them the way they are, and understands how they feel, and is actively helping, these are the characteristics of the therapeutic alliance.

What about the professional training of a psychotherapist? Being a good therapist has more to do with personal qualities and training than with professional discipline.

If you have been given a diagnosis of a psychotic disorder, or other severe, disabling disorder it is important to establish that the proposed therapist has had substantial experience with people with your diagnosis. Experience with more common, less severe problems is not a sufficient basis for a therapist to hold themselves out as appropriate for patients who suffer with severe mental illness. Major mental illness is different from other psychological problems and requires specific expertise for its treatment.

This discussion has been about individual psychotherapy.

Online, there are therapists who describe themselves as offering couples or family or group psychotherapy as well as individual. If you are uncertain about whether one of these may be the best for you, your choice is more difficult. With a good therapist, any of these can be helpful, but as with any therapy you should feel the therapist's unconditional positive regard.

Another comment on choice: if you are a member of a minority group or one that is treated with prejudice by mainstream society – LGBTQ, African American, Muslim, Asian, or women—you may want to choose a therapist who is a member of your group. A member of your group likely will have experienced some of the same prejudice or harsh treatment that you have experienced, and this can be valuable. But the most important question in choosing a therapist is not whether the therapist shares your group membership. The most important question is whether the person has the characteristics of a good therapist, and is a person with whom you are comfortable, and it is this that you ought to evaluate. If you can find a therapist who shares your social experience and who has these characteristics, so much the better. If you have a therapist who shares your social experience, but about whom you have questions, listen to your gut.

Leaving Therapy

In the best case, you and the therapist agree that the work is done, but sometimes there is a disagreement: the patient is dissatisfied, but the therapist wants to continue. Because of the power imbalance it can be hard for the patient to raise the issue. Here, a consultant can be helpful, perhaps even essential.

Children and Adolescents

Everything I have written about seeking help for an adult applies to seeking help for a child or adolescent, but with the unfortunate caveat that there are far less professionals available to treat young people then there are to treat adults. There are whole states in which there is not a single child psychiatrist, and in other states there are counties with no child therapist.

Internet Therapy

The observation that nothing is new under the sun goes back at least to the Book of Ecclesiastes, but internet therapy is genuinely new: therapy that is effective with no face-to-face patient contact. I am writing this during the pandemic when internet therapy is the new norm. When a colleague did an informal survey, more than two thirds of patients said they preferred internet to face-to-face. These new enforced conditions may dramatically change future mental health service delivery.

* * *

Psychotherapy has the potential to be greatly helpful when it is successful. There is another old saying that, 'money doesn't buy happiness; but it helps you look for it in a lot more places'. Psychotherapy may represent the experience that probes this rule. In contrast to almost every other experience, psychotherapy, when it works, can help buy happiness. For those of you who begin therapy, I hope you find what you are looking for.

#####

Endnotes

1. Mack, J., *A Prince of Our Disorder: The Life of T.E. Lawrence.* 1976, Boston: Little, Brown.

2. Sadock, B.J., V.A. Sadock, and P. Ruiz, eds. *Kaplan & Sadock's Comprehensive Textbook of Psychiatry.* 10th ed. 2017, Philadelphia, PA: Lippincott Williams & Wilkins

3. Kahn, R.S., et al., *Schizophrenia.* Nature Reviews Disease Primers, 2015. **1**: p. 15067.

4. Correll, C.U., et al., *Prevalence, incidence and mortality from cardiovascular disease in patients with pooled and specific severe mental illness: a large-scale meta-analysis of 3,211,768 patients and 113,383,368 controls.* World Psychiatry, 2017. **16**(2): p. 163-180.

5. Jayatilleke, N., et al., *Contributions of specific causes of death to lost life expectancy in severe mental illness.* European Psychiatry, 2017. **43**: p. 109-115.

6. Amadeo, K. *Deinstitutionalization, Its Causes, Effects, Pros and Cons: How Deinstitutionalization in the 1970s Affects You Today.* The Balance, 2018. https://www.thebalance.com/deinstitutionalization-3306067 Accessed on: July 17, 2019.

7. Torrey, E.F., et al. 2014. The treatment of persons with mental illness in prisons and jails: A state survey.

8. Powers, R., *No One Cares About Crazy People: The Chaos and Heartbreak of Mental Health in America*. 2017, New York, NY: Hachette Book Group.

9. Ebert, A. and K.-J. Bar, *Emil Kraepelin: A pioneer of scientific understanding of psychiatry and psychopharmacology*. Indian journal of psychiatry, 2010. **52**(2): p. 191-192.

10. Ashok, A.H., J. Baugh, and V.K. Yeragani, *Paul Eugen Bleuler and the origin of the term schizophrenia (SCHIZOPRENIEGRUPPE)*. Indian Journal of Psychiatry, 2012. **54**(1): p. 95-96.

11. Kadiyala, P.K. and L.D. Kadiyala, *Anaesthesia for electroconvulsive therapy: An overview with an update on its role in potentiating electroconvulsive therapy*. Indian Journal of Anesthesia, 2017. **61**(5): p. 373-380.

12. Ray, A.K., *How bad was unmodified electroconvulsive therapy! A retrospective study*. Indian Journal of Psychiatry, 2016. **58**(2): p. 212-215.

13. Jones, K., *Insulin coma therapy in schizophrenia*. J R Soc Med, 2000. **93**(3): p. 147-9.

14. Fink, M., *A Beautiful Mind and Insulin Coma: Social Constraints on Psychiatric Diagnosis and Treatment*. Harvard Review of Psychiatry (Taylor & Francis Ltd), 2003. **11**(5): p. 284.

15. Jansson, B. *Egas Moniz*. The Nobel Prize. https://www. nobelprize.org/prizes/medicine/1949/moniz/article/ Accessed on: July 8, 2019.

16. Caruso, J.P. and J.P. Sheehan, *Psychosurgery, ethics, and media: a history of Walter Freeman and the lobotomy.* Journal of Neurosurgery, 2017. **43**(3): p. 1-8.

17. Sheffield, W. *The Community Mental Health Act of 1963: Still Pursuing the Promise of Reform Fifty Years Later.* 2013. https://www.ymadvocacy.org/the-community-mental-health-act-of-1963/ Accessed on: September 16, 2019.

18. Rosenbloom, M., *Chlorpromazine and the psychopharmacologic revolution.* JAMA, 2002. **287**(14): p. 1860-1.

19. Adams, C.E., et al., *Chlorpromazine for schizophrenia: a Cochrane systematic review of 50 years of randomised controlled trials.* BMC Medicine, 2005. **3**(1): p. 15.

20. Sneader, W., *Drug Discovery: A History.* 2005, West Sussex, ENGLAND: John Wiley & Sons, Ltd.

21. Meltzer, H.Y., et al., *A randomized trial comparing clozapine and typical neuroleptic drugs in non-treatment-resistant schizophrenia.* Psychiatry Research, 2010. **177**(3): p. 286-293.

22. Manschreck, T.C. and R.A. Boshes, *The CATIE schizophrenia trial: results, impact, controversy.* Harv Rev Psychiatry, 2007. **15**(5): p. 245-58.

23. Meltzer, H.Y. and G. Okayli, *Reduction of suicidality during clozapine treatment of neuroleptic-resistant schizophrenia: impact on risk-benefit assessment.* Am J Psychiatry, 1995. **152**(2): p. 183-90.

24. Hennen, J. and R.J. Baldessarini, *Suicidal risk during treatment with clozapine: a meta-analysis.* Schizophr Res, 2005. **73**(2-3): p. 139-45.

25. Hartwell, C.E., *The schizophrenogenic mother concept in American psychiatry.* Psychiatry, 1996. **59**(3): p. 274-97.

26. Chou, I.J., et al., *Familial Aggregation and Heritability of Schizophrenia and Co-aggregation of Psychiatric Illnesses in Affected Families*. Schizophrenia Bulletin, 2017. **43**(5): p. 1070-1078.

27. Susser, E.S. and S.P. Lin, *Schizophrenia after prenatal exposure to the Dutch Hunger Winter of 1944-1945*. Arch Gen Psychiatry, 1992. **49**(12): p. 983-8.

28. Brown, A.S. and P.H. Patterson, *Maternal Infection and Schizophrenia: Implications for Prevention*. Schizophrenia Bulletin, 2011. **37**(2): p. 284-290.

29. Labrie, V. and L. Brundin, *Harbingers of Mental Disease— Infections Associated With an Increased Risk for Neuropsychiatric Illness in Children*. JAMA Psychiatry, 2018.

30. Morgan, C. and H. Fisher, *Environment and Schizophrenia: Environmental Factors in Schizophrenia: Childhood Trauma—A Critical Review*. Schizophrenia Bulletin, 2007. **33**(1): p. 3-10.

31. Fearon, P. and C. Morgan, *Environmental Factors in Schizophrenia: The Role of Migrant Studies*. Schizophrenia Bulletin, 2006. **32**(3): p. 405-408.

32. Kendell, R.E., J.E. Cooper, and A.G. Gourlay, *Diagnostic criteria of American and British psychiatrists*. Archives of General Psychiatry, 1971. **25**: p. 123-130.

33. Sartorius, N., *The International Pilot Study of Schizophrenia*. Schizophrenia Bulletin, 1974. **11**: p. 21-34.

34. Mubarik, A. and H. Tohid, *Frontal lobe alterations in schizophrenia: a review*. Trends Psychiatry Psychother, 2016. **38**(4): p. 198-206.

35. Husa, A.P., et al., *Lifetime antipsychotic medication and cognitive performance in schizophrenia at age 43 years in a*

general population birth cohort. Psychiatry Res, 2017. **247**: p. 130-138.

36. Beck, J.C., S. Golden, and F. Arnold, *An empirical investigation of psychotherapy with schizophrenic patients.* Schizophr Bull, 1981. **7**(2): p. 241-7.

37. Beck, A.T., *Cognitive therapy and the emotional disorders.* 1976, New York: International Universities Press.

38. Fowler, D., P. Garety, and E. Kuipers, *Cognitive Behaviour Therapy for Psychosis: Theory and Practice.* 1995, Chichester, UK: John Wiley & Sons

39. *Daniel B. Fisher, M.D., Ph.D.* 2019. https://power2u.org/dan-fisher/ Accessed on: July 8, 2019.

40. Fisher, D.B., *Health care reform based on an empowerment model of recovery by people with psychiatric disabilities.* Hosp Community Psychiatry, 1994. **45**(9): p. 913-5.

41. Poloni, N., et al., *A naturalistic study on the relationship among resilient factors, psychiatric symptoms, and psychosocial functioning in a sample of residential patients with psychosis.* Psychology Research and Behavior Management, 2018. **11**: p. 123-131.

42. Drake, R.E., et al., *Research on the individual placement and support model of supported employment.* Psychiatric Quarterly, 1999. **70**(4): p. 289-301.

43. Drake, R.E. and G.R. Bond, *IPS Support Employment: A 20-Year Update.* American Journal of Psychiatric Rehabilitation, 2011. **14**(3): p. 155-164.

44. Bond, G.R., R.E. Drake, and K. Campbell, *Effectiveness of individual placement and support supported employment for*

young adults. Early Intervention in Psychiatry, 2016. **10**(4): p. 300.

45. Swartz, M., et al. *New York State Assisted Outpatient Treatment Program Evaluation.* 2009. https://omh.ny.gov/omhweb/resources/publications/aot_program_evaluation/ Accessed on: June 27, 2009.

46. *Tarasoff v Regents of the University of California, 529 P2d553, 118 Cal Rptr 129.* 1974, Cal Sup Ct. p. 914.

47. *Tarasoff v Regents of the University of California, 551, P2d 334, 17 Cal3d 425* 1976, Cal Sup Ct.

48. McClelland, M. *When 'Not Guilty' Is a Life Sentence.* The New York Times Magazine, 2017. https://www.nytimes.com/2017/09/27/magazine/when-not-guilty-is-a-life-sentence.html Accessed on: February 12, 2020.

49. Rogers, J.L., J.D. Bloom, and S.M. Manson, *Insanity defenses: contested or conceded?* Am J Psychiatry, 1984. **141**(7): p. 885-8.

50. McCracken, D. *TRUST BETRAYED.* Chicago Tribune, 1992. https://www.chicagotribune.com/news/ct-xpm-1992-09-27-9203270891-story.html Accessed on: March 26, 2019.

51. Psychiatric Rape: Assaulting Women and Children, ed. Citizens Commission on Human Rights. 2004. https://files.ondemandhosting.info/data/www.cchr.org/files/booklets/psychiatric-rape_en.pdf?_=8b32df5

52. Noel, B. and K. Watterson, *You Must be Dreaming.* 1993, United Kingdom: Poseidon Press. 333.

53. Sato, C., *Gender and Work in the American Aircraft Industry during World War II.* The Japanese Journal of American Studies, 2000. **11**: p. 147-172.

54. Lundberg, F. and M.F. Farnham, *Modern woman: the lost sex.* 1947, New York: Harper & Brothers. vii, 497 p.

55. Strecker, E.A., *Their mothers' sons: The psychiatrist examines an American problem.* [New ed., with additional chapter] ed. 1951, Philadelphia: Lippincott.

56. Fromm-Reichmann, F., *Notes on the development of treatment of schizophrenics by psychoanalytic psychotherapy.* Psychiatry, 1948. **11**(3): p. 263-73.

57. Escalona, S., *Some considerations regarding psychotherapy with psychotic children.* Bulletin of the Menninger Clinic, 1948. **12**: p. 126-134.

58. Lidz, T., *Schizophrenia and the family.* 2nd ed. / Theodore Lidz, Stephen Fleck, with the collaboration of Alice R. Cornelison ... [et al.]. ed, ed. S. Fleck. 1985, New York: International Universities Press.

59. Kanner, L., *Autistic disturbances of affective contact.* Nervous Child, 1943. **2**: p. 217-250.

60. Distel, M.A., et al., *Genetic covariance structure of the four main features of borderline personality disorder.* J Pers Disord, 2010. **24**(4): p. 427-44.

61. Franklin, B. and et al. 1785. Report of Dr. Benjamin Franklin, and Other Commissioners, Charged by the King of France, with the Examination of the Animal Magnetism, as Now Practised at Paris. Translated from the French. With an Historical Introduction.

62. Wohlberg, J., *Personal Interview.* 2014. Interviewed by J.C. Beck on September 30, 2014.

63. *TELL: Therapy Exploitation Link Line (About TELL).* 2019. https://www.therapyabuse.org/about_us.htm Accessed on: July 15, 2019.

64. Sturdivant, S., *Therapy with women: A feminist philosophy of treatment.* 1980, New York: Springer Publishing Company.

65. Herman, J.L., et al., *Psychiatrist-patient sexual contact: results of a national survey, II: Psychiatrists' attitudes.* The American Journal of Psychiatry, 1987. **144**(2): p. 164.

66. Gartrell, N., et al., *Psychiatrist-Patient Sexual Contact: Results of a National Survey, I: Prevalence.* The American Journal of Psychiatry, 1986. **143**(9): p. 1126-1131.

67. Celenza, A., *Sexual boundary violations: Therapeutic, supervisory, and academic contexts.* 2007, Lanham, MD, US: Jason Aronson.

68. Rezendes, M., *'I own you': Prominent psychiatrist accused of sexually exploiting patients,* in *The Boston Globe.* 2019.

69. Milar, K.S., *The Myth Buster.* Monitor on Psychology, 2011. **42**(2): p. 24.

70. Hooker, E., *A Preliminary Analysis of Group Behavior of Homosexuals.* The Journal of Psychology, 1956. **42**(2): p. 217-225.

71. Hooker, E., *The adjustment of the male overt homosexual.* J Proj Tech, 1957. **21**(1): p. 18-31.

72. Bieber, I., et al., *Homosexuality: A Psychoanalytic Study.* 1962, New York, NY: Basic Books.

73. Faderman, L., *The Gay Revolution: The Story of the Struggle.* 2016, New York, NY: Simon & Schuster.

74. Kernberg, O., *Borderline Conditions and Pathological Narcissism.* 1975, New York, NY: Jason Aronson, Inc.

75. *Basic Right to consent to medical care – Schoendorff v. Society of New York Hospital*, in *211 N.Y. 125; 105 N.E. 92, 93*. 1914, Court of Appeals of New York.

76. Kendell, R.E., et al., *Diagnostic criteria of American and British psychiatrists*. Arch Gen Psychiatry, 1971. **25**(2): p. 123-30.

77. Ruffalo, M.L. *The Psychoanalytic Tradition in American Psychiatry: The Basics*. Psychiatric Times, 2018. https://www.psychiatrictimes.com/view/psychoanalytic-tradition-american-psychiatry-basics Accessed on: June 1, 2020.

78. Whitaker, R. and L. Cosgrove, *Psychiatry Under the Influence*. 2015, New York: Palgrove McMillan.

79. Greenberg, G., *Not Diseases, but Categories of Suffering [The D.S.M.'s Troubled Revision]*, in *The New York Times*. 2012.

80. *Product Search: American Psychiatric Association Publishing*. https://www.appi.org/home/search-results?FindMeThis=dsm March 6, 2019

81. Andreasen, N.C., *DSM and the Death of Phenomenology in America: An Example of Unintended Consequences*. Schizophr Bull, 2007. **33**(1): p. 108-12.

82. Shen, W.W., *A history of antipsychotic drug development*. Compr Psychiatry, 1999. **40**(6): p. 407-14.

83. National Alliance on Mental Illness. *Early Psychosis and Psychosis*. [cited 2018 June 29]; Available from: https://www.nami.org/earlypsychosis.

84. Kane, J.M., T. Kishimoto, and C.U. Correll, *Non-adherence to medication in patients with psychotic disorders: epidemiology, contributing factors and management strategies*. World Psychiatry, 2013. **12**(3): p. 216-26.

85. CBC Radio *Miltown: a game-changing drug you've probably never heard of.* 2017. https://www.cbc.ca/radio/ondrugs/miltown-a-game-changing-drug-you-ve-probably-never-heard-of-1.4237946 Accessed on: April 11, 2019.

86. Wick, J.Y., *The history of benzodiazepines.* Consult Pharm, 2013. **28**(9): p. 538-48.

87. Cooper, A. *An Anxious History of Valium.* The Wall Street Journal, 2013. **November 15, 2013**. https://www.wsj.com/articles/an-anxious-history-of-valium-1384547451 Accessed on: November 15, 2013.

88. Ramachandraih, C.T., et al., *Antidepressants: From MAOIs to SSRIs and more.* Indian J Psychiatry, 2011. **53**(2): p. 180-2.

89. Taylor, D., *The Pharmaceutical Industry and the Future of Drug Development*, in *Pharmaceuticals in the Environment.* 2015, Royal Society of Chemistry. p. 1-33.

90. Mojtabai, R. and M. Olfson, *Proportion of antidepressants prescribed without a psychiatric diagnosis is growing.* Health Aff (Millwood), 2011. **30**(8): p. 1434-42.

91. Smith, B.L., *Inappropriate Prescribing.* Monitor on Psychology, 2012. **43**(6): p. 36.

92. Pratt, L.A., D.J. Brody, and G. Qiuping. 2017. Antidepressant Use Among Persons Aged 12 and Over: United States, 2011-2014. Center for Disease Control and Prevention National Center for Health Statistics. August 2017

93. Mark, T.L., K.R. Levit, and J.A. Buck, *Datapoints: psychotropic drug prescriptions by medical specialty.* Psychiatr Serv, 2009. **60**(9): p. 1167.

94. Angell, M., *The Truth About the Drug Companies.* 2004, New York, NY: Random House.

95. Thase, M.E., *Are SNRIs more effective than SSRIs? A review of the current state of the controversy.* Psychopharmacology Bulletin, 2008. **41**(2): p. 58.

96. Bech, P., et al., *The Hamilton Depression Scale.* Acta Psychiatrica Scandinavica, 1981. **63**(3): p. 290-299.

97. Cipriani, A., et al., *Comparative efficacy and acceptability of 21 antidepressant drugs for the acute treatment of adults with major depressive disorder: a systematic review and network meta-analysis.* The Lancet, 2018. **391**(10128): p. 1357-1366.

98. Rabinowitz, J., et al., *Initial depression severity and response to antidepressants v. placebo: patient-level data analysis from 34 randomised controlled trials.* Br J Psychiatry, 2016. **209**(5): p. 427-428.

99. Whiteford, H.A., et al., *Estimating remission from untreated major depression: a systematic review and meta-analysis.* Psychol Med, 2013. **43**(8): p. 1569-85.

100. Zimmerman, M., I. Chelminski, and M.A. Posternak, *Generalizability of antidepressant efficacy trials: differences between depressed psychiatric outpatients who would or would not qualify for an efficacy trial.* Am J Psychiatry, 2005. **162**(7): p. 1370-2.

101. Grigoriadis, S., et al., *Benzodiazepine Use During Pregnancy Alone or in Combination With an Antidepressant and Congenital Malformations: Systematic Review and Meta-Analysis.* J Clin Psychiatry, 2019. **80**(4): p. 18r12412.

102. Banov, M. and A.J. Harrison *When is it Safe to Stop Antidepressants? An Evidence-Based, Patient-Physician Collaborative Approach to Medication Discontinuation.* Relias Media, 2003. https://www.reliasmedia.com/articles/24906-

when-is-it-safe-to-stop-antidepressants-an-evidence-based-patient-physician-collaborative-approach-to-medication-discontinuation Accessed on: March 15, 2019.

103. Hiles, S.A., et al., *Bidirectional Prospective Associations of Metabolic Syndrome Components with Depression, Anxiety, and Antidepressant Use.* Depression and Anxiety, 2016. **33**(8): p. 754-764.

104. Renoir, T., *Selective serotonin reuptake inhibitor antidepressant treatment discontinuation syndrome: a review of the clinical evidence and the possible mechanisms involved.* Front Pharmacol, 2013. **4**: p. 45.

105. American Psychiatric Association, *Practice Guideline for the Treatment of Patients with Major Depressive Disorder.* 3rd ed. 2010, Washington, DC: American Psychiatric Association.

106. Schatzberg, A. and C. Nemeroff, eds. *Textbook Of Psychopharmacology.* 5th ed. 2017, Arlington, VA: The American Psychiatric Association Publishing

107. Offidani, E., et al., *Efficacy and tolerability of benzodiazepines versus antidepressants in anxiety disorders: a systematic review and meta-analysis.* Psychother Psychosom, 2013. **82**(6): p. 355-62.

108. Salzman, C., *Do Benzodiazepines Cause Alzheimer's Disease?* American Journal of Psychiatry, 2020. **177**(6): p. 476-478.

109. Balon, R., et al., *The rise and fall and rise of benzodiazepines: a return of the stigmatized and repressed.* Braz J Psychiatry, 2020. **42**(3): p. 243-244.

110. Zito, J.M., et al., *Off-label psychopharmacologic prescribing for children: history supports close clinical monitoring.* Child Adolesc Psychiatry Ment Health, 2008. **2**(1): p. 24.

111. Nisen, M. *The 10 Best Selling Prescription Drugs In The United States*. Business Insider, 2012. https://www.businessinsider.com/10-best-selling-blockbuster-drugs-2012-6 Accessed on: March 1, 2019.

112. Hampton, L.M., et al., *Emergency department visits by children and adolescents for antipsychotic drug adverse events*. JAMA Psychiatry, 2015. **72**(3): p. 292-4.

113. Government Accountability Office (GAO), Antipsychotic Drug Use: HHS Has Initiatives to Reduce Use Among Older Adults in Nursing Homes, but Should Expand Efforts to Other Settings. 2015, Washington, DC: GAO. https://www.gao.gov/products/GAO-15-211

114. Olfman, S. and B.D. Robbins, eds. *Drugging Our Children: How Profiteers are Pushing Antipsychotics on Our Youngest, and What We Can Do to Stop It*. 2012, Santa Barbara, CA: ABC-CLIO, LLC.

115. Maglione, M., et al., Off-Label Use of Atypical Antipsychotics: An Update. 2011, Rockville, MD: Agency for Healthcare Research and Quality. http://www.ncbi.nlm.nih.gov/books/NBK66081/

116. Maher, A.R., et al., *Efficacy and comparative effectiveness of atypical antipsychotic medications for off-label uses in adults: a systematic review and meta-analysis*. JAMA, 2011. **306**(12): p. 1359-69.

117. Hwang, Y.J., et al., *Atypical antipsychotic drugs and the risk for acute kidney injury and other adverse outcomes in older adults: a population-based cohort study*. Ann Intern Med, 2014. **161**(4): p. 242-8.

118. Maust, D.T., et al., *Antipsychotics, other psychotropics, and the risk of death in patients with dementia: number needed to harm.* JAMA Psychiatry, 2015. **72**(5): p. 438-45.

119. El-Saifi, N., et al., *Quetiapine safety in older adults: a systematic literature review.* J Clin Pharm Ther, 2016. **41**(1): p. 7-18.

120. Driessen, J., S.H. Baik, and Y. Zhang, *Trends in Off-Label Use of Second-Generation Antipsychotics in the Medicare Population From 2006 to 2012.* Psychiatric Services, 2016. **67**(8): p. 898-903.

121. Semla, T.P., et al., *Off-Label Prescribing of Second-Generation Antipsychotics to Elderly Veterans with Posttraumatic Stress Disorder and Dementia.* J Am Geriatr Soc, 2017. **65**(8): p. 1789-1795.

122. Law Offices of Robert Vaage, *Latest Open Payments Data Reveals Strong Financial Ties Between Doctors and Drug Makers,* in *Our Blog.* 2015.

123. Carlat, D., *Confessions of a former 'drug rep': A doctor in thrall to a multibillion-dollar marketing juggernaut.(Finance).* 2007, International Herald Tribune. p. 13.

124. Trudo, H. and T. Meyer *Dollars for Docs: The Top Earners.* ProPublica, 2013. https://www.propublica.org/article/dollars-for-docs-the-top-earners Accessed on: January 22, 2019.

125. Tigas, M., et al. *Dollars for Docs.* Updated June 28, 2018, ProPublica:New York, NY. https://projects.propublica.org/docdollars/ January 28, 2019

126. Brauser, D. *Psychiatrists Top List of Big Pharma Payments Again*. Psychiatry News, 2013. https://www.medscape.com/viewarticle/780835 Accessed on: January 22, 2019.

127. Ornstein, C., M. Tigas, and R.G. Jones *Now There's Proof: Docs Who Get Company Cash Tend to Prescribe More Brand-Name Meds*. ProPublica, 2016. https://www.propublica.org/article/doctors-who-take-company-cash-tend-to-prescribe-more-brand-name-drugs Accessed on: June 29, 2018.

128. Levy, D.M., *Maternal overprotection*. 1943, New York: Columbia university press. ix, 417 p.

129. Huang, F.Y., et al., *The association of pharmaceutical company promotional spending with resident physician prescribing behavior*. Acad Psychiatry, 2005. **29**(5): p. 500-1.

130. Kowalczyk, L., *Massachusetts General moves to curb drug vendors*, in *Boston Globe*. 2002, Boston, MA: Boston Globe Media Partners, LLC

131. Wake, N., *Private practices: Harry Stack Sullivan, the science of homosexuality, and American liberalism*. 2011, New Brunswick, N.J.: Rutgers University Press. xiii, 263 p.

132. Hartzband, P. and J. Groopman, *Money and the changing culture of medicine*. N Engl J Med, 2009. **360**(2): p. 101-3.

133. Breggin, P., *Toxic Psychiatry: Drugs and Electroconvulsive Therapy: The Truth and Better Alternatives*. 1993, London, England: Fontana.

134. Hoberman, J.M., *Black and blue : the origins and consequences of medical racism*. 2012, Berkeley: University of California Press. 293.

135. Sullivan, H.S., *The interpersonal theory of psychiatry*. [1st] ed. 1953, New York: Norton. xviii, 393 p.

136. Spiegel, A. *Selling Sickness: How Drug Ads Changed Health Care.* Morning Edition, 2009. https://www.npr.org/templates/story/story.php?storyId=113675737 Accessed on: March 6, 2019.

137. Kravitz, R.L., et al., *Influence of patients' requests for direct-to-consumer advertised antidepressants: a randomized controlled trial.* JAMA, 2005. **293**(16): p. 1995-2002.

138. Arndt, M. *Eli Lilly: Life after Prozac.* Bloomberg Businessweek, 2001. https://www.bloomberg.com/news/articles/2001-07-22/eli-lilly-life-after-prozac Accessed on: March 3, 2019.

139. Schriever, N. *Ranking the biggest industries in the US economy – with a surprise #1!* [cited 2018 June 29]; Available from: http://bluewatercredit.com/ranking-biggest-industries-us-economy-surprise-1/.

140. Kongstvedt, P.R.P.R., *Essentials of Managed Health Care.* 6th ed. 2013, Burlington, MA: Jones and Bartlett Learning.

141. The Physicians Foundation. 2018. 2018 Survey of America's Physicians: Practice Patterns and Perspectives. T.P. Foundation.

142. Wallace, J., J. Lemaire, and W. Ghali, *Physician wellness: a missing quality indicator.* The Lancet, 2009. **374**(9702): p. 1714-21.

143. Shanafelt, T.D., et al., *Burnout and medical errors among American surgeons.* Ann Surg, 2010. **251**(6): p. 995-1000.

144. Balch, M.C., et al., *Distress and Career Satisfaction Among 14 Surgical Specialties, Comparing Academic and Private Practice Settings.* Annals of Surgery, 2011. **254**(4): p. 558-568.

145. Dyrbye, L.N., et al., *Relationship Between Burnout and Professional Conduct and Attitudes Among US Medical Students.* JAMA, 2010. **304**(11): p. 1173-1180.

146. Shanafelt, T., et al., *Why Do Surgeons Consider Leaving Practice?* Journal of the American College of Surgeons, 2011. **212**(3): p. 421-422.

147. Molfenter, T., *Reducing appointment no-shows: going from theory to practice.* Subst Use Misuse, 2013. **48**(9): p. 743-9.

148. Burke, T., *The health information technology provisions in the American Recovery and Reinvestment Act of 2009: implications for public health policy and practice.* Public Health Rep, 2010. **125**(1): p. 141-5.

149. Colligan, L., et al. *Sources of physician satisfaction and dissatisfaction and review of administrative tasks in ambulatory practice: A qualitative analysis of physician and staff interviews.* 2016. https://www.ama-assn.org/sites/ama-assn.org/files/corp/media-browser/public/ps2/ps2-dartmouth-study-111016.pdf Accessed on: May 5, 2019.

150. Jha, A.K., et al., *A Crisis in Health Care: A Call to Action on Physician Burnout.* Partnership with the Massachusetts Medical Society, Massachusetts Health and Hospital Association, Harvard T.H. Chan School of Public Health, and Harvard Global Health Institute, 2018.

151. Arndt, B.G., et al., *Tethered to the EHR: Primary Care Physician Workload Assessment Using EHR Event Log Data and Time-Motion Observations.* Ann Fam Med, 2017. **15**(5): p. 419-426.

152. Domaney, N., J. Torous, and W. Greenberg, *Exploring the Association Between Electronic Health Record Use and Burnout*

Among Psychiatry Residents and Faculty: a Pilot Survey Study. Academic Psychiatry, 2018. **42**(5): p. 648-652.

153. Drees, J. *KLAS: Epic, Cerner dominate EMR market share.* Becker's Hospital Review, 2019. https://www. beckershospitalreview.com/ehrs/klas-epic-cerner-dominate-emr-market-share.html Accessed on: May 15, 2019.

154. *"Fast Facts" – America's Health Insurance Plans.* HealthDecisions.org, 2005. https://web.archive.org/web/20070928204630/http://www.healthdecisions.org/LearningCenter/Facts.aspx Accessed on: 01/24/19.

155. American Psychiatric Association. 2009 (Reaffirmed). Position Statement on Carve-Outs and Discrimination. APA.

156. Bishop, T.F., et al., *Acceptance of insurance by psychiatrists and the implications for access to mental health care.* JAMA Psychiatry, 2014. **71**(2): p. 176-81.

157. Spector, J.M., B. Studebaker, and E.J. Menges. 2015. Provider Payment Arrangements, Provider Risk, and Their Relationship with the Cost of Health Care (Milliman Report). Society of Actuaries.

158. Meadows, T., et al., *Physician "costs" in providing behavioral health in primary care.* Clin Pediatr (Phila), 2011. **50**(5): p. 447-55.

159. Mandros, A. *Understanding The Medicaid Behavioral Health Carve-Out Map – Step One In Health Plan Contracting.* Open Minds: Executive Briefing, 2017. https://www.openminds.com/market-intelligence/executive-briefings/understanding-the-medicaid-behavioral-health-carve-out-map-step-one-in-health-plan-contracting/ Accessed on: June 29, 2018.

160. Goodman, J.D. *Chirlane McCray, de Blasio's Wife, Is Questioned Over His 'Revolutionary' $1 Billion Mental Health Plan.* The New York Times, 2019. https://www.nytimes.com/2019/03/22/nyregion/thrivenyc-mental-health-.html Accessed on:

161. Wallerstein, R.S., *The future of psychotherapy.* Bull Menninger Clin, 1991. **55**(4): p. 421-43.

162. Lapidos, A., J. Lapedis, and M. Heisler, *Realizing the Value of Community Health Workers – New Opportunities for Sustainable Financing.* N Engl J Med, 2019. **380**(21): p. 1990-1992.

163. Shortell, S.M., *Occupational prestige differences within the medical and allied health professions.* Social Science and Medicine, 1974. **8**(1): p. 1-9.

164. Yager, J., et al., *Medical students' evaluation of psychiatry: A cross-country comparison.* The American Journal of Psychiatry, 1982. **139**(8): p. 1003-1009.

165. Katschnig, H., *Are psychiatrists an endangered species? Observations on internal and external challenges to the profession.* World Psychiatry, 2010. **9**(1): p. 21-28.

166. Angermeyer, M.C., et al., *Public attitudes towards psychiatry and psychiatric treatment at the beginning of the 21st century: A systematic review and meta-analysis of population surveys.* World Psychiatry, 2017. **16**(1): p. 50-61.

167. Mercier, A., et al., *Why do general practitioners prescribe antidepressants to their patients? A pilot study.* BioPsychoSocial Medicine, 2014. **8**: p. 17-17.

168. Melek, S., D. Perlman, and S. Davenport. 2017. Addiction and mental health vs. physical health: Analyzing disparities in network use and provider reimbursement rates. Milliman.

169. Burns, A.M., D.H. Erickson, and C.A. Brenner, *Cognitive-behavioral therapy for medication-resistant psychosis: a meta-analytic review.* Psychiatr Serv, 2014. **65**(7): p. 874-80.

170. Association of American Medical Colleges *New Findings Confirm Predictions on Physician Shortage.* AAMC News, 2019. https://news.aamc.org/press-releases/article/2019-workforce-projections-update/ Accessed on: September 5, 2019.

171. Hasin, D.S., et al., *Epidemiology of Adult DSM-5 Major Depressive Disorder and Its Specifiers in the United States.* JAMA Psychiatry, 2018. **75**(4): p. 336-346.

172. Harrington, A., *Mindfixers: Psychiatry's Troubled Search for the Biology of Mental Illness.* 2019, New York, NY: Norton.

173. Boccuti, C., et al. *Primary Care Physicians Accepting Medicare: A Snapshot.* Medicare, 2015. https://www.kff.org/medicare/issue-brief/primary-care-physicians-accepting-medicare-a-snapshot/ Accessed on: May 3, 2020.

174. 1997. Managed Care Quality: Hearing Before the Subcommittee on Health and Environment of the Committee on Commerce, Serial No. 105-63. House of Representatives – One Hundred Fifth Congress – First Session. October 28, 1997

175. Larrabee Sonderlund, A., T. Thilsing, and J. Sondergaard, *Should social disconnectedness be included in primary-care screening for cardiometabolic disease? A systematic review of*

the relationship between everyday stress, social connectedness, and allostatic load. PloS One, 2019. **14**(12): p. e0226717.

176. Johansson, R., R.J. Frederick, and G. Andersson, *Using the Internet to Provide Psychodynamic Psychotherapy.* Psychodynamic Psychiatry, 2013. **41**(4): p. 513-540.

CPSIA information can be obtained
at www.ICGtesting.com
Printed in the USA
FSHW021130031120
75420FS